Me Too, Feminist Theory, and Surviving Sexual Violence in the Academy

Me Too, Feminist Theory, and Surviving Sexual Violence in the Academy

Laura A. Gray-Rosendale

LEXINGTON BOOKS
Lanham • Boulder • New York • London

Published by Lexington Books
An imprint of The Rowman & Littlefield Publishing Group, Inc.
4501 Forbes Boulevard, Suite 200, Lanham, Maryland 20706
www.rowman.com

6 Tinworth Street, London SE11 5AL

Excerpt from Bloom, Lynn. "Teaching College English as a Woman," *College English* Nov. 1992 pp. 824-825. Reprinted with permission from NCTE.

British Library Cataloguing in Publication Information Available

Library of Congress Cataloging-in-Publication Data Available

ISBN 978-1-7936-1112-3 (cloth: alk. paper)
ISBN 978-1-7936-1114-7 (pbk.: alk. paper)
ISBN 978-1-7936-1113-0 (electronic)

This book is dedicated to survivors of sexual violence in all of its forms—the many ones I have been fortunate enough to meet and work with over the years as well as those who I may never meet. Thank you for your strength in the face of seemingly insurmountable odds. Thank you for your bravery even in those moments when you have felt less than brave. And thank you always for sharing your stories in your own time and in your own ways. I am forever grateful to you.

And thanks always to Steve who has long supported all of my work on these issues. Your love, understanding, intelligence, sense of humor, and kindness make it all possible.

Contents

Introduction

Laura Gray-Rosendale

In the last few years survivors of various kinds of sexual harassment and violence have spoken up perhaps more loudly than ever before. There has been significant public mobilization around the Me Too movement and Time's Up, especially concerning Brett Kavanaugh's appointment to the Supreme Court in the face of the chilling testimony offered by Dr. Christine Blasey Ford, Harvey Weinstein's harassment and rape of well-known actresses, Jeffrey Epstein's various atrocities involving underage girls, R. Kelly's sexual abuse of girls and women, as well as the actions of many other high-profile perpetrators within arenas such as entertainment, politics, education, and religion. As a result, right now survivors' voices are being heard more often on television shows, at protest rallies and speak outs, as well as at academic conferences across the country.

As part of this turn in public discourse, we have seen the publication of quite a number of crucial books on the subject of sexual violence both in the popular press and within academic quarters. Here I will mention but a few key examples. And many more are sure to follow. Books addressed to a more popular audience include Kate Harding's superb *Asking for It: The Alarming Rise of Rape Culture—and What We Can Do About It* (2015) in which Harding makes the case that higher education as well as other institutional contexts help to promulgate a rape culture and proposes how we might best fight against it. Jon Krakauer penned the excellent *Missoula: Rape and the Justice System in a College Town* (2016), a text that examines the problem of campus rape by investigating one town and one academic institution, drawing on the stories of a number of survivors as well as interviewing various others involved in the justice system. Vanessa Grigoriadis's *Blurred Lines: Rethinking Sex, Power, and Consent on Campus* (2017) offers a very thoughtful treatment of changes in campus sexuality and the ways in which

1

sexual violence operates. Acclaimed writers Jodi Kantor and Megan Two-hey, two Pulitzer Prize–winning reporters from the *New York Times*, came out with their *She Said: Breaking the Sexual Harassment Story That Helped Ignite a Movement* (2019), a *New York Times* bestseller that traces the many abuses of Harvey Weinstein and the ways in which they were discovered. Robyn Warshaw published a new edition of her groundbreaking *I Never Called It Rape* (2019) that centers specifically on acquaintance and date rape, this time with a foreword written by Gloria Steinem.

Books addressed to a somewhat more scholarly audience include Sara Carrigan Wooten and Roland W. Mitchell's collection *The Crisis of Campus Sexual Violence: Critical Perspectives on Prevention and Response* (2015), a strong text that examines the sorts of policies and practices that surround rape issues in higher education and does so from a variety of valuable perspectives. Jessica C. Harris and Chris Linder's edited book *Intersections of Identity and Sexual Violence on Campus: Centering Minoritized Students' Experiences* (2017) furnishes a thorough understanding of how sexual violence influences the lives of campus survivors too often left out of our discussions. Authors in this text interrogate how sexual violence intersects with issues like homophobia, transphobia, racism, and classism. Kelly Oliver's excellent *Hunting Girls: Sexual Violence from the Hunger Games to Campus Rape* (2017) examines how popular culture texts are impacting perceptions about sexual violence in our culture and are also shaping how campus sexual violence operates. Linda Martín Alcoff's pivotal *Rape and Resistance* (2018), drawing on feminist philosophy, takes a strong stand on the value of all survivors' voices and argues for reading survivors' stories within their specific cultural, social, and political contexts. Donna Freitas also came out with her *Consent on Campus: A Manifesto* (2018), a very important text that considers how issues of consent are taken up within higher education, advancing suggestions for how we might better understand the complexities surrounding consent as well as teach our students about it. Laurie Collier Hillstrom also published *The #MeToo Movement* (2018), a vital text that traces the history of the movement, featuring both historical events and profiles of some crucial activists and thinkers who have been critical in spearheading it.[1]

Significantly, during this same time frame we have also seen the publication of a series of influential edited books and anthologies that actually feature survivors' own collective voices. These books have spoken to a wide range of audiences as well. Again, I mention just some of them here. There are absolutely essential texts such as *We Believe You: Survivors of Campus Sexual Assault Speak Out* (2016) by Annie Clark and Andrea Pino, a book that provides both resources for survivors as well as reveals the voices of student survivors from various universities and colleges. There is *Queering Sexual Violence: Radical Voices from Within the Anti-Violence Movement*

(2016) edited by Jennifer Patterson, a tremendous book that includes a wide range of very important survivor voices too often relegated to the margins and addresses the larger institutional forces that undermine such voices. *#MeToo: Essays About How and Why This Happened, What It Means, and How to Make Sure It Never Happens Again* (2017) edited by Lori Perkins thoughtfully joins together voices of those fighting against sexual violence in fundamental ways, arguing that we need to make substantive changes in our workplaces and in culture in general. There is *Things We Haven't Said: Sexual Assault Survivors Speak Out* (2018) edited by Erin Moulton, a book that features gorgeous writings across different genres from survivors who experienced sexual violence at early points in their lives. We have also seen *Written on the Body: Letters from Trans and Non-Binary Survivors of Sexual Assault and Domestic Violence* (2018) edited by Lexie Bean, a collection of very impactful letters by survivors written to various body parts in a collective effort to bring themselves back together after trauma, to become whole once more. Along with the publication of Roxane Gay's stellar memoir *Hunger* that charts her own experiences with sexual violence, Gay came out with the beautifully-written anthology *Not That Bad: Dispatches from Rape Culture* (2018). This text offers a wide range of survivors' viewpoints and experiences as well, reaching a mass audience and becoming a *New York Times* best seller. More recently, we have seen *Drawing Power: A Comics Anthology* (2019) edited by Diane Noomin, with a foreword provided by Gay, a book that links survivors' stories to raw and haunting visuals. The intriguing collection *Indelible in the Hippocampus: Writings From the Me Too Movement* (2019) edited by Shelly Oria also includes the invaluable writings of survivors from a wide variety of backgrounds and with diverse experiences, sharing their thoughts through poetry, fiction, and essays.

In spite of these very important developments both in the socio-political sphere and within the writing world, as we have seen time and time again, at the very historical moments when survivors' voices seem to emerge with the greatest force, they have also sometimes been met with just as much if not more resistance. As Linda Martín Alcoff and I argued some years ago now in our essay "Survivor Discourse: Transgression or Recuperation," survivors' speech and writings have "great transgressive potential to disrupt the maintenance and reproduction of dominant discourses as well as to curtail their sphere of influence. Dominant discourses can also, however, subsume survivor speech in such a way as to disempower it and diminish its disruptive potential" (270). In that essay we asserted that survivors' discourses were sometimes being used against them, to attempt to undermine the expertise of their own experiences or to satiate the voyeuristic impulses of readers and viewers. It is when survivors exercise the disruptive potential of their own discourses and stories that survivors have the ability to challenge mainstream conceptions about gender and violence against women, we contended. However, simply privileging the suggestion that survivors speak out or share their stories is not enough since

> this formulation leaves unanalyzed the conditions of speaking and thus makes us too vulnerable to recuperative discursive arrangements. Before we speak we need to look at where the incitement to speak originates, what relations of power and domination may exist between those who incite and those who are asked to speak, as well as to whom the disclosure is directed. We must also struggle to maintain autonomy over the conditions of our speaking out if we are to develop its subversive potential. (284)

If we are to challenge typical formulations of a dominant rape culture and how survivors' speech and writings are taken up, we must consider who is asking us to share our stories, within what contexts, and with what potential political effects.

Today survivors' stories continue to be recuperated in very troubling ways by the mainstream media, academic institutions, and our larger culture. Too often survivors' voices have been rewritten, reorganized, and repackaged as things that are not to be taken seriously, as part of "he said, she said" situations, or as downright falsehoods. We find ourselves in a moment when white men in power—chief among them President Trump—would seek to reduce if not reject outright survivors' traumatic experiences so that they become little more than easily ignorable sound bites in the otherwise static-free, smooth, and inevitable rise of men's positions of power and prestige.

Like many other survivors of sexual violence, I have found the last few years to be rather difficult, at times simply frustrating and at times downright infuriating. Many of us who share such a background have felt powerless in the face of a culture that would seek to silence women's voices about their traumatic experiences at every turn. I am a survivor of a sexual assault perpetrated by a stranger while I was an undergraduate student attending Syracuse University. Early one November morning the perpetrator broke into the apartment I shared with two other women, opened the door to my room while I slept, and leapt hard onto my back. To this day I distinctly remember the smell of his leather jacket, the feeling of my hands clumsily searching around for my glasses in the dark as I tried to shake off my sleepiness. He repeatedly suffocated me with my pillow, stuffed my own sock in my mouth, bound my hands with cord, and held an object against my neck that he claimed was a knife. I would later learn that it was the sharp edge of a screwdriver. All of this time he threatened to kill me. I screamed against his blows to my cracked nose, my bruised cheeks, my bloodied lips. I screamed against the sock wedged in my mouth. I screamed into the pillow into which he kept pushing my face. My screams were swallowed by those cottony cloths. He raped me and sodomized me repeatedly in that terrible darkness. Lurching vomit rose in my stomach, chunks of spaghetti and sauce that I had hastily eaten the night before squeezing out from the sides of my sock. I came dangerously close to dying. For some period during this time I blacked out. During much of the assault I could barely breathe.

Unlike for many survivors, though he tried very hard to escape and broke various police officers' bones in the process, the rapist in my case was caught by the police in the act and at the scene. However, because he came from a well-connected, privileged family—he was the grandson of the President of the Board of Trustees at my university and his family owned the major employer in town, a company responsible for the university's famous sports arena—I had to fight hard to find justice. Throughout this process, I was also dissuaded from pursuing charges against him by a university administrator. In the end, he did serve jail time for his crime—eight years out of a seven- to twelve-year sentence. Today the same crimes would likely have resulted in a several decades-long sentence, attorneys have told me. And every year I had to write letters to a parole board to explain why he should not be released. I was desperately trying to finish my doctoral work at Syracuse University before he got out and moved back to the town where he was from, the very next town over.

I published my story in an award-winning memoir titled *College Girl*. Since then I have found myself traveling to many campuses to speak about issues of sexual violence, addressing how we can best honor survivors' experiences as well as navigate the difficult issues posed by Title IX reporting. Sexual violence remains one of the key experiences that has shaped my life as a person, as a woman, and as a scholar.

In the face of the many disturbing instances of the recuperation of survivors' voices, during these last months I determined that I wanted to bring to the fore a series of survivor stories that, I believe, have heretofore received far too little attention. As Clark and Pino's work especially makes clear, many who work in academic institutions are loath to really look closely at how sexual violence is rampant within our high schools, colleges, and universities. And, in those very rare moments when they do, students' voices alone have usually been highlighted. But many of our faculty members and administrators are also survivors of crimes of sexual violence. Too often we do not hear the stories of both female students and scholars who have experienced this kind of abuse either within or in connection to academic institutional contexts, and we have not typically heard about the ways in which they have tried to negotiate their complex identities within such spaces. In addition, when we do hear these voices, too often they can be somewhat decontextualized and not theorized in terms of larger social, cultural, and political issues.

Me Too, Feminist Theory, and Surviving Sexual Violence in the Academy gathers together a range of survivors' stories that are powerfully and creatively written as well as theoretically grounded. The chapters include analyses of the events that the survivors recall as well as their varied effects. These analyses are located within discussions of recent cultural events and larger contexts of race, ethnicity, class, age, gender, sexuality, region, and nation. Writers draw on research within various scholarly arenas including feminist, autobiographical, rhetorical, political, and sociological theories.

Me Too, Feminist Theory, and Surviving Sexual Violence in the Academy offers something unique. It is a volume produced within the contemporary Me Too movement moment in which survivors from various areas of academic culture—students, faculty, and administrators (and from across the academic disciplines)—describe their own personal experiences with various forms of sexual harassment and violence. Some writers in the book tell stories of growing up with sexual violence and then later learning to negotiate academic life. Some writers tell stories of sexual violence on their way to entering academic culture. Some writers tell stories of sexual violence within academic culture in both high school and college. Some writers tell stories of sexual violence that span from their childhoods through to their adulthoods. All of these writers provide superb examples of courageous writing and politics in action. And they work toward ending the cultural conditions that make sexual violence within and around academic institutions possible.

The book begins with a very significant chapter by Melinda Mills, "Seeing Through the Lens of Troublesome Tropes: Refusing to See Brown and Black Women as Victims of Sexual Violence." Mills is currently an Associate Professor of Women's and Gender Studies, Sociology, and Anthropology and Coordinator of Women's and Gender Studies at Castleton University as well as a Visiting Instructor in the Women's and Gender Studies Department at the University of South Florida. Mills's superb essay examines her experiences of sexual harassment in light of scholarship on the intersectionality of race and gender issues. Mills describes how various examples of sexual harassment in her workplace, the university, impacted her ability to function in her job, constantly undermining her sense of herself as a person and an intellectual. Mills situates her own experiences within larger historical and cultural contexts, describing how African-American women have historically been marginalized time and time again within the academy as well as in recent discussions around the Me Too movement. Meticulously researched and beautifully written, Mills's essay asks the reader to face her experiences of sexual violence as well as to address systemic power inequities related to race and gender in the academy that make such violence possible. Mills's piece indicates that the survivor voices of people of color are too often silenced, even by those very people who profess to consistently make room for them. Finally, Mills reveals that the costs of speaking out for women of color are often high indeed. The costs of losing female faculty of color to forms of sexual violence in the university workplace, she argues, need to be a greater part of everyone's consciousness. At every turn we must fight against this—for ourselves, for our students, and for the future integrity of academic institutions altogether.

Chapter 2, written by Ari Burford, is titled "My Grandfather Is Dying, Kavanaugh Just Got Appointed Supreme Court Justice, and I Should Probably Not Tell You These Stories." Burford is a Senior Lecturer in Women's and Gender Studies at Northern Arizona University who created a Queer Studies minor, and teaches a wide variety of courses on feminism, autobiography, and queer studies. In this exquisite essay, Burford tells the story of how they were raped by their grandfather, how they had to fight to have others in their life believe their story, and how they aid their students in telling their own stories of trauma and violence. Burford's essay is a study not just in making sense of experiences of sexual violence and theorizing about them but also in better understanding the intersectionality of violence against women, racism, and the colonizing of native lands. Burford explains the ways in which other stories of trauma and sexual violence, among them those experienced by many in the LGBTQ and Native American communities, have long been silenced in troubling ways. In the end, Burford's essay both powerfully interrogates and reveals what it really means to be a survivor—to choose to live in spite of those harrowing experiences that would seek to destroy us.

Lena Ziegler offers chapter 3, "A Revisionist History of Loving Men: Exploring Consent and Sexual Violence in Romantic Relationships." Ziegler is a doctoral candidate in Rhetoric and Writing Studies at Bowling Green State University. In her valuable essay, Ziegler traces her own history of the sexual violence she experienced in a number of romantic relationships and the various ways in which men force women they know to endure trauma repeatedly. She also takes the reader through her experience of being raped by a stranger. The essay grapples with the various truths around sexual violence as well as the ways in which our rape culture encourages women to think of some forms of sexual violence as more "real" than other forms. Ziegler also invites the reader to reconsider the meanings of terms like "consent" and how they presuppose a binary yes/no configuration when consent is actually a far more complicated issue. Toward her conclusion, she explains that contextualizing our stories is absolutely fundamental. And Ziegler suggests that in telling her various stories of sexual violence now, she is writing herself and her experiences more fully into being.

Hélène Bigras-Dutrisac, a doctoral candidate in the department of Women's Studies and Feminist Research at the University of Western Ontario, provides chapter 4, "'I Don't Know What's Real and What's Not': How Journaling Helped Me Cope with Trauma." In this thoughtful chapter, Bigras-Dutrisac makes the argument that journals focusing on traumatic experiences such as sexual violence can be deeply empowering for their female writers. Utilizing contemporary theory about autobiography and journal writing as well as her own experiences with sexual violence, Bigras-Dutrisac takes the reader on a reflective journey through her own journals as she tries to make sense of the sexual assaults and other forms of violence that she endured from her boyfriend while she was an undergraduate student. She also uses these reflections to theorize about as well as to build a fuller life and identity beyond those experiences. In the end, Bigras-Dutrisac's essay advocates that such journal writing can be an essential step toward making structural changes in our patriarchal culture that challenge violence against women in all of its forms.

"Jailbait: At the Intersection of Teenage Desire and Statutory Rape" by Marissa Korbel is chapter 5. Korbel now works as a public interest attorney, supporting campus and minor sexual assault survivors. However, Korbel's crucial essay is about adolescent female desire, about the cultural taboos against expressing it, and about men—especially teachers—who objectify and take further advantage of girls and young women. Korbel's essay traces her early interactions with older men online—both her fascination with older men and the ways in which she was exploited by them. In particular, she describes her sexual experiences with one older male teacher. Her positions on mandatory reporting are complex. She understands why it is valuable and believes that it saved her. And it is a key part of the important work she now does in the world. Yet Korbel also reveals that the experiences she had with mandatory reporting were themselves deeply traumatic. While what she experienced was labeled statutory rape, she also believes that it was in some ways consensual, making the experiences she had all the more confusing. Moving between feminist theory and research on female desire, Korbel provides an intimate portrait of the complicated issues surrounding girls' embodied desires, uneven power relations between males and females, and gender-based sexual violence. While her teacher was ultimately fired and prosecuted for statutory rape, Korbel's story indicates that surviving sexual violence can mean different things to different people and that the erasure and policing of girls' sexuality is a key, often uninterrogated part of the equation.

Sally J. Kenney offers chapter 6, "Does Any Woman Have Just One Survivor Story? One Vagina's Monologue." Among other posts, Kenney holds the Newcomb College Endowed Chair at Tulane University and is a Professor of Political Science. However, her path to get there was extremely difficult. As she notes, she is the survivor of various crimes of sexual violence, including "sex discrimination, sexual harassment, domestic violence, sexual assault, abandonment, and bullying" (see page 105 of this book). Kenney's important chapter leads the reader through a set of different experiences she has had—including being harassed by her mother's boyfriend, a very controlling, "Dirty John"-type person. Her essay also addresses much contemporary literature and theory about sexual violence. But at the center of

Kenney's powerful narrative is one story that is especially difficult to tell and that she addresses only toward the end of her piece—her sexual abuse by her father. She describes how tremendously difficult it is to love and respect a person who also abuses you. Kenney closes her piece with a call to action for all survivors, indicating that now is the time for revolution.

Chapter 7 is "Survival Stories: Transforming Terror to Power" by Lynn Z. Bloom. Lynn Z. Bloom is the Emerita Board of Trustees Distinguished Professor and Aetna Chair of Writing at the University of Connecticut and has taught autobiography, creative nonfiction, and rhetoric for many years. In this dynamic essay, Bloom tells the story of her narrow escape from a would-be rapist years ago. She then explains how she teaches texts that represent sexual violence in her courses and addresses some of the positives and negatives of bringing these materials into the classroom environment. Bloom also offers decisive suggestions for how survivors might beneficially narrate their own experiences to others through speech and writing.

Katrina M. Powell gives us chapter 8, "Layers: Academia, Autobiography, and Narrative as Refuge and Struggle." Powell is now a professor of rhetoric and writing and former director of Women's and Gender Studies. In this intriguing piece, Powell offers the reader an Appendix that details twenty-four instances in her life during which she experienced sexual harassment and violence. This powerful list makes clear that events of sexual violence are pervasive in many women's lives and that each one emerges within a certain context and set of circumstances. As just one example, Powell details her assault while attending the United States Air Force Academy. She outlines how studying and teaching rhetorical theory, feminist theory, and autobiography helped her to make sense of her own experiences. Though Powell had been concerned about sharing her story, her students' own courage in telling their stories propelled her to do so. In the end, Powell's chapter relays the various difficulties of telling one's story and the various reasons one might choose to tell as well as not to do so.

In chapter 9, Tanya Serisier offers an essay titled "Speaking Out, Public Judgments, and Narrative Politics: Researching Survivor Stories and (Not) Telling My Own." Serisier is a senior lecturer in Criminology at Birkbeck College, University of London. While Serisier has published very well-regarded research on the subject of sexual violence before, she has never told her own story. In this very thoughtful piece she details her own experiences of sexual violence when she was an undergraduate student and how they have informed her research as well as how she theorizes about survivors sharing their stories. Drawing on works such as Roxane Gay's *Not That Bad: Dispatches from Rape Culture*, Serisier makes the case that in order to fully acknowledge the value of survivors' narratives, we also need to read such narratives within the contexts of survivors' larger lives and other experiences. In addition, we must seek to examine these stories within the broader discursive structures that in fact make them possible.

Chapter 10 is written by Donna L. Potts and titled "Professing to Power." Now a professor and chair of the English Department at Washington State University, where she teaches Irish literature, in this wonderful essay Potts recounts her various experiences with sexual violence. In particular, she describes how she was raped as an undergraduate student by her German professor around the very same time that her father had committed suicide. Vulnerable and afraid, her rapist forced her into silence, a silence that she began breaking as she made her way through graduate school and eventually became a professor. During this time she was also trafficked by a boyfriend who facilitated her gang rape by a group of men, further traumatizing her and resulting in yet greater levels of PTSD. Joining together her thoughts on feminist theory, her analyses of other survivors' testimonies and experiences, as well as her teaching on Irish Literature and Trauma, Potts presents a beautifully written and carefully theorized piece that exposes the insidious nature of all forms of sexual harassment and violence, especially those that occur within universities. Since Potts is herself a survivor of a college rape and now is a professor, she is in a position to offer a thorough critique of how survivors' language is often taken up within such contexts.

Chapter 11, "Beaches, Books, Baseball, and Being One of the Guys," is written by a doctoral candidate at the University of California, San Diego, Katherine Chelsea, whose experiences of sexual violence are relatively recent. Chelsea's gorgeously written piece tells her own experiences of rape, taking the reader not only into what she went through but also her struggles with the medical establishment that followed the assault. She also traces the various triggers that she has experienced as a graduate student, explaining the ways in which reading literature about rape has become crucial to her in her recovery. She describes how the Me Too movement has also impacted her reactions to what happened to her. Chelsea then details how she finally sought solace and comfort in playing baseball, only to be raped again, this time by one of her teammates, a person she trusted. Chelsea closes by indicating that she is still very much healing from her two experiences of sexual assault. Still, she chooses to embrace life and to not be defined by these experiences alone.

Chapter 12, "The Past Is Always Present: Social Media and Survival," is written by Lee Skallerup Bessette. Bessette's insightful piece takes the reader into the world of social media, a world that she is very skilled at negotiating as a Learning Design Specialist at the Center for New Designs in Learning and Scholarship (CNDLS) at Georgetown University and a professional blogger for *Inside Higher Ed* and *ProfHacker*. She describes how she found an identity and a purpose working within social media platforms only to be contacted by a previous boyfriend who had raped her. Bessette explains the difficulties that come with naming "rape" as "rape" when one is in a relationship with that person. She also reveals the ways in which her experiences of sexual violence have impacted her teaching. In the end, Bessette champions the fact that women are now using social media as a place to share their voices and to gain empowerment. Bessette also argues that we must change the cultural conditions that make sexual violence possible if we are ever to begin to eradicate it.

Chapter 13 is "Claiming Conclusively: Speaking Back to Campus Title IX" by Courtney Cox. Cox is currently a doctoral student. In this compelling chapter, she reveals that her undergraduate advisor in Anthropology sexually harassed her. She tells the story of deciding to come forward with her story as well as the ways in which Title IX both helped and hindered her ability to share her experiences. She also explains the ways in which her experiences with sexual violence and being involved in a Title IX report changed the trajectory of her academic life. Her essay moves deftly between theorizations about trauma and sexual violence and her own experiences. In the end, Cox reveals that while Title IX reporting has been valuable in some ways, we need not turn to Title IX and its various mandates alone as ways to make sense of our experiences of trauma. Instead, we should search out many diverse ways to speak out.

Taken together, these survivor stories weave within, around, and through academic culture decisively, overtly challenging those dominant cultural discourses that would seek to recuperate, co-opt, or silence them. These survivor stories provide windows into how sexual violence in all of its forms invariably impacts the lives of those who experience it, undermining our senses of ourselves and our abilities to function and succeed in this world. Finally, these survivor stories stand as a testament to the fact that together survivors are radically changing the discussion about sexual violence within our culture.

Right here.
Right now.
This is *our time*.

NOTE

1. *Me Too, Feminist Theory, and Surviving Sexual Violence in the Academy* does not focus a great deal on male student or faculty experiences of survivorship. While such stories are absolutely crucial, they also deserve their own full attention. One especially noteworthy book published in recent years about such concerns is Raymond M. Douglas's text *On Being Raped*. Written by a male professor who shares his experiences of sexual violence, it is truly a must-read for anyone concerned with male survivor experiences and issues.

REFERENCES

Alcoff, Linda Martín. 2018. *Rape and Resistance*. Cambridge: Polity Press.
———, and Laura Gray-Rosendale. 1993. "Survivor Discourse: Transgression or Recupera-tion?" *Signs: Journal of Women in Culture and Society* 18 (2): 260–290.
Bean, Lexie, ed. 2018. *Written on the Body: Letters from Trans and Non-Binary Survivors of Sexual Assault and Domestic Violence*. London: Jessica Kingsley Publishers.
Clark, Annie and Andrea Pino. 2016. *We Believe You: Survivors of Campus Sexual Assault Speak Out*. New York: Holt Paperbacks.
Douglas, Raymond M. 2016. *On Being Raped*. Boston: Beacon Press.
Freitas, Donna. 2018. *Consent on Campus: A Manifesto*. London: Oxford University Press.
Gay, Roxane. 2018. *Hunger: A Memoir of (My) Body*. New York: Harper Perennial.
———, ed. 2018. *Not That Bad: Dispatches from Rape Culture*. New York: Harper Perennial.
Gray-Rosendale, Laura. 2014. *College Girl: A Memoir*. Albany: SUNY Press.
Grigoriadis, Vanessa. 2017. *Blurred Lines: Rethinking Sex, Power, and Consent on Campus*. New York: Eamon Dolan/Houghton Mifflin Harcourt.
Harding, Kate. 2015. *Asking for It: The Alarming Rise of Rape Culture—and What We Can Do About It*. Boston: Da Capo Lifelong Books.
Hillstrom, Laurie Collier. 2018. *The #MeToo Movement*. Santa Barbara: ABC-CLIO.
Harris, Jessica C. and Chris Linder, eds. 2017. *Intersections of Identity and Sexual Violence on Campus: Centering Minoritized Students' Experiences*. Sterling: Stylus.
Kantor, Jodi and Megan Twohey. 2019. *She Said: Breaking the Sexual Harassment Story That Helped Ignite a Movement*. New York: Penguin Press.
Krakauer, Jon. 2015. *Missoula: Rape and the Justice System in a College Town*. New York: Knopf Doubleday.
Moulton, Erin, ed. 2018. *Things We Haven't Said: Sexual Assault Survivors Speak Out*. Minne-apolis: Zest Books TM.
Noomin, Diane, ed. 2019. Foreword by Roxane Gay. *Drawing Power: A Comics Anthology*. New York: Harry N. Abrams.
Oliver, Kelly. 2017. *Hunting Girls: Sexual Violence from the Hunger Games to Campus Rape*. New York: Columbia University Press.
Oria, Shelly, ed. 2019. *Indelible in the Hippocampus: Writings From the Me Too Movement*. San Francisco: McSweeney's Publishing.
Patterson, Jennifer, ed. 2016. *Queering Sexual Violence: Radical Voices from Within the Anti-Violence Movement*. Riverdale: Riverdale Avenue Books.
Perkins, Lori. 2017. *#MeToo: Essays About How and Why This Happened, What It Means, and How to Make Sure It Never Happens Again*. Riverdale: Riverdale Avenue Books.
Warshaw, Robyn. 2019. Foreword by Gloria Steinem. *I Never Called It Rape*. New York: Harper Perennial.
Wooten, Sara Carrigan and Roland W. Mitchell, eds. 2015. *The Crisis of Campus Sexual Violence: Critical Perspectives on Prevention and Response*. New York: Routledge.

Chapter One

Seeing Through the Lens of Troublesome Tropes

Refusing to See Brown and Black Women as Victims of Sexual Violence

Melinda Mills

"You're gorgeous."

—White male senior colleague, to me

"If I was a student, I would want to date you."

—White male senior colleague, to me

The "MeToo" Movement was first introduced as a MySpace hashtag by Tarana Burke. Over the last decade, the movement has built momentum, extending its reach, as advocates, survivors, and/or allies have joined the fight for social justice. Finally, analyses of sexual violence within academia are within reach, facilitating a critical interrogation of the once ivory tower. In this essay, I discuss how academic institutions—while slow to change—have become more (but still minimally) diverse. Such diversity, however small and significant, has been met with mixed reactions.

As the quotes above allude to, academia remains, for many black women, a space of intellectual inquiry *and* hostility, a place where people can enact violence or exercise their "power over" as a means of maintaining hierarchies and shaping black women's experiences much differently than their white colleagues (see Houston 2015; Prois and Moreno 2018). This essay reckons with academic rape culture and the violence I encountered and experienced therein. It speaks to patterns of disappearing and/or silencing, black women.

IN THE ACADEMY

By extension, this essay explores the forces that facilitate and encourage the silencing of black and brown women faculty in the academy. It considers the way in which educational institutions create and/or reproduce oppression, often tokenizing experiences for its multiply marginalized faculty (see hooks 1984). Typically, educational institutions enjoy the benefits of faculty bodies with intersectional identities that symbolize "diversity" (Ahmed 2012).

Yet, universities neglect to fully protect faculty from any real or imagined threats to their humanity (Rankine 2014), productivity, vitality (Maparyan 2011), longevity, and/or sustainability (Muñoz 1999) personally or professionally speaking (Delgado 1982). Educational institutions, with programs and policies to respond to sexualized violence and harassment, also enable assaultive conditions (Matsuda 1993). These conditions adversely impact underrepresented faculty, protect perpetrators, and uphold systems and social environments that remain not only uninviting but hostile to black and brown women faculty (Ahmed 2012).

Within *academic* rape culture (Buchwald, Fletcher, and Roth 2005), black and brown women faculty are seen as "public texts" (Holloway 2011), our bodies regarded tenuously, positive yet problematic. Our bodies signal our traumatic, if applauded, entrance into and presence within the academy (Walters et al. 2011). Historically, black women's bodies have been sexually assaulted, exploited for reproduction (Hesse-Biber and Carter 2005), scientific research, medical experimentation, and a number of other nefarious reasons (Roberts 1998). Denied privacy, bodily autonomy, and freedom, black women have "coded social identities that have an embedded vulnerability" (Holloway 2011, 8). The vulnerabilities black women experience differ from those that people generally experience, primarily because of the "public unveiling," or surveillance and spectacularity surrounding black bodies in general, and black women's bodies specifically. In the United States, Holloway posits, "the bodies of women and blacks are always and already public" (2001, 15).

Other scholars agree. Consider the work of Sharlene Hesse-Biber and Gregg Carter who describe the "double oppression" that enslaved black women faced in Southern colonies—"exploited not only as workers but as breeders of slaves" (2005, 24). The legacy of slavery, that "peculiar institution," persists in society and the academy. The "double jeopardy" (Beal 1971) of being black and a woman means managing gendered racism (Essed 1991), or sexism, racism, or other interlocking oppressions (Collins 1991).

A HISTORY AND LEGACY OF HATE

The legacy of slavery is evidenced in the persistent (mis)treatment of black women in the US. Black women are at greater risk of violence in society. Not only have black women been denied typical patriarchal protections offered to women (categorically speaking), they have also faced various forms of violence. Dominant (racist, hetero/sexist) logic has accommodated, if not normalized and encouraged, white men's physical, sexualized violence toward black women. Thus, the historical sexual and corporal exploitation of black women left a residue—of violence, hatred, and misogyny—specific to them. That is, black women experience "misogynoir" (see Bailey 2017), a racialized misogyny (or hatred of women) that is *specific* to black women.

In the academy, the "misogynoiristic" dynamics are expansive, nebulous, and dangerous to black women faculty (Hanson and Richards 2019) who are deemed "out of place" and in need of being "kept in our place" (Epstein 1997). Academic misogynoir feeds on ideas about black women's bodies as "public," abject, inhumane even. Black women experience the deleterious effects partially through the university's very refusal to acknowledge misogynoir. Seldom, too, do they acknowledge the continuing significance of race and racism (Feagin 1991; Thompson-Miller and Feagin 2014); (hetero)sexism; and patriarchy. The consequent and nefarious entanglements often get little recognition, much less serious consideration.

Within and beyond the academy, many black women get entangled in what I call the "web of violence." The web exposes them to violence across time and space. Black women are violently victimized in various settings, including the street, schools, and their homes (Jones 2008; McGuire 2010; Nash, S. 2005; O'Toole, Schiffman, and Kiter Edwards 2007; Roberts 1998; Smith, Huppuch, and van Deven 2011). In historical and contemporary moments, black and brown women who leave the (presumed) protection of the domestic sphere (private spaces designated for them) risk injury and compromise their own safety. Consider the 1950s, when black women encountered harassment and violence largely from white men agitated by black women's use of public transportation (McGuire 2010). Buses facilitated black women's road to freedom, offering them mobility, not only geographically (from home to work), but often socioeconomically (from insecurity/precarity to stability).

During this time, heightened racial tensions, coupled with emergent and convergent social movements, meant that many white people were feeling increased anxiety and hostility toward black people. Black women bore the brunt of much of this animosity. White men who assaulted, harassed, and/or raped black women terrorized them; used violence and force to punish black women for stepping out of line; and wanted to regulate black women.

In their attempts to lead autonomous lives, preserve their "bodily integrity" (McGuire 2010, 77), and walk "in dignity and pride" (95), black women "demanded that they be treated like human beings worthy of protection and respect" (95). The racialized and gendered aggression and violence they faced operated as a form of social control, an attempt to maintain racial and gender boundaries, to continue tracking, regulating, and disciplining black bodies.

Not only did black women face this violence in public spaces and with regard to public accommodations. They also experienced it in both informal and formal workplaces where they labored. When the academy is the workplace, what are the experiences of black women faculty? The question rhetorically suggests that black women, as typical targets, will likely not escape the effects of any violence that lives there (as expressed individually and/or embedded institutionally). The question suggests the difficulty in confronting and even encountering sexual assault and harassment in the academy. The various *other* sites of violence black women experience compound this challenge.

An exploration of and reflection upon the ways in which black women experience sexual assault and harassment in the academy also reveals a different iteration of violence: silence. In my experience, "the silence of violence" included a refusal to reasonably respond to my accounts of encountering questionable behavior by male colleagues twenty-plus years my senior. Thus, this essay operates as an intervention, a way of naming violence that is not always nor necessarily life-threatening, but rather soul-crushing, distracting, depleting, exhausting, and stunning (especially in terms of the aforementioned silence). In writing this work, I acknowledge, and potentially disrupt institutional, and even individual, impulses to ignore black and brown women, and the violent conditions in which we labor. Next, I explore the statistical reality of marginality of black women in the academy, first by presenting a broader view and then drilling down into some particularities.

MANAGING MARGINALITY AS AN OUTSIDER WITHIN THE ACADEMY

Educational institutions have a history of exclusion and selective inclusion. Nationally, the disproportionate number of white faculty speaks to the centrality of whiteness in academia and reflects broader patterns of white hegemony or dominance in society. Consider, for example, that, in 2016, among the 1.5 million faculty members, white men constituted the majority of full-time faculty (US Department of Education, National Center for Education Statistics 2018). Under 20 percent of these positions were occupied by faculty members of color, with black women accounting for 2 percent of full-time professors, and multiracial people (or individuals of two or more races) constituting about 1 percent of full-time faculty (NCES 2018). Based on these data, higher education institutions reflect racial and gender inequality in relation to rank. Far more white males and females are present at all ranks. The ratio of white faculty to black faculty is about 10:1, while that of white faculty to multiracial faculty is about 35:1.

Dr. Adia Harvey Wingfield corroborates these data. In asking, "Where are black women sociologists today?" this sociologist draws attention to the scant number of African Americans (about 6 percent) who earn doctorates in the discipline (only 31 went to black women in 2016) (Wingfield 2019). The view of tenure-track and tenured faculty is no more encouraging, with black women constituting less than 5 percent of faculty (of any rank) (Wingfield 2019). That the numbers dwindle as doctorates in Sociology enter the tenure-track in pursuit of tenure and promotion suggests that faculty of other racial groups 1) are less likely to have black women faculty colleagues (at any rank) at their respective institutions, and 2) by extension, are arguably less hospitable to them.

Increasingly, many black women faculty report experiencing marginalization, even misrecognition and invalidation. Some misrecognition can arguably appear "complimentary," with others mistaking or misreading black women faculty as students. Rather than being viewed as highly trained experts with specialized knowledge in their respective discipline/s, black women faculty are "presumed incompetent" (Gutierrez y Muhs, Niemann, Gonzalez, and Harris 2012), read as unqualified or lacking the requisite credentials typically needed to meet the basic criteria for their faculty positions. They are denied authority as credible intellectuals or the status and prestige associated with their esteemed professorships. Black women are viewed through a distorted lens (Harris-Perry 2012) that ignores, diminishes, or altogether dismisses their expertise (that which was likely hard-won in the process of securing the requisite advanced degree/s).

Given their dearth, the presence of an absence of black women faculty can be felt in the halls of academia by students of color seeking representations and role models who mirror/approximate them; such students likely find few faculty that fit. The consistently disproportionate faculty ratios reflect gendered racism and other structural oppressions/inequities. The national faculty body fails to reflect 1) the student body, with black women graduating at historically high numbers, according to Reeves and Guyot (2017) and 2) the broader society, with its increasingly diverse population predicted to soon become a majority minority nation (Toppo and Overberg 2014).

WAYS OF SEEING BLACK WOMEN IN THE ACADEMY

Many double-edged swords exist regarding ways of seeing black women faculty. Building on Collins's "controlling images" work (1991), feminist scholars Aimee Marie Cox (2015) and Jennifer Nash (2019) explore some of the persistent, or "enduring," troublesome tropes of black and brown women. In *Shapeshifters*, Cox argues that our national fears get "projected onto Black women and actualized through the discursive and material control of their bodies" (2015, 56). Black women are viewed as partial subjects or social citizens, abject, always already "not" women, denied their humanity and feared for being "freaks, gold diggers, divas" (Stephens and Phillips 2003). In her book *Black Feminism Reimagined*, Jennifer Nash further engages controlling images to illustrate the double-sided ways black women are dis/regarded in the academy.

Nash's work explores the complexities and contradictions of black women serving the academy in material, ideological, and symbolic ways. To the latter point, Nash argues that within the field of Women Studies "the symbol of black woman is incessantly called upon to perform intellectual, political, and affective service work in women's studies and across the university" (2019, 15). Consequently, black women are not taken seriously, their contributions neglected or taken for granted, their experiential heterogeneity flattened. In this way, black women academics signal progress (inclusion), symbolic evidence of remedied problems ("past" exclusions). This "illusion of inclusion" obscures how the academy (and society) denies black women faculty full citizenship.

THE COSTS OF ADMISSION

What are the costs of being a black woman in the academy? Research indicates that the costs "of being included" can be high for certain groups, especially women of color (Ahmed 2012; see also Gutierrez y Muhs et al. 2012; Martin 2016). This research speaks to the harsh realities faculty of color face. These scholars challenge the idea that institutional initiatives of *aspirational* inclusion create *actual* experiences of inclusion.

A significant cost of being included is workplace harassment. Uggen and Blackstone argue, "Sexual harassment can serve as an equalizer against women in power, motivated more by control and domination than by sexual desire. Interviews point to social isolation as a mechanism linking harassment to gender non-conformity and women's authority, particularly in male-dominated work settings" (2012, 625). Workplace harassment is the impetus for many women targets to change jobs within a few years (post-incidence) (see McLaughlin et al. 2017).

Itself a social institution, higher education sets its own price of admission. For black women faculty, being present in educational spaces not designed with them in mind increases their precarity and vulnerability. Sara Ahmed, the aforementioned feminist scholar, speaker, and activist, acknowledged these points in a keynote address at a National Women's Studies conference a few years ago. There, as well as in her book *On Being Included*, Ahmed (2012) has candidly discussed the ways in which institutional dynamics perpetuate violence while protecting its perpetrators from repercussions. She, among other feminists, attempts not only to narrate, but document and ideally dismantle, the deleterious effects of the university on women of color. For example, Ahmed writes about the extent to which educational institutions nominally advocate diversity and inclusivity, yet undermine or oppose these efforts or initiatives. One of Ahmed's interviewees notes, "'[N]ot everyone has an interest in equity and diversity issues" (2012, 30). Ahmed's work is about the price of admission, and the costs of fighting for these institutional goals or aspirations. She suggests, "[D]iversity workers must be persistent" in their efforts to transform institutions but that there is a catch: "The more you persist, the more the signs of resistance. The more resistance, the more persistence is required" (30).

If black women in the academy (not necessarily solely within the disciplines of Sociology and Women's and Gender Studies) are seen as "diversity workers," they come to symbolize some accomplishment aligned with that aspiration. That is, the mere presence of black women in the academy, irrespective of their actual areas of expertise, training, and/or interest in these institutional aspirations, signals "diversity." The dilemma of this disinterest is that black women are generally disallowed this decision, and by default, are implicitly or explicitly expected to take on this work. Our bodies are "marked" in this way, as always already "diverse" and ourselves as not only naturally interested in, but capable of, diversity work.

Following Ahmed's point, then, people who are resistant to the sort of institutional aspirations of diversity, inclusivity, and equity (or processes that require change), will be, by extension, potentially and/or actually resistant to the people who signal that change, those processes, and that transformative potential. Consequently, many black women face a variety of injuries and indignities in academic workplaces, their everyday realities often vastly different than those of their colleagues. Wingfield describes some of the challenges that tenured and tenure-track black women encounter in predominantly white institutions, including the following:

> [M]arginalization, micro (or macro) aggressions, difficulties finding mentors and sponsors who can facilitate their career advancement. As academics, black women professors also must confront colleagues' tendencies to denigrate or dismiss their research (this is particularly present in the inclination to label

work that focuses on race and/or gender as "me"search). There are also the
heavy service burdens that come with being underrepresented, ranging from
mentoring students of color to helping universities resolve their issues with
diversity and inclusion. (2019)

Wingfield's observations speak to a variety of ways in which black wom-
en face invalidation, hostility, the devaluation of themselves and their work,
and other obstacles in the social environment that suggest their presence is
provocative and problematic at best, and unappreciated and undesired at
worst. How might black women faculty be seen and regarded differently
within predominantly white institutions, where these women largely remain
ignored, marginalized, and silenced? When seen and/or heard, black women
are often viewed through dominant and distorted frames. Nash notes,

> Indeed, black feminist theory has a long history of *both* tracking the violence
> the university has inflicted on black female academics (often by demanding
> black women's labor) *and* advocating for institutional visibility and legibility.
> While black feminists have long traced the violence of the university, few have
> advocated for abandoning the institutional project of black feminism, despite
> long-standing and widely circulating texts theorizing how the academy quite
> literally cannibalizes black women, extracts their labor, and renders invisible
> the work they perform to establish fields. (2019, 16)

Yet, in many ways, black women's presence in educational institutions is
indeed shapeshifting, through the offering of enriching educational experiences for students; the generation of innovative ideas and knowledge production; a continuation of service that proves rewarding but feels exhausting and
frequently gets diminished, overlooked, and eventually normalized, at their
expense. That is, the university visits violence upon black women's bodies,
while making false promises (much like any abusive relationship) about its
"capacity to be remade, reimagined, or reinvented in ways that will do less
violence to black feminist theory and black feminists' bodies" (Nash 2019,
16). Next, I explore the impact of these effects on my own experience.

DISAPPEARING DANGEROUS WOMEN

As a black feminist practicing black feminism and teaching various aspects
of black feminisms to my students in related courses, I contend that my
experience within the university feels very much like Nash's narration. Here
I explore some of the frictions I felt as a black biracial sociologist doing
black feminist work in the academy. I engage Nash's idea that black women
(feminist) faculty are simultaneously viewed as a threat (an anomaly, outside,
outlier) and are curiously concurrently devalued and dismissed. In the latter
view, members of the dominant group may disparage black feminism and its

practitioners, devalue our labor, and deny us opportunities to feel included, to be recognized as meaningful and important members of a university community, and to be celebrated for our often tireless efforts to improve conditions for everyone. They may exploit, tokenize, and/or objectify us; then, they rely upon whatever discursive strategies facilitate the denial of their actions (to exploit, tokenize, objectify . . .). Through these discourses, they can make our bodies ones that matter (or not), and they can make our labor in/conveniently dis/appear.

What does it mean to be considered endangered and dangerous at once? To remain relatively unseen, invisible in most social contexts in your workplace environment, to have colleagues deny that the reality you choose to narrate actually exists even as they experience the social world completely differently? What does it mean to feel endangered, to look around your university at the senior faculty and search for faces that resemble your own, or mirror your race and gender, only to find a few at first, and then eventually none? What does it mean to know that your presence on a predominantly white campus in an almost exclusively white state makes you feel endangered and in danger? What does it mean to expect to be seen as dangerous but seldom to be sincerely seen otherwise?

As a feminist sociologist, I have become familiar with the troublesome tropes and discursive practices generated, circulated, and upheld by the dominant group. I have come to understand that what is truly troublesome about these tropes is their inaccuracy and their persistence. For the dominant group, the discourses that they develop can be more dangerous than the misperception of black women as dangerous or threatening.

Throughout my professional career, I have learned how to manage these potential views, to find ways to mitigate the adverse impact of being viewed as dangerous, scary, or angry (Wingfield 2007). In my training, I have learned to examine social worlds and interrogate social inequalities. I have researched topics close enough to my lived experience to be considered "me-search." This topic is no different.

ON BEING HARASSED

Despite my own extensive research on the topic of (street) harassment, I never anticipated experiencing harassment in academia, or at least in the ways that it surfaced. It began when I was a graduate student, with the casual flirtations of men my senior. These men engaged in this flirtation with such ease and nonchalance that at first I questioned whether their intention was at all malicious. A charming kind of harassment? This was new. The kind that I was used to, or at least encountered more frequently, was much easier to recognize: a loud shout here, a quick compliment there, but always outside, on the street or the sidewalk. This kind of harassment was public, for others to witness, if they wanted, or to ignore altogether.

But the kind of harassment that I would continue to experience over the course of my early career had a gentler tone, which made it harder to detect, obtuse enough to feel curiously tangible and elusive. I brushed aside the incidents that occurred in graduate school, because, after all, "I was *just* a graduate student," not yet a real person, as Tressie McMillan Cottom writes in her new book, *Thick*: "Graduate students are not people. In the academic hierarchy, graduate students are units of labor. They can be students, but not just students. They are academics in the making. They do not have any claim to authority among scholars. In fact, the most surefire way to get a real, minted academic to speak to you when you are just a graduate student is to introduce yourself by proxy" (2019, 160–61). For me, the rub was that I felt just as Cottom described, largely insignificant in the structural scheme of things, relevant mostly through my working relationship with my dissertation chair.

If I extend the logic stemming from Cottom's experiences (ones that feel incredibly familiar, I might add), graduate students who are regarded as "not" people may run the risk of *never* being regarded as people. The sobering history of black people's humanity being denied, coupled with graduate school status and social locations regarded as "not human," followed me to Vermont where I took my first tenure-track position. In the chase toward tenure, I hustled hard to win the respect of my colleagues, and ultimately, tenure. I did as many things as humanly possible, and then some. I introduced new classes, taught during the interim between the fall and spring semesters, worked to create a major program, served on multiple search committees, secured a book contract by my tenure year, and published said book at the start of the following year.

Yet none of those accomplishments or acts of service would buffer me from the "benevolent" sexism and racism I would experience while there: the intrusive questions about my personal life; the seemingly perpetual reference to my physical appearance, as well as the apparent *difference* of my appearance (the thinly veiled reminder of my status as a racial outsider, "not a Vermonter," and the like). There was also the unwanted but glaringly positive attention elicited from my effective performance of emphasized femininity (a patriarchal bargain, or act which I engaged in, ironically enough, as a strategy for minimizing said attention and harassment, and that resulted in *heightened* attention and attendant celebration of my conformity to these expectations).

Relatedly, casual "compliments" came from some white men in powerful leadership positions on campus (and in the community); they enthusiastically congratulated me on my appearance (of emphasized femininity) as opposed to any of my scholarly publications or accomplishments. One of these men made other inappropriate comments (to the tune of "I'd much rather be your complexion than mine"). I found these comments exoticizing and fetishizing, the conversational dynamics concerning, given him openly discussing with me the aesthetic appeal of the color of my skin, immediately outside of my office, in our workplace.

The same individual (a white male senior colleague) who made this observation that mine was, in his interpretation, such a lovely shade of brown, in contrast to his own self-described pale skin, also did not hesitate on multiple occasions to offer variations of these sorts of comments and personal observations. In fact, he once used the conditional sentence ("if you and I were dating") made at one of the monthly faculty meetings. The gist of the comment involved casual reference to a theoretical possibility that did not seem at all possible *under any circumstances*, which is perhaps why it felt so startling. There was no apparent understanding of the potential discomfort this might provoke for me. Perhaps that was the point.

The comment felt so callous and jarring to me in its presumptive coolness and indifference to my feelings. Innocuous words, really, just a thought. Nothing actually between us but an idea, a mere suggestion or *mention* of an idea. Yet the idea loomed, not so much as a threat or directive, but more of a menace or nuisance. Here, a white man attempted to assert whatever power he could through traditional expressions of masculinity: interactional violence in an institutional setting (Kaufman 2007). The toxicity was suffocating (Kimmel 2009), the speaker so comfortable in his efforts to entertain, connect, or communicate with me (perhaps to demonstrate his ability to relate to people of color) that he never registered his words as weapons—unjust, injurious. He never would have understood his behavior as harassment. Any efforts to prove himself not racist and/or sexist failed in that moment. His comments clearly felt racialized and gendered, supported within systems of power asymmetries that silenced me and emboldened him.

In response, I sat in silence, weighing my options carefully. I would go up for tenure in a few short years. I could make a big deal about it, or I could play along, "go with the joke." Perhaps I could participate in the romanticized or "sexualized camaraderie" (Lerum 2004) for kicks? If I chose the former, I might risk ever winning tenure. If I chose the latter, I might appear appealing for different reasons, pliable, "easy to get along with," or any of the other invisible criteria especially requisite for the handful of people of color who become faculty members, and certainly for those seeking tenure (Gay 2017). Speaking up, ironically, might have meant losing my voice in other ways (i.e., tenure denial). That is, the academy accommodates questions of a personal nature from a man positioned with attendant privileges; when I began to ask a lot of questions about the process of protection from others, including said senior colleague, I was the one shushed and silenced, explicitly directed to consider his privileged position (individually and institutionally) as a tenured white male senior colleague (McIntosh 1998). I was effectively asked to anticipate the cost of speaking truth to power. I registered these conversations as the way universities 1) protect perpetrators and 2) gesture to potential "retaliation" as a distraction from always already existing violence. That various institutional members framed said violence *in the future* meant that repercussions would *likely* follow; this tactic worked to silence me. If speaking up about *in the now* violence would *amplify* violence visited upon me, not speaking up might mean that I risk losing (or at least severely eroding) my integrity, shrinking my voice, under the guise of complicity. This was a lose-lose situation for me.

What I learned in the moments when I encountered harassment is that those moments are sticky. They linger. They have a long shelf life, as they can take up a lot of mental space, require psychic energy. And those moments also thread together. They weave into the web of violence made up of various incidents, here, there, maybe everywhere. They connect both within and across settings, not stopping at the halls of the academy, but taking on a particular sound and shape there. They make work difficult, and taking your senior colleagues seriously even more challenging. They permeate the spaces where you try to think for a living, and they inhabit your mind and body. They can begin to take up enough space that a person needs to tell someone what the harassment feels like, or that it happened. So that is what I did.

TELLING TO LIVE AND LIVING TO REGRET IT

After another incident of harassment, one where the same white male senior colleague made a reference to me looking "like a student" and said that if he was a student, "I would want to date you," I decided to approach a mutual colleague about the offense. Instead of being met with support from this white woman colleague whose own work relates to advocacy and support for survivors and trauma victims, I was met with words that worked to normalize our colleague's bad behavior. "You know how he is, always saying something silly. That's just [name]!" Oh, the incredulity. I often imagined that I would have received better care were I to have been able to make my injuries visible, like cuts, scrapes from falling down, scarring knees. Perhaps I should have known better. History, of course, hinted at how my experiences would unfold. But I had not braced myself for further injury in the course of seeking support.

Instead, what resulted was additional injury, trauma compounded by a refusal to make space for my story. I already had an open wound from feeling somewhat infantilized by a comment that disregarded/discarded my age in celebration of the appearance of youth. My concerns about my colleague were not met with the same care and attention I have witnessed students receiving in moments of crisis. I wondered, "What would it take to register my discomfort as important? How would I need to narrate the story to convey the depth of the injury?" In that moment, in that casual, almost indifferent response, I experienced a different but attendant kind of trauma—the trauma of not being seen, heard, or believed. Feeling like "We Believe You" (following Clark and Pinto 2016) might only be for a select, "respectable," few (Higginbotham 1993), I learned the hard way that people's refusal to take black women's pain seriously causes additional suffering (Sacks 2019; Cottom 2019), or what I call "multiplicative trauma." It feels like an isolating, lonely place, made all the more intense from the realization that people in positions to serve students and support them through their trauma have no idea, or no interest, in supporting you. It should not have come as any surprise that telling my story, searching for support, was met with a virtual non-response. A veritable normalization of the process, it aimed to effectively "put me in my place."

As if the initial offense was not enough, the reaction (or non-reaction) of this senior female colleague stunned me. In her role in the university, this person works as an advocate for survivors. She herself often faces scrutiny from skeptics, or people who see the broader scope of her advocacy work as part of what Patai dubs the "Sexual Harassment Industry" (2000, 33). Despite facing a variety of dubious reactions from colleagues, students, and even community members, this colleague chose in that moment to normalize the male senior colleague's comments, rather than to afford me the same spirit of advocacy so generously offered to students. Rather than risk protecting me in that moment, the female senior colleague chose to side with the male colleague. Her actions told me everything I needed to know about my putative value in society and in that university. It was also a painful reminder that I was perceived as not being capable of feeling much pain. It also suggested that I would be much better served in continuing to serve others, rather than attending to my own pain.

Internalizing this view would only validate the myth that black people feel no pain, that black lives do not matter, that black faculty should be "grateful" for their positions, having been "lucky" enough to enter the academy, much less securing tenure so that they can stay in such positions. Internalizing this view would also endorse the kind of silence that is violent, and it would work to silence me. My faculty status would not make my victimization more important, more necessary to pay attention to, not even equivalent to that which student survivors of sexual violence and harassment experienced. Instead, that moment made clear that the energies expended on helping to support students would not be extended to me. As faculty, or maybe (and more likely) as a brown woman, my victimization would remain illegible, unintelligible. I could not be seen as a victim, so the encounters of harassment from my colleague I had recounted *had to be* met with indifference. That was the way to normalize the inappropriateness of the comments, to diminish their impact on me, and to altogether disregard their impact on me. They were, after all, "just words." But, to me, they were not "just" words. They were far from *just*. These were my once-trusted colleagues in the fight for social justice. Instead, their words became a kind of betrayal, a departure from any kind of justice I imagined for myself and others in this world.

I had been here before, however, speaking truth to power about my experiences as a brown woman living in Vermont, a state with a predominantly white population. Rather than hold space for my reality to differ from that of any dominant groups, most people failed to do so. They denied the interlocking oppressions that differently impacted my everyday life and failed to see the harassment I was experiencing as part of a broader pattern of encounters with individual and institutional racism and sexism (and xenophobia, to a lesser degree). Refusals to recognize reality (and the attendant injury of a reality that accommodates harassment) speak to how silence becomes violence, too.

Like many victims of workplace harassment, I felt like my experiences were minimized and marginalized. The harassment I encountered made visible my precarious presence in the academy, but also highlighted my invisibility as a victim. I was simultaneously seen and unseen. I was in an ostensibly powerful institutional position, yet I personally felt disempowered. My presence, as a brown woman in a white space, was precarious at best, provocative at worst (see Horton 2006). Following Ahmed, I *must* 1) *be* a beneficiary of the affirmative action that does *not* exist as university policy; and 2) have been hired to do "diversity work," not by virtue of my extensive training in the social sciences, but naturally, as a brown woman.

The harassment I encountered partially stemmed from the frequency of being seen as an outsider, with "partial citizenship," not *really* American, or an academic. Being seen—only to be objectified—resulted from a perpetual inability to see me as human, as deserving of similar protections afforded students, or even white women faculty colleagues.

THE AFTERMATH

In the months following each of the incidents of harassment, I grew disconnected from my work and working environment. I nestled even further into my reading and my research, likely in search of affirmation, understanding, even escape. To fend off the isolation of my experience, I read (or re-read) a variety of books including Laura Gray-Rosendale's (2014) *College Girl.* Books renewed my spirit; they creatively (yet soberly) reassured me of the ubiquity of my experience. My recent reading of *Thick* reminded me of this.

Even in writing about another topic (poverty), Cottom's words resonate: "Much as we interrogate what a woman was wearing when she was raped, we look for ways to assign personal responsibility for structural injustices to bodies we collectively do not value" (2019, 161). Our collective tendency to victim-blame broadly applies.

In a rape culture, men, even ones not closely conforming to heteronormative and hegemonic expectations, can still rely upon and deploy whatever privileges they can access by virtue of their valued positions and particular intersections of race (white) and gender (man). For those of us situated in more precarious social locations (as women of color), we have fewer protections and arguably different strategies for survival. The men who harassed me also failed to protect me, their comments likely registered as benign, innocuous, inconsequential. Imagine the reverse, where I make a comment about "dating" a colleague, a senior member of the faculty where I was (at the time) untenured? What risks to my reputation would I incur for such a suggestion?

Despite knowing Audre Lorde's words, "Your silence will not protect you," I was ill-prepared for the way speaking my truth would be met with silence that *would* protect my harasser (2007, 41). I learned that being unseen means that your injuries and pain remain unseen, that the institutional forces that enable this harassment also remain unseen. Within the aforementioned web of violence, I learned that this web is sticky and hard to escape, unscathed. I learned that there is power in departing from assaultive spaces (for self-protection), and also in refusing to run. I learned the limits of some sisterhood, that "living to tell" (The Latina Feminist Group 2001) does not mean that everyone can sincerely listen to or hear us; they do not believe black women or honor our truths. As a result, I learned to linger over questions: Are we worth it? Are we worth fighting for, or dismantling oppressive conditions over, in the academy and the broader society?

DISCUSSION AND CONCLUSION

Throughout history and into contemporary society, black women's relationship to work has been entangled with violence. As "outsiders within" the academy, black women faculty continue to cultivate survival or subsistence strategies, at work and in the world (Collins 1991). Black women rely upon a DuBoisian "double consciousness" to anticipate the needs and demands of others (including white students and colleagues) (2017/1903). That is, they look "both from the outside in and from the inside out [to] understand both" (hooks 2000, vii). Black women's experiences have "differed dramatically from those of white women" largely because "these women of color suffered a double oppression of sexism and racism" (Hesse-Biber and Carter 2005,

24). In noting whites' refusal to see black humanity, then and now, these scholars point to the racial ideology of supremacy guiding the views that support the superiority of whiteness and the inferiority of blackness; they highlight how interlocking oppressions intensify in impact on black women.

If being an "outsider within" provides a unique vantage point for producing distinctive analyses of race, class, and gender, then the presence of black women in academia remains beneficial to society. Creating space for black women entails believing black women; valuing our lives; respecting our bodies (of work); and ultimately eradicating oppressive systems that harm.

The dismantling of oppressions invites serious consideration of the persistent patterns of inequality evident in higher education institutions. Intersectional inequalities persist when underrepresented faculty encounter social forces in the workplace environment that heighten any real or imagined personal and/or professional risks incurred in the process of being present in spaces not designed with them in mind. The denial of the oppressive conditions of many educational institutions, coupled with the assaultive behavior of academic colleagues, can incentivize the departure of black women faculty at various institutions. In my own experience, I requested professional leave to help mitigate the soul-crushing harassment and its cumulative, residual impact.

At virtually every turn, I was informed in one way or another to consider the costs of speaking out. Here, however, I want to turn the question around, or perhaps upside down. What is the cost to academic institutions to risk losing black women faculty, sometimes the only black women faculty at these institutions? When will the cost to the institution, through the loss of black women faculty, be registered as a far greater price to pay than any individual (or collective) suffering we face? When will universities stop silencing black women and really listen to our experiences? When will we cease to be tokens and commence being seen, as colleagues making meaningful contributions to our workplaces and thus, by extension, to society? When will we be recognized in our full humanity (Rankine 2014), rather than as having "partial social citizenship" (Cox 2019, 57)? When will our stories matter enough to suggest that we, too, matter?

REFERENCES

Ahmed, Sara. 2012. *On Being Included: Racism and Diversity in Institutional Life.* Durham: Duke University Press.
Bailey, Moya. 2017. "They Aren't Talking About Me." Accessed November 30, 2017. http://www.crunkfeministcollective.com/2010/03/14/they-arent-talking-about-me/.
Beal, Frances M. 1971. *Double Jeopardy: To Be Black and Female.* New York: Radical Education Project.
Buchwald, Emilie, Pamela Fletcher, and Martha Roth, eds. 2005. *Transforming a Rape Culture* (Revised Edition). Minneapolis: Milkweed Editions.

Clark, Annie E. and Andrea L. Pino. 2016. *We Believe You: Survivors of Campus Sexual Assault Speak Out.* New York: Holt Paperbacks.

Collins, Patricia Hill. 1991. *Black Feminist Thought: Knowledge, Consciousness, and the Politics of Empowerment.* New York: Routledge.

Cottom, Tressie McMillan. 2019. *Thick: And Other Essays.* New York: The New Press. Kindle.

Cox, Aimee Marie. 2015. *Shapeshifters: Black Girls and the Choreography of Citizenship.* Durham: Duke University Press.

Delgado, Richard. 1982. "Words That Wound: A Tort Action for Racial Insults, Epithets, and Name Calling." *Harvard Civil Rights-Civil Liberties Law Review* 17: 133–84.

DuBois, W. E. B. 1903/2017. *The Souls of Black Folk.* New York: CreateSpace Independent Publishing Platform.

Essed, Philomena. 1991. *Understanding Everyday Racism: An Interdisciplinary Theory.* Thousand Oaks: Sage.

Epstein, Debbie. 1997. "Keeping Them in Their Place: Hetero/sexist Harassment, Gender and the Enforcement of Heterosexuality." In *Sexual Harassment: Contemporary Feminist Perspectives*, edited by Alison M. Thomas and Celia Kitzinger, 154–71. Philadelphia: Open University Press.

Feagin, Joe. 2009. *The White Racial Frame: Centuries of Racial Framing and Counter-Framing.* New York: Routledge.

———. 1991. "The Continuing Significance of Race: Anti-Black Discrimination in Public Places." *American Sociological Review* 56 (1): 101–16.

Gay, Roxane. 2017. *Hunger: A Memoir of (My) Body.* New York: Harper Perennial.

Gray-Rosendale, Laura. 2014. *College Girl: A Memoir.* Albany: SUNY Press.

Gutierrez y Muhs, Gabriella, Yolanda Flores Niemann, Carmen G. Gonzalez, and Angela P. Harris, eds. 2012. *Presumed Incompetent: The Intersections of Race and Class for Women in Academia.* Logan: Utah State University Press.

Hanson, Rebecca and Patricia Richards. 2019. *Harassed: Gender, Bodies, and Ethnographic Research.* Los Angeles: University of California Press.

Harris-Perry, Melissa. 2012. *Sister Citizen: Shame, Stereotypes, and Black Women in America.* New Haven: Yale University Press.

Hesse-Biber, Sharlene Nagy and Gregg Lee Carter. 2005. *Working Women in America: Split Dreams* (2nd Ed.). New York: Oxford University Press.

Higginbotham, Evelyn Brooks. 1993. *Righteous Discontent: The Women's Movement in the Black Baptist Church, 1880–1920.* Cambridge: Harvard University Press.

Holloway, Karla F. C. 2011. *Private Bodies, Public Texts: Race, Gender, and a Cultural Bioethics.* Durham: Duke University Press.

hooks, bell. 2000. *Feminism is for Everybody: Passionate Politics.* Boston: South End Press.

———. 1984. *Feminist Theory: From Margin to Center.* Boston: South End Press.

Horton, Hayward Derrick. 2006. "Racism, Whitespace, and the Rise of the Neo-Mulattoes." In *Mixed Messages: Multiracial Identities in the "Color-Blind" Era*, edited by David Brunsma, 117–24. Boulder: Lynne Rienner Press.

Houston, Shannon M. 2015. "Respectability Will Not Save Us: Black Lives Matter Is Right to Reject the 'Dignity and Decorum' Mandate Handed Down to Us From Slavery." *Salon*, August 15, 2015. https://www.salon.com/2015/08/25/respectability_will_not_save_us_black_lives_matter_is_right_to_reject_the_dignity_and_decorum_mandate_handed_down_to_us_from_slavery/.

Jones, Nikki. 2008. *Between Good and Ghetto: African-American Girls and Inner-City Violence.* New Brunswick: Rutgers University Press.

Kaufman, Michael. 2001. "The Construction of Masculinity and the Triad of Men's Violence" in *Men's Lives* (5th Ed.). Edited by Michael Kimmel. Boston: Allyn and Bacon.

Kimmel, Michael S. 2009. *Guyland: The Perilous World Where Boys Become Men.* New York: Harper Perennial.

Lerum, Kari. 2004. "Sexuality, Power, and Camaraderie in Service Work." *Gender and Society* 18 (6): 756–76. https://doi.org/10.1177/0891243204269398.

Lorde, Audre. 2017. *Your Silence Will Not Protect You: Essays and Poems.* London: Silver Press.

———. 2007. "The Transformation of Silence into Language and Action." *Sister Outsider: Essays and Speeches by Audre Lorde*. San Francisco: Crossing Press, 40–44.

Maparyan, Layli. 2011. *The Womanist Idea*. New York: Routledge.

Matthew, Patricia A., ed. 2016. *Written/Unwritten: Diversity and the Hidden Truths of Tenure*. Chapel Hill: The University of North Carolina Press.

McGuire, Danielle. 2010. *At the Dark End of the Street: Black Women, Rape, and Resistance— A New History of the Civil Rights Movement from Rosa Parks to the Rise of Black Power*. New York: Vintage.

McIntosh, Peggy. 1998. "White Privilege and Male Privilege: A Personal Account of Coming to See Correspondences Through Work in Women's Studies." Working Paper 189. Wellesley, MA: Wellesley College Center for Research on Women.

McLaughlin, Heather, Christopher Uggen, and Amy Blackstone. 2017. "The Cost of Sexual Harassment." Gender & Society (blog), June 7, 2017. https://gendersociety.wordpress.com/2017/06/07/the-cost-of-sexual-harassment/.

———. 2012. "Sexual Harassment, Workplace Authority, and the Paradox of Power." *American Sociological Review* 77 (4): 625–47.

Matsuda, Mari. 1993. *Words That Wound: Critical Race Theory, Assaultive Speech, and the First Amendment*. New York: Routledge.

Muñoz, Jose. 1999. *Disidentifications: Queers of Color and the Performance of Politics*. Minneapolis: University of Minnesota Press.

Nash, Jennifer. 2019. *Black Feminism Reimagined: After Intersectionality*. Durham: Duke University Press.

Nash, Shondrah Tarrezz. 2005. "Through Black Eyes: African American Women's Construction of Their Experiences with Intimate Male Partner Violence." *Violence Against Women* 11 (11): 1420–40.

O'Toole, Laura, Jessica R. Schiffman, and Margie L. Kiter Edwards, eds. 2007. *Gender Violence: Interdisciplinary Perspectives* (2nd Ed.). New York: New York University.

Patai, Daphne. 2000. *Heterophobia: Sexual Harassment and the Future of Feminism*. Lanham: Rowman and Littlefield.

Prois, Jessica and Carolina Moreno. 2018. "The Me Too Movement Looks Different for Women of Color. Here Are 10 Stories." *Huffington Post*, January 2, 2018. https://www.huffingtonpost.com/entry/women-of-color-me-too_us_5a442d73e4b0b0e5a7a4992c?utm_campaign=hp_fb_pages&utm_source=main_fb&utm_medium=facebook&ncid=fcbklnkushpmg00000063.

Rankine, Claudia. 2014. *Citizen: An American Lyric*. Minneapolis: Graywolf Press.

Reeves, Richard V. and Katherine M. Guyot. 2017. "Black Women Are Earning More College Degrees, but That Alone Won't Close Race Gaps." *Brookings*, December 4, 2017. https://www.brookings.edu/blog/social-mobility-memos/2017/12/04/black-women-are-earning-more-college-degrees-but-that-alone-wont-close-race-gaps/.

Roberts, Dorothy. 1998. *Killing the Black Body: Race, Reproduction, and the Meaning of Liberty*. New York: Vintage.

Sacks, Tina. 2019. *Invisible Visits: Black Middle-Class Women in the American Healthcare System*. New York: Oxford University Press.

Smith, Joanne, Meghan Huppuch, and Mandy van Deven. 2011. *Hey Shorty! A Guide to Combating Sexual Harassment and Violence in Schools and on the Streets*. New York: The Feminist Press.

Stephens, Dionne P. and Layli D. Phillips. 2003. "Freaks, Gold Diggers, Divas, and Dykes: The Sociohistorical Development of Adolescent African American Women's Sexual Scripts." *Sexuality & Culture* 7 (1): 3–49.

"Testimony of Emily J. Martin, National Women's Law Center, General Counsel and Vice President for Workplace Justice." Hearing of March 16, 2016—Public Input into the Proposed Revisions to the EEO-1 Report. Published by the Equal Employment Opportunity Commission. https://www.eeoc.gov/eeoc/meetings/3-16-16/martin.cfm.

The Latina Feminist Group. 2001. *Telling to Live: Latina Feminist Testimonios*. Durham: Duke University Press.

Thompson-Miller, Ruth and Joe Feagin. 2014. *Jim Crow's Legacy: The Lasting Impact of Segregation*. New York: Rowman and Littlefield.

Toppo, Greg and Paul Overberg. 2014. "The Changing Face of America: Diversity Reshapes Nation." *The Shreveport Times*, November 1, 2014. https://www.shreveporttimes.com/story/news/local/2014/11/01/changing-face-america-diversity-reshapes-nation/18359819/.

Uggen, Christopher and Amy Blackstone. 2004. "Sexual Harassment as a Gendered Expression of Power." *American Sociological Review* 69 (1): 64–92.

US Department of Education. 2018. National Center on Education Statistics. "Fast Facts: Race/Ethnicity of College Faculty." Accessed October 20, 2019. https://nces.ed.gov/fastfacts/display.asp?id=61.

Walters, Karina, Selina A. Mohammed, Teresa Evans-Campbell, Ramona Beltran, David H. Chae, and Bonnie Duran. 2011. "Bodies Don't Just Tell Stories, They Tell Histories." *DuBois Review* 8 (1): 179–89.

Wingfield, Adia Harvey. 2019. "Does Sociology Silence Black Women?" Gender & Society (blog), June 4, 2019. https://gendersociety.wordpress.com/2019/06/04/does-sociology-silence-black-women/.

———. 2007. "The Modern Mammy and the Angry Black Man: African American Professionals' Experiences with Gendered Racism in the Workplace." *Race, Gender & Class* 14 (1/2): 196–212.

Chapter Two

My Grandfather Is Dying, Kavanaugh Just Got Appointed Supreme Court Justice, and I Should Probably Not Tell You These Stories

Ari Burford

I don't want to spend another summer writing about how I was raped by my grandfather when I was fifteen. Or how maybe it happened when I was eight. Or how it also (maybe) happened when I was 5, 4, 3, 2, and 1. I thought I'd want to publish my memoir that names *EVERYTHING* before he dies, but I don't want to write about my grandfather anymore.

My mother calls one morning soon after Kavanaugh is appointed Supreme Court Justice to tell me about her father.

"He can't walk anymore. Ever since he broke his hip. He's just given up."

I like the picture this conjures in my mind of him suffering. I've written in detail about the gruesome ways I'd like to see him suffer. It was cathartic.

Now though I'd rather not have to picture anything at all. I interrupt her.

"I don't want to hear any details about him. Just tell me when he's dead. And if he ever acknowledges what he did. Tell me that."

That was eight months ago.

I've been waiting for him to die all my life.

I don't want to keep writing about what he did to me. I've been writing about it for seven years. I'm done. I'm out. I wanna break up with this story via text message. Pretend it never happened. I'd rather spend my summer trying to find romance. Or at least good sex. Wouldn't that be fun? I'd rather spend this summer not thinking about trauma. Not deeply anyway—because, as trauma survivors, we know it never just goes away. I'd rather take a hike.

Build that fence I keep trying to finish. Drink margaritas in the sunshine. Crank up the top forty hits and daydream of lost loves. *Anything* but this.

When I first started talking about incest, nobody in my family believed me. I had to write so I could feel heard. Fast forward seven years: my parents and sister believe me. I've written my memoir. But maybe if I quit before publishers tell me my story doesn't stand out, that nobody will want to read it, that the writing is not good enough . . . maybe if I quit first—like breaking up with someone before they break up with you—then I won't be confused, lonely, brokenheartednothingnobodygirl without words to say what happened to her. I want to quit first.

Yet here I am on a Tuesday in May, writing. The semester just ended and I'm sitting on the balcony of the house my friends and I rented in Puerto Peñasco, Mexico. I look up at the bright turquoise blue of the Sea of Cortéz. The sun begins to warm the sand. I shiver in my jeans. Because "behind every story I tell is the one I don't. Behind the story you hear is the one I wish I could make you hear" (Allison 1996, 42).[1]

I'm not ready to let the story go.

When I write I imagine you all. All you survivors. The ones who are listening. I write because it makes me feel less crazy. Actually, sometimes it makes me feel *more* crazy: re-telling the details of brutal sexual exploitation and the aftermath of trauma. But then something shifts. One person reads it (or hears me at a reading) and feels strength from it. Another person taps into their own grief. Someone writes me or tells me their story and says, "I've never told anyone before but . . ." and then I'm not alone.[2] We are not alone in this.

It's kind of Dorothy Allison's fault that I am writing at all. I had read Dorothy's[3] groundbreaking book *Bastard Out of Carolina* in my first-year composition course back in college. I'd devoured it even though I had no idea why (it was a story about incest and I hadn't recovered my blocked memories yet). Years later, when I attended a workshop with her I couldn't believe she was my teacher.

On the first day she looked right into our eyes and told us we would *have* to write our stories and to do so we would *have* to become like sharks. "The part of you that wants the story told, even though people want you to shut up: that's your shark writer brain. You have to be sharks. This means telling the real stories, even if your family doesn't want you to," she would say.

In a one-on-one meeting with Dorothy, she asked what I did for a day job. I said I taught at a university.

"You have an incredible way with words. But academia will be your biggest block to writing," she said.

I had written a three-hundred-page dissertation, so I figured the biggest block to writing would be the literary critic I was trained to be to get my PhD in Literature. How that critic would stand in my way, keep me from accessing my creativity. I would later realize that the biggest block would be questions about how I should censor myself. Should I try to keep—or at least not damage—the respect of colleagues? How would I do this and still write the truth of my story? I decided to write all of it. The blood and guts of it. The bare-boned nakedness of my truth. Some may respect me for it. Some will think it's inappropriate. I am not supposed to tell my story. But I'm doing it anyway.

Maybe I'm more afraid *not* to write for real. Because writing honors my life. Not writing feels like the ultimate silence. It feels like death. Like his hands wrapped around my throat.

Dorothy writes, "For years, every time I said it, said 'rape' and 'child' in the same terrible sentence, I would feel the muscles of my back and neck pull as taut as the string of a kite straining against the wind" (Allison 1996, 42). People don't like to hear these words in the same sentence. Rape. He. Child. My grandfather raped me as a child. I survived incest.

Not all of us do.

Survive.

It doesn't make us any better than the rest.

My mother still blames herself for all that he did to me. To my sister. If she's reading this I'm sure she's blaming herself right now too. *Please don't. It was not your fault. It was his fault. What he did.* Like Dorothy says, "Of all the stories I know, the meanest stories are the stories the women I loved told themselves in secret—the stories that sustained and broke them" (Allison 1996, 69). When my mother blames herself she tells some of the meanest stories. When I write, I get to rewrite them. Maybe all along I've been writing for you, Moo.[4] To try to heal the broken parts of both of us.

My experience with writing creatively as a professor is that I've had to prove to some colleagues and bosses that stories matter. That the research of creative production *is* research. This story is a true *and* researched story. Even if my memory betrays me sometimes, I have these facts: I was raped by my grandfather. He's still alive. It's 2019 and the US has a known sexual predator as Justice of the Supreme Court, appointed by a president who encourages "pussy grabbing" and bragged about his own pedophilia on the Howard Stern show in 2005, about "inspecting" kids—girls under eighteen—while they were naked in dressing rooms at the Miss Teen America beauty pageant (which he also owned).[5] It's not the first time sexual predators have held public office.[6]

My right shoulder clenches and tightens as the pain shoots up my neck into my jaw, remembering the way he held me down. For all the times he had his hands around my throat. For that. I keep writing for that.

And then the grip. His grip on me. It loosens.

He didn't kill me. I thought what he did to me might—for a lot of years. A few years ago, when I was in the thick of writing the story, I told my close friends to burn my journals if I died suddenly. "You know, like if I'm in a car accident," I'd say, to assure rather than scare them. My best friend Barb always knew otherwise. She would check in on me. She made me dinner once a week and asked about the pain. She listened. I'm alive because of her, really. I'm alive because I have one good friend who listened to the story and didn't doubt my truth. In this heteropatriarchal culture, to not be discounted and victim blamed—it's life saving.

Every time I hear of a survivor who survived—until they didn't—I'm reminded of the intensity of the pain. The emotional spin. The longing to make the story stop. It's right here—with us—*all* the time. It never goes away.

Like I said, I want to quit writing this story.

Every time I choose to stay here, with you, I think of those who haven't. I think of genderqueer writer Andrea Gibson's words:

> Let me say right now for the record, I am still gonna be here asking this world to dance even if it keeps stepping on my holy feet.
> Each of us at each other's backs whispering over and over and over, "Live, live." (Gibson 2012, stanza 21)

Mine is a story of staying. It is a story of finding my push back. I believe in our push back. I believe you. I believe in you. I believe us.

Right before Kavanaugh was appointed Supreme Court Justice, in the fall of 2018, I sat with students in my Women's and Gender Studies courses and asked them why rape survivors don't often speak out. I've been doing this lesson with students for over a decade. There are always passionate answers about the ways people are threatened by perpetrators into silence. We talk about rape culture, slut shaming, heteropatriarchy, power, and the way heterosexual men are taught to use women and people assumed to be women. We talk about silence, economic necessity, and surviving capitalism—jobs, security, bosses, partners—all of which often cause people not to speak out. We talk about what the word "survivor" means. How it's not just about surviving the actual incident of violence: it is, in part, about staying here and not taking our own lives. We talk about racism, homophobia, about not being sure you'd be believed because you are queer and your rapist was a woman. About the difficulty for all men—including trans men—to speak about being raped because of the oppressiveness of toxic masculinity and how it is enmeshed in homophobia. We talk about the way women of color are judged and constructed as hypersexual and thus not believed in a way that's different than white survivors.

We read Kimberlé Crenshaw's famous article "Mapping the Margins" and listen to her more recent talk "The Urgency of Intersectionality." We discuss what she says about how because of anti-black racism it is difficult for Black women to speak out. We talk about how survivors who are Black experience anti-black racism by the police and, if their rapists were Black, this information can also be used by anyone who wishes to demonize Black communities. We talk about how people with disabilities are targeted. How people are raped crossing the border. We discuss how sex workers are often seen as not rape-able.[7] We talk about rape on college campuses. At home. In places of worship. How it's hard to speak when that very breaking of silence causes people to be deported. How trans people in detention are systematically raped and how these systems are built on violence.[8] We talk about Transformative Justice in contrast to the Prison Industrial Complex and ideas students have for healing in their communities.[9]

We also talk about how it's hard to speak out as a non-binary person because your gender can be used as a weapon against you. Even if it's an attempt at inclusion, us non-binary people often get misgendered. For example, women will often say things like "we're all so strong as women!"—assuming everyone in the room at a survivor speak out is a woman when some of us, like me, are non-binary (or some in the room are trans masculine)—we get misread and misgendered as women.

During the fall of 2018, when I asked the same question about rape I've been asking for nearly two decades it was different. One reason is that it was shortly before Kavanaugh's appointment as Supreme Court Justice—despite two women coming forward and speaking about him sexually assaulting them. It was also different because I read the first chapter of my memoir to them because I wanted to share not just my story by my writing. I have told students that I'm a survivor of incest, but I had not yet ever read the first chapter of my memoir. In doing this, I began to claim the importance of my story and the way I tell it on the page. I was ready to be even more vulnerable. I was honoring my story and my writing, which meant honoring my life. So in a basement classroom with no windows, shaking and guttural, I spoke the raw of my story. I looked up at their faces. Paused. It was quiet for a moment. Some of them looked me in the eye. Others looked down. Then they began sharing their stories with an urgency to speak that I've never before witnessed. One after another. Many told us they were telling their stories for the first time. Others had told their stories before, but weren't believed. This time it was to a room full of people who believed them. One of these students, a woman of color, had already told her story in a court of law where her truth had not been heard due to systematic racism intersecting with sexism.

"I believe you," someone told her, with presence, eye contact, connection. Then she told her own story.

"It was not your fault," someone said.

"Thank you for sharing your story. I'm not brave enough to share mine," another said.

"There are many ways to be brave," I said. She blinked back tears.

Their stories are not mine to tell, but creating a space where survivors' stories can be heard is a form of collective healing that I believe deeply in. When we share our stories it's one way we can fend off the isolation that comes with surviving sexual assault. On these days I feel the beauty and healing of collectively pushing back in the deepest places of my brokenness. Via teaching, I'm doing something about the violence that happened to me. This is the opposite of paralyzed nobodynothinggirl.

I do think students' willingness to talk more is in part because of the #MeToo movement. However, as Leah Lakshmi Piepzna-Samarasinha and many other feminists of color have pointed out, a decade before the #MeToo movement "officially" began a Black woman named Tarana Burke was calling for such a rising up and naming it (Piepzna-Samarasinha 2018, 227). As Gillian White, a Black woman who is an editor at *The Atlantic* wrote: "Though the #MeToo movement has made clear the insidiousness and prevalence of sexual harassment and assault, it has also been centered mostly on the experiences of white, affluent, and educated women" (White 2017).

Not decentering white people's stories is another form of oppressive erasure and silencing: for any classroom setting or speak out the question "Who is this erasing?" must be asked.

When I get home from teaching, I'm exhausted. I turn on a TV series. Dig out leftover soup from the freezer. Wonder how long I can keep doing this. I wake up in the middle of the night short of breath, with my mind spinning, feeling the weight of it all. I often wonder if I'm pushing myself too much. That's when I know I have to reset. Get into nature. Go through my elaborate rituals and routines to restore. Similar to the dilemma about writing, teaching about rape—particularly as a non-tenure-track faculty member (i.e., high teaching load, precarious job security)—involves an element of burnout and exhaustion: when this happens I want to quit.

Sometimes I feel like I fail the students completely. For example, what happens next, after the sharing of a story? They have a long road ahead of them to try to survive, much less make it through college with tens of thousands of dollars in student loans. There are not many resources in this world for people who are poor, who are trans, who are Brown, Black and Indigenous, people with disabilities. Still, when a student reads their story and you can hear their voice tremble; when you hear them becoming more and more fierce with the telling—that is something. It's not nothing. This experience— many students who are survivors have told me, sometimes years later—kept them in this life. That is not nothing. To be clear it is not me saving them: it is us, together, creating spaces of collective healing. And yet, I don't believe the university setting, especially with predominantly white students, is always a "safe" space for students of color. So it's important to not glorify this space. Yet there are fissures where something different can and does happen. There are spaces that my colleague Ikaika Gleisberg calls "brave" spaces— not savior spaces, not white cis-centered spaces . . . but spaces of collective healing.[10]

When Kavanaugh was being questioned about his predatory actions, I purposely didn't listen to his voice. It's too triggering to hear the total disregard for the people they have violated in perpetrators' voices. Us survivors can hear this in the voice of many others too, like the current president of the United States.[11] Despite trying to protect myself by how I take in news, it was while Kavanaugh was being appointed that I woke one night and didn't know where I was or who I was. I moved my head around but couldn't see anything. My eyes were open but I still couldn't see the usual lights filtering through my bedroom window. I didn't know how old I was. I had no body. It felt kind of like floating, but in a lost kind of way. Like haunted ghosts must feel. I don't know how long I remained like this: the paralysis of limbs reliving being raped by my grandfather in Europe, too roofied up and drunk on sangria to move. What the body does when you are being touched somewhere you don't want to be and you can't get away—you're just trapped so you go into nowhere nothing nobodygirl.

Like Lidia Yuknavitch said, "I didn't feel crazy. I just felt gone away." (Yuknavitch 2011, 27).

I don't know how long nothingnobodynowhere girl lasted. Shaking and crying, I was fifteen-years-old-lost-drunk-roofied-girl unable to find her way home. Then a loud thundering explodes over my house, shaking the walls. As this happens I register that I'm in my bed. I reach for my phone. Sobbing, I call the guy I'm dating. I'm bisexual and non-binary. I feel the need to say this because it often gets lost when I mention facts like this and then *I* get lost and misgendered in my own story. It's 5 a.m. in Colorado where he lives. He usually wakes up at 5 a.m. for work. He doesn't answer. I call my best friend Barb. It's 4 a.m. in Arizona. She picks up. She reminds me I'm ok and that it's "ok to not be ok." This is one of her favorite phrases from a suicide prevention organization of that name. She gently listens, says it's PTSD brain, that it will pass. I inhale. The guy I'm newly dating calls. I let it go to voicemail. I text him that I'm ok—just super triggered from a thunderstorm and talking to my besty. I talk to Barb for two hours. He gets mad that I don't make time for him before he has to go to work, especially after texting so early. Little do I know that morning that I will never see him again. Every time a relationship ends I wonder how many relationships trauma has destroyed.

Sometimes it's really obvious things that trigger PTSD. Like having to hear a person I assume is a woman at a restaurant talking about how "*that woman*"—insert derogatory tone—just made stuff up to get attention. Sometimes, it's a smell. Those are the worst triggers. Like Old Spice cologne. Especially anything like the brand my grandfather wore. Sometimes it's the good things that are triggering. Like orange blossoms—the smell of Southern California springtime. Or a really good orgasm with another person.

I know. That's probably not appropriate to say.

Maybe that was too much. If that wasn't too much, then maybe the parts of my longer memoir where I write about how incest has messed with my sex life and how I've reclaimed my body and pleasure *is* too much to share. Or deciding to go off and on and back off my antidepressant. Maybe I shouldn't write about those things. It can be used against you. Professors are not supposed to talk about our personal lives. We are supposed to be like steel. Impenetrable. If we talk about hard things we've been through, it should always be past tense—we're stronger now, over it. We should not publish things like this. Students might read them! Deans might read them. In class we should not say anything about our personal lives beyond quaint stories about our cats or anecdotes for comic relief during lectures. Definitely not the *real* stories. Maybe other peoples' stories. Ethnographies. Yes! We can definitely write about other peoples' stories and safeguard our own that way.

In her 2012 book *Depression: A Public Feeling*, feminist theorist Ann Cvetkovitch writes about being an academic, a lesbian, and her experiences with depression—all woven into her analysis of art and literature. In her earlier 2003 book, *An Archive of Feelings*, Cvetkovitch writes against label-ing trauma PTSD. She writes against the medicalization and othering that happens in the psychiatric industrial complex. Cvetkovitch points out that the third edition of the *Diagnostic and Statistical Manual of Mental Disorders* calls trauma "outside the range of usual human experience" (Cvetkovitch 2003, 18). Instead of diagnosis, she explains: "I treat trauma instead as a social and cultural discourse that emerges in response to the demands of grappling with the psychic consequences of historical events" (Cvetkovitch 2003, 18). She doesn't point out that trauma is *everyday common.* Or that the wording of the manual makes it seem unusual to have trauma. But rape is common. Incest is common. What Cvetkovitch calls the "psychic conse-quences" of trauma are, for me, *directly* related to the way violence is *not* dealt with—and most certainly not deeply grappled with—in rape culture. In contrast to Cvetkovitch, what's useful for me about claiming PTSD is that it recognizes the continued effects and impacts we experience in the aftermath of violence. Rape survivors are survivors of a war. As Barb says, "It's a war that terrorizes the targets long after the bombs happen."

Conversations about rape need to always be contextualized in the ways Brown, Black, and Indigenous writers are (and have been for centuries) naming what it means to survive (and not). For example, in *Queer Indige-nous Studies*, Indigenous scholar Chris Finley writes about the aftermath and continued impacts of white colonizers' rape and genocide of Native women.

She argues that silence about sexual abuse in Indigenous communities is part of the trauma of colonialism. The day after the election of Trump, at the National Women's Studies Association Conference in Montréal, Leanne Betasamosake Simpson spoke about how Indigenous people have been surviving the trauma of continued colonialism, rape, and targeting of gender non-conforming folks for over 500 years. Simpson emphasized that they will "continue to survive." Their 2015 book *Islands of Decolonial Love* addresses the difficulty of not just surviving but loving in the midst of continued violence of rape and genocide against Indigenous people. The collection *Queer Indigenous Studies* addresses the impacts of colonialism on Native people, and the targeting by white colonizers of non-binary, non-Western genders and sexualities. [12] This anthology makes a case for honoring and respecting histories/stories/research by Indigenous people to counter the "knowledge" produced by white academics, as part of what the editors call "intellectual sovereignty" (Driskill et al. 2011, 8). That these writers had to make these arguments evidences that stories—especially as told by those oppressed by settler colonialism and white supremacy—are still not often seen as truth, particularly in university settings.

As most feminists know, some of the work of Women's and Gender Studies—a field historically founded on the re-written histories of feminists—is to counter what constitutes "truth" and knowledge production. Black feminists such as Angela Davis, Toni Morrison, and Patricia Hill Collins have paid homage to the work of writers like Harriet Jacobs—whose 1861 memoir *Incidents in the Life of a Slave Girl* bears witness to the systematic raping of Black women by white men during slavery as well as the complicity of white women with this violence. Gloria Anzaldúa has been cited prolifically for having written about rape, land theft, and the impact of colonialism on gender systems and heteropatriarchy on Xichanx people as well as the connection of these realities to the literal and metaphorical construction of borders that function to create an "us" and a "them." Saidiya Hartman's *Lose Your Mother* weaves her own family history and memoir together with research about the slave trade in the US. In *Loving in the War Years* Cherríe Moraga wrote about her own experiences as a white passing lesbian daughter of a brown Xicana woman who was a farmworker, and the impact of colonialism on her sense of self and sexuality. In *A Life in Trans Activism*, Revathi writes of British-imposed colonialist laws about gender and sexuality in India, the impacts on trans women, and her experience being sexually assaulted as a child, as an adult, and as a sex worker. [13] These writers are just a few of many who, long before the #MeToo movement, have contextualized the trauma of rape in relation to colonialism and slavery and told their stories, all the way through.

It's hard to tell the whole story all the way through when memories are blurry. Sometimes that loss of memory *is* the story. Staceyann Chin writes about her experience with the violence of incest as a biracial Black lesbian growing up in Jamaica. Black feminist lesbian Audre Lorde asks a question about the uncertainty regarding the cause of her friend Gennie's suicide, while also stating that Gennie's father "was using that girl for I don't know what" (Lorde, 101). Toni Morrison's *The Bluest Eye* traces the (fictionalized) history of a Black girl surviving incest. All of these were before the #MeToo movement and all of these Black authors are naming the hard things, particularly in the contexts of anti-black racism and its intersections with heterosexism.

When I teach these stories, I am compelled to apply what Crenshaw writes about in relation to domestic violence and Black women to address how stories of incest often get racialized. White perpetrators of incest are seen by many white readers as individuals and not racialized, leaving hetero-patriarchy and white supremacy intact while, simultaneously, incest/rape/violence in Black communities is often read in racialized ways. When consuming stories by white authors about incest many white people fail to see incest as connected to power, entitlement, and white supremacy and rather as individual acts.

I argue that writing about incest as a white person necessitates locating it in the context of colonialism, entitlement, and taking that the above authors (and many more) have named. Without doing so, I am complicit in those systems. My whole dissertation was a way to avoid writing about my own trauma and to also not think about my ancestors. I wrote about literature that represented rape, and pointed to ways white women in the nineteenth century—in what was named/called the United States—were often, but not always, in collusion with white men as settlers. I also wrote about fissures within this, moments when they resisted white supremacy. For many academics, it's a less vulnerable way to write about the trauma of others that's not our own (and also not have to look at our own potential accountability as perpetrators).[14] I don't want to write this part of the story either. Underneath the story I tell of myself as a survivor is another story. Maybe this is the story beneath the story.

When I write the word "survivor" I want to trouble it. I want to trouble the idea of calling myself a survivor on stolen land. As Roxanne Dunbar-Ortiz names in *An Indigenous People's History*, "Inherent in the myth we've been taught is an embrace of settler colonialism and genocide. The myth persists, not for a lack of free speech or poverty of information but rather for an absence of motivation to ask the questions that challenge the core of the scripted narrative of the origin story" (Dunbar-Ortiz 2015, 2). I was asking some questions about my past. But I wasn't asking these questions, the ones that challenge the scripted narrative of colonialism. Of my family's origin story.

I have survived specifically *because* other people haven't. When I started researching my family history I found that on the incest side of my family they stole land from Bannock and Shoshone people. My mother told me that her great-grandparents simply filed paperwork with the US government and the land was "theirs." My grandmother had always just said that her family "moved" to Idaho. This is the scripted narrative of my family's history, the origin story that is settler colonialism. My family on the incest side, culminating with me, has owned property (i.e., stolen land) for over a hundred years. I did not literally inherit it—but growing up as a white person in this country I internalized the mindset of entitlement and erasure that comes with unsettled settler identity, land ownership, and whiteness (Morgensen 2011, 163). My ancestors' taking put me here: My grandmother was alive to reproduce *because* so many people weren't. Because of the Bannock wars against Indigenous people that land became "open" for my ancestors to file a land claim. So my question to white survivors of rape is this: What does it mean to claim ourselves as survivors when *because* of our ancestors' taking so many Indigenous people didn't?

In the poem "Cycle Undone," Ahimsa Timotéo Bodhrán writes, "I write as a person coming out of genocide, survivor . . ." (Bodhrán 2013, 35). Bodhrán identifies as of Kanien 'kehaka, Onondowaga, Puerto Rican, Irish, and German/Moroccan Jewish descent, and says that: "Perhaps our rapture is / surviving the rape, the mindfuck of living" (35). Speaking of the ways rape is linked to the taking of land, Bodhrán asks, "Who knows what we would do if we owned our own lands? Perhaps live / or be free, rather than simply on sale. If we spoke our own languages / owned our own bodies. If / If" (35). Bodhrán names the linkages between colonialism, rape, and the impacts of colonialism on gender non-conforming Indigenous people. Writing with fierce resilience that "we are supernovas" and "we are not going away" Bodhrán refuses erasure (28). The "we" in this poem is not just rape survivors or Indigenous or trans people—it refers specifically to gender-nonconforming Indigenous rape survivors of colonialism and the aftermath of transphobia and gender binaries imposed on gender non-conforming people by white people during violent processes of colonialism.

I want to make clear the relationship between a lack of accountability in my family about stolen land that enabled their/our life and the violence of incest. Denial is part of colonialism and white supremacy. I am trying to interrupt the dangerous lies of my ancestors. This is something white people should do to not be complicit with rape culture, which very much goes hand in hand with settler colonialism: all of these feed off denial, erasure, and silence. I refuse to hide the lies of my ancestors. As part of this, I am trying to complicate the concept of survivor. There are harder, deeper questions than this to think about too. Like how this is not enough. What other actions am I willing to take as a white person, to "throw down," as Diné activist Spike Manning puts it, when giving guest lectures to students?

My grandmother was oppressor and oppressed—for a long time I didn't see this, but I now recognize her as a woman who was in an abusive relationship under patriarchy. The man who raped my grandmother's granddaughter and groped other women in her family. . . . I'm sure that this man did not practice consent for the seventy-five years he shared my grandmother's bed. To tell that story I would have to fill in the gaps. My grandmother was also complicit with the rape of her granddaughter(s) and with the myth of settler colonialism. Telling us it was all okay. Denying everything.

To tell the story of my gender in relation to all this violence I have to keep filling in the gaps. Beneath the story I tell is always the one I don't. There's always the story that never makes it to the page. I'm trying to write that story. Here's part of it: I hate how hard I always tried to be a pretty girl for him. My grandfather. I used to wear a deep dark shade of maroon lipstick for him. He would compliment me on it. After Europe, when he no longer had access to me at night there was something about the way he looked at me when I had it on: Europe was over, I wasn't sharing a bed with him anymore, and I knew he couldn't get to me. Finally *I* had power. I know, it's fucked up. It's not liberation. But that's what incest does. It fucks with our sense of ourselves, even in our attempts to claim power.

There's not a way for me to know the cause/effect of my genderqueerness and sexuality in relationship to being raped/violated/assaulted by my grandfather. I don't know when the abuse started so I can't claim he targeted me *because* of my queerness. Trans theorist Eli Clare writes in an illuminating way about this:

> Most feminist and queer activists reject these [cause and effect] linkages and for good reason. Conservatives use them to discredit lesbian, gay, bi, and trans identities and to argue for conversion rather than liberation. But this strategy of denial, rejecting any possibility of connection between abuse and gender identity, abuse and sexuality, slams a door on the messy reality of how our bodies are stolen. (Clare 2015, 145–46)

If we cannot speak about the possibility of cause and effect—including the messiness of the questions we have about our lives—without it threatening our right to exist as trans and non-binary people, as queer people, then our bodies keep getting stolen, ironically, for the cause of equality and rights.[15] And then, the liberation we might have found in speaking our stories can get lost in the process.

Clare concludes by stating, "I want to say, 'My father raped me for many reasons, and inside his acts of violence I learned about what it meant to be female, to be a child, to live in my particular body, and those lessons served the larger power structure and hierarchy well'" (Clare 2015, 150). If we cannot speak, we are being disciplined by our non-binary genders, even if it's supposed to liberate us from binaries. We need to speak freely about our survival as trans and non-binary people, but as long as our stories are used and manipulated to write us out of existence, it is difficult to speak. In his piece "No Longer Small and Lonely," Clare fiercely writes:

> The man I used to call father, let him tumble forever. I have stormed his bunker, picked the lock, found my heart amidst the rubble, laughed him off the edge of the world. NO longer small and lonely, I live among the furious and the joyful. We dance, sing, drum, limp, fall, walk, swish, howl our way through the world. The next 10,000 miles await, wild open of sky. I'll no longer pretend, no longer be afraid: neither girl nor boy, I am a boulder that splits the current and dreams. (Clare 2015, 115)

Clare writes of his disability and existence as a non-binary person in a way that refuses erasure, even in the midst of hard questions. Perhaps he *can* exist *because* he allows the hard questions to exist on the page.

Additionally, *Written on the Body: Letters from Trans and Non-Binary Survivors of Sexual Assault and Domestic Violence* exists as a collection to counter the way discourses about gendered violence often normalize gender binaries and erase the realities of trans and non-binary existence. One author writes that they told their lover that "I didn't like these lumps on my chest" (*Written on the Body* 2018, 86). In response, "she promised me she loved them . . . [and] three months later, she held me down, this time with clenched fists instead of prayers reminding me how she loved the woman in me" (*Written on the Body* 2018, 86). This particular anonymous writer names something I have felt for years about the way some lesbians tried to "woman" me into a gender. If I wasn't a woman, then (some) of my lesbian lovers felt they couldn't be lesbians.

"You don't want to start testosterone do you, Ari?" a lesbian lover I'd had for nearly four years asked.

"Because I wouldn't be ok with that."

Again, I'm not supposed to say this, but the truth is sometimes lesbians reenact the cissexism of the world we live in. Trans activist and writer Dean Spade writes that "witnessing others holding all the complexity of our survival inside brutal systems gives me relief and strength" (Spade 2018, 12). Statements like this make me want to write the real stories. Not silence myself. Another writer of the collection asks: "Sometimes I wonder if I want to erase you because we were assaulted. That is to say, what if I'm not really trans . . ." (*Written on the Body* 2018, 40). I wonder that too. Maybe I want to erase myself as a woman because if I wash his idea of woman off me—and thus our heterosexist patriarchal culture's notion of "woman"—then maybe I can scrub the smell of his Old Spice off me too. Forever. But what does it mean to be "really trans" anyway?

Some will say I'm a fake non-binary person just looking for attention, especially as a person assigned female at birth whose hair is currently growing longer with each day (until I pull out my clippers and shave it again). I might—especially now—be taken for a fraud. I do worry that my words could harm those who could have my story hurled at them. Maybe my questions will create some messed-up message that healing would mean not to exist as non-binary anymore. People have told me this before. It's messed up. My words should not be taken that way. I just want the freedom to ask the hard questions without having to talk about intimate details of my body and how sometimes in the spaces between my legs I have a dick and I like it. I don't want to have to prove that I qualify as non-binary or tell everyone about my dreamscapes where my body sometimes feels free to be a guy who is also kind of but not really a girl. I want to be able to say out loud that I'm pretty certain I would be fine with being called "she" and "woman" if I hadn't been raped by my grandfather. This is the first time I've said this so directly.

Still. Don't tell me to be a strong woman and reclaim it. I don't want to.

In Leah Lakshmi Piepzna-Samarasinha's groundbreaking essay "Not Over It, Not Fixed, and Living a Life Worth Living," they name the "Survivor Industrial Complex" (SIC) as "the web of institutions, practices, and beliefs that work to manage, contain, and/or offer resolution to survivors of sexual violence" (Piepzna-Samarasinha 2018, 229). The "good survivor" in this system is the one who has gotten a few months of therapy and "moved on" (229). However, Piepzna-Samarasinha brilliantly points out the danger of these beliefs and practices: "That model and its harsh binary of successful and fixed or broken and fucked is part of what contributes to suicidality and struggle in long-term survivors" (231). Playing the "good survivor" game is a fake, unrealistic goal that harms our communities and ourselves. It's compelling. It's one we want to believe, as Piepzna-Samarasinha explains. Instead of suggesting that to have hope means getting beyond trauma, they write, "What if some trauma wounds never will go away—and we might still have great lives?" (235). *This* is real. They suggest "map[ping] a new model of survival where my scars and still being crazy in adulthood are not signs that I've failed" (231). When I'm in a spin about a thought and it won't stop, it helps to name the impact of trauma and ride the wave of it. Trying to escape my crazy just makes it worse. [16]

I wish I could tell my students that a decade spent on healing has gotten me "over it." Still, it's true that when my heart is full, and I can let love in—the love for life, the joy I feel from the sun, the ocean, the wind, my heart flat on the sand: this is part of being a survivor too. I can tell students that there are new pathways in my mind toward peace. I can find them more easily. Neuroscience has proven this: how we can reset our brains. [17] It's not easy and requires a lot of work. But it's worth it. I have learned how to slow down enough in the spaces between the PTSD thunder jolts and the inflammation flare-ups of chronic pain that mirror my waves of anxiety and trauma. I can live here, too, with all of it: the hard story, the real story, the story beneath the story. And I sure as hell won't deny the truth of any of it, whether by omission or euphemism.

When I write, his hands around my throat loosen. They tighten. The asthma flares. Dies down. I put my hand up to my throat—remind myself that it's only *my* hands here, now. I take a deep breath.

I teach. It matters. I fuck up. I try harder. This doesn't always solve it. These are the harder stories to tell.

I wish that when my grandfather dies, the memories would die too. That I'd feel safe to fall asleep by myself more often than not. That I'd feel safe to fall asleep with someone else in my bed more often than not. I can't predict how I will feel when my grandfather finally dies. He's dragged it out this far at the age of ninety-six. How do you bury the hope that accountability on the part of your rapist will finally, maybe one day come?

In any case, no matter what happens in my life I commit to feeling all of it. This will include the times of not being okay, being okay, and even the times of feeling great. I'm glad I spent a good amount of my summer writing my story. Summer is not over and I met a new lover and I'm having healing, beautiful, sweet connection and amazing, delicious sex (something that has previously been hard to enjoy). I'm letting myself be present enough in my body to take in all of the joy, fully. I finally know how. This has been a long healing process, and it's not done. It's not linear. I'm not "over it." I also commit to feeling pain. This trauma body—full of breakdowns and flare-ups and freak-outs and singing to top forty and feeling *incredible* pleasure—this is the body I live in. As I promised my best friend in a commitment more binding than the marriage certificate I made with a man and the government decades ago: I commit to this life. I promise you this, Barb and Ari: as hard as it may ever get I will not give up on us.

Like I said. Some of us don't. Survive. It doesn't make us any better than you, Hollie Vargas.[18] But it does make us here. And while we are here, for this short time, if we benefit from systems of oppression that have enabled us to exist and survive, will we look the other way? I, for one, will keep troubling what it means to survive. As lesbian incest survivor Mary Oliver asks in her poem "Summer Day," *What is it you plan to do with this one wild and precious life?* (Oliver, 1990).

NOTES

1. I would like to thank Laura Gray-Rosendale for encouraging me to write my memoir, inviting me to contribute to this collection, and always reminding me that our stories as survivors matter. I would like to thank my best friend, Barb White, who was the first person to encourage me to write about incest. Her friendship saved my life more than once: she persistently, peacefully, lovingly, patiently, and with great tenderness and wisdom guided me to keep doing the work to heal. Finally, even though my memoir itself names so much of the pain from

my parents not believing me for many years, having written the memoir and done years of work and having hard conversations I am so relieved to say that my parents and sister *without a doubt* believe me now. I would like to thank them for opening their eyes to things that were, at first, almost too painful to look at . . . things that might have tested their own survival processes. Thank you, Moo, Dad, and Sis for doing the hard work of healing together: I love you.

2. I use "their" here to refer to a student who might be a woman, a man, or a non-binary person—in other words I'm using "their" as a general, non-gendered singular term to refer to a student rather than saying "he, she, or they." I do this throughout the essay to emphasize that people of all genders speak out about rape, for example.

3. I can't call her by her last name because I know her and it feels too formal.

4. I call my mother Moo—when referring directly to her I can't call her mother.

5. See "E. Jean Carroll Accuses Trump of Sexual Assault in Her Memoir," "These Women Have Accused Trump of Sexual Harassment," and "Donald Trump boasted about meeting semi-naked teenagers in beauty pageants."

6. See the 2016 book review by Jean Zimmerman in the National Public Radio article, where the rape of Sally Hemmings by Thomas Jefferson is referred to as a "relationship"—she is also referred to as his "companion." Never once is Thomas Jefferson referred to as a rapist in this article. Thomas Jefferson was a rapist and even though there's DNA evidence linking him as the father of Sally Hemmings' offspring, a Black woman who he legally owned.

7. Just one example is the 2007 case in Philadelphia where a judge ruled a case of rape against a sex worker "theft" because a "prostitute can't be raped."

8. See Dean Spade's *The Trouble with Normal* and "ICE allows rape of transgender woman at Eloy: Save Marichuy." http://www.notonemoredeportation.com/portfolio/marichuy/. She is not an isolated example but more a story documenting systemic violence.

9. *The Revolution Starts at Home* shaped how I understand Transformative Justice as another way of holding communities accountable to prevent and heal from violence. This anthology argues the necessity for it because, in contrast, the Prison Industrial Complex is set up to punish, traumatize, and target Black, Brown, and Indigenous communities.

10. Ikaika Gleisberg said this at the roundtable discussion we were both on at the National Women's Association Conference in Montreal in 2016.

11. I resonated with Kim Curtis's point about taking in the news and post-traumatic stress disorder (PTSD) when she spoke at the Planned Parenthood survivor speak out at Northern Arizona University before Kavanaugh was appointed in the Fall of 2018.

12. See specifically the introduction and conclusion chapters as well as Qwo-Li Driskill's chapter 5.

13. Her book was published before the 2018 rescinding of the law that criminalized queer sex (an old law resulting from British colonialism).

14. All too often the power dynamic involved in researchers without the experiences of those they are writing about is ignored. When heterosexual and/or cisgender people write about us as queer and trans people—without naming their distance from the struggles of our lived experience—it is a messed-up enactment of power. Like Bodhrán says trans people are used to "gain tenure on" (24). Scott Morgensen also points out that as a white person writing about Indigenous people, "my translations necessarily tell as much or more about me and the power I retain as they do about two-spirit organizing" (134).

15. In other words, if we don't tell a story of "born this way," our lives as non-binary and/or trans people are often seen as "fake," "made up," or "curable." Curing our existence suggests we should go away. It suggests something is broken or wrong about our identities and the way we know our genders if we don't tell the "born this way" story (which of course for many people is true, and I'm not discounting that).

16. Earlier in a chapter in their stunning book *Carework: Dreaming Disability Justice* they write that "queer people of color never say we are disabled if we have any choice about it" (184) because survival depends on that. I don't use this word lightly (and am attempting to reclaim it, while also recognizing that, as Piepzna-Samarasinha has pointed out, the privilege in claiming such a weighted word as this one).

17. See *The Body Keeps the Score* by Van der Kolk for the neuroscience of trauma and its aftermath.

18. Hollie Vargas was a survivor who worked with an activist organization for rape survivors in Flagstaff, Arizona, where I live. For years she supported countless victims of rape in crisis intervention. She was a survivor, until she took her life in March, 2019.

REFERENCES

Allison, Dorothy. 1996. *Two or Three Things I Know for Sure.* London: Penguin Books.
Alter, Alexandra. 2019. "E. Jean Carrroll Accuses Trump of Sexual Assault in Her Memoir." *New York Times*, June 21, 2019. https://www.nytimes.com/2019/06/21/books/e-jean-Carroll-trump.html (accessed May 1, 2019).
Anzaldúa, Gloria. 1987/2012. *Borderlands: La Frontera.* 4th Edition. San Francisco: Aunt Lute Books.
Bean, Lexie, ed. 2018. *Written on the Body: Letters from Trans and Non-Binary Survivors of Sexual Assault and Domestic Violence.* Philadelphia: Jessica Kingsley Publishers.
Blau, Max and Megan Vasquez. 2019. "These Women Have Accused Trump of Sexual Harassment." *CNN*, June 24, 2019. https://www.cnn.com/2016/10/14/politics/trump-women-accusers/index.html (accessed July 1, 2019).
Bodhrán, Ahimsa Timotéo. 2013. "Cycle Undone." In *Troubling the Line: Trans and Genderqueer Poetry and Poetics*, edited by TC Tolbert and Tim Trace Peterson, 24–35. Brooklyn: Nightboat Books.
Chin, Staceyann. 2009. *The Other Side of Paradise.* New York: Simon and Schuster.
Clare, Eli. 2015. *Exile and Pride: Disability, Queerness, and Liberation.* Durham: Duke University Press.
Crenshaw, Kimberlé. 2016. "The Urgency of Intersectionality." *TED* Talk. https://www.youtube.com/watch?v=akOe5-UsQ2o (accessed July 1, 2019).
Cvetkovitch, Ann. 2003. *Archive of Feeling.* Durham: Duke University Press.
Driskill, Qwo-Li, Chris Finley, Brian Joseph Gilley, and Scott Lauria Morgenson. 2011. "Introduction." In *Queer Indigenous Studies*, edited by Qwo-Li Driskill, Chris Finley, Brian Joseph Gilley, and Scott Lauria Morgensen, 21–28. Tucson: University of Arizona Press.
Dunbar-Ortiz, Roxanne. 2015. *An Indigenous Peoples' History of the United States.* Boston: Beacon Press.
Finley, Chris. 2011. "Decolonizing the Queer Native Body (and Recovering the Native Bull-Dyke): 'Bringing Sexy Back' and Out of Native Studies Closet." In *Queer Indigenous Studies*, edited by Qwo-Li Driskill, Chris Finley, Brian Joseph Gilley, and Scott Lauria Morgensen, 31–42. Tucson: University of Arizona Press.
Gibson, Andrea. 2012. "The Nutritionist." *Pansy.* Long Beach: Write Bloody Publishing.
Hartman, Saidiya. 2008. *Lose Your Mother: A Journey Along the Atlantic Slave Trade.* New York: Farrar, Straus and Giroux.
Lorde, Audre. 1982. *Zami: A New Spelling of My Name.* Trumansburg: Crossing Press.
Marshall, Jake. 2012. "Can a Prostitute Be Raped?" *Ethics Alarms*, November 2012. https://ethicsalarms.com/2013/11/02/can-a-prostitute-be-raped/ (accessed July 1, 2019).
Moraga, Cherríe. 1985. *Loving in the War Years: Lo que nunca pasó por sus labios.* Troy: Southend Press.
Morgensen, Scott. 2011. "Unsettling Settler Colonialism in Queer Studies." In *Queer Indigenous Studies*, edited by Qwo-Li Driskill, Chris Finley, Brian Joseph Gilley, and Scott Lauria Morgensen, 163–79. Tucson: University of Arizona Press.
Oliver, Mary. 1990. "The Summer Day." *House of Light.* Boston: Beacon Press.
Piepzna-Samarasinha, Leah Lakshmi. 2018. *Care Work: Dreaming Disability Justice.* Vancouver: Arsenal Pulp Press.
———, Jai Dulani, and Ching-In Chen, eds. 2016. *The Revolution Starts at Home.* London: AK Press.
Revathi, A. 2016. *A Life in Trans Activism.* Delhi: Zubaan Books.
Revesz, Rachel. 2016. "Donald Trump boasted about meeting semi-naked teenagers in beauty pageants." *Independent*, October 12, 2016. https://www.independent.co.uk/news/world/

americas/donald-trump-former-miss-arizona-tasha-dixon-naked-undressed-backstage-ho-ward-stern-a7357866.html (accessed July 1, 2019).

Simpson, Leanne Betasomosake. 2013. *Islands of Decolonial Love.* Winnipeg: Arbeiter Ring Publishing.

Spade, Dean. 2015. *The Trouble with Normal: Administrative Violence, Critical Trans Politics, and the Limits of the Law.* Durham: Duke University Press.

Van der Kolk, Bessel A. 2015. *The Body Keeps the Score: Brain, Mind, and Body in the Healing of Trauma.* London: Penguin.

White, Gillian. 2017. "The Glaring Blind Spot of the Me Too Movement." *The Atlantic*, November 22, 2017. https://www.theatlantic.com/entertainment/archive/2017/11/the-glaring-blind-spot-of-the-me-too-movement/546458/ (accessed July 1, 2019).

Yuknavitch, Lidia. 2011. *The Chronology of Water.* Portland: Hawthorne Books.

Zimmerman, Jean. "The Agonizing Collision of Love and Slavery in 'Thomas Jefferson.'" *NPR*, April 6, 2016. https://www.npr.org/2016/04/06/471619275/the-agonizing-collision-of-love-and-slavery-in-thomas-jefferson (accessed July 1, 2019).

Chapter Three

A Revisionist History of Loving Men

*Exploring Consent and Sexual Violence in
Romantic Relationships*

Lena Ziegler

In my car, on a crisp Tennessee-winter night, I first told Shane I had been raped. It happened three years ago, I explained, the first time I moved to this state. It happened when I was just turning twenty-three and already getting divorced, when I was lonely and afraid, when I was trying to celebrate my birthday with a stranger from the internet. It happened when I was crushed beneath the weight of his body on top of me—his ashy tongue probing my mouth, his calloused hands flipping me to my stomach and his dick pushing inside of me while I cried for him to stop. And, it kept happening after that, too. It happened when he said *you can't tell anyone you invited me over. I didn't rape you. I didn't do anything wrong.* It happened when, in the end, I somehow apologized to him.

I told this story as it happened and Shane held my hand as I spoke, watching me cry right there in the empty parking lot of the Carrabba's where we had spent over four hours talking about things that must have made me trust him.

"I've never told anyone this," I said. "But every time I hear the word 'rape' I go right back to that moment."

I don't remember what he said, just how he said it. With tears in his eyes and a gentle pain in his smile, a smile creased in the corners from the decades of living he had over me. I was twenty-six at the time and he was fifty-two. We had just ended our second date.

We all have damage we'd prefer rattle around our own brains than turn into stories to tell other people. But when and how do you break the silence around a history with sexual violence when it comes to pursuing consensual sex and intimacy? For example, how do you tell a new partner that you have been a victim of sexual violence? How do you tell this new partner that you were not only victimized by a stranger on your twenty-third birthday that first time you moved to Tennessee, but also in three out of four of the past relationships you once considered serious? How do you blend the histories of your life, the stories you tell about yourself and the parallel truths of what you wish never happened in the first place, when you are seeking both intimacy and protection from it?

It'd be easier and far less complicated to say I was raped on my twenty-third birthday by a stranger and only began to acknowledge it years later once I learned more about rape culture through the cultural commentary filling social media, telling me that consent is a black and white concept, clearly recognizable to any adult with halfway decent communication skills. But nothing about sexual violence is easy, most especially, telling the truth. And one of the truths of my story is that the rape I experienced on my twenty-third birthday took three years for me to acknowledge. It took me years, in part, because living as a woman in a culture that normalizes and even celebrates unbridled male obsession with sex, while shaming the same in females, told me that simply inviting this man over that night was an invitation to, if not a promise of sex. It also told me that what happened is not only what I should have expected from any red-blooded American man, but it's what I deserved as a woman brazen enough to invite the *possibility* of physical connection.

This is one truth.

Another is that at the point in my life when I first acknowledged this as rape, it was also the only experience I felt even remotely *allowed* to call rape, and even then, just barely. Of all the names associated with sexual violence—"assault," "misconduct," "violation," etc.—"rape" is the only one with a powerful enough linguistic energy to communicate the pain of the experience. However, the word "rape" also "prescribes behaviors" for victims, challenging "their abilities to see themselves as agents" by implying that there are certain ways they should feel and behave after being raped, all while reducing "the complexity of their experiences" to one catch-all term (Harris 2011, 46).

A broader, more global truth would be to say loudly, and clearly, that this was *not* the first time I had been raped and was not, in that moment, even the most *recent* time I had been raped, and that this would not be the last time I'd experience sexual violence. It was, however, the only time I would ever experience it with a stranger, and because of this, the only one I felt justified in using the word.

There are many truths in every story. I am trying to tell it as it happened.

I started researching sexual violence in early 2017 while finishing the final semester of my master's degree in creative writing. I was just beginning my second workshop in memoir, a genre with which I still had little familiarity. During my first workshop the previous year, so much of what I wrote was composed with a thin film of protective language blanketing it. I was afraid to be too vulnerable, or go too far within myself for fear that I might find something ugly. The first year of an MFA program can feel a lot like learning to swim, but limiting your lessons to the shallow end, wearing floaties and pool shoes, trying not to get too wet. But a year later, a lot about my personal life had changed. My relationship with Shane had blown up in a dramatic, public way that had left me reeling in the vacuum of his absence. I was left alone to make sense of the wounds of the relationship. I had spent the previous semester writing raw, angry poetry that had revealed, in minute details, the nature of our psychologically and sexually abusive relationship, but I had yet to delve into the circumstances of what had happened, or what role I played in it.

As the second workshop started, we read powerful essays and books written by Lidia Yuknavitch, Maggie Nelson, and Elissa Washuta who all, in some form or another, touched on sexual violence. I loved each one of these readings in different ways, finding inspiration in the language, the raw storytelling. Each week we submitted drafts of essays, missives composed with the readings in mind. My writing was more direct and visceral than anything I had written before. Yet it felt disconnected from fluid narrative, still searching for focus. However, when we read our third full text, *College Girl* by Laura Gray-Rosendale, a powerful and devastating memoir about the trauma endured after a brutal rape, and the journey toward understanding and healing from it, all sense of calm, safety, and protective language blanketing me fell away. Suddenly, memories of my own violations, and the internal conflicts and wounds I had learned to live with erupted through me, as I measured them against the experiences I was reading about. But for every scene, line, or word from *College Girl* that I related to, I felt a palpable, mounting guilt for believing I knew anything at all about suffering. Once again, I was reeling.

I want to tell you stories of violation.

I want to tell you how I hovered above myself, disembodied from the girl on the futon mattress. I want to tell you about her drunken husband crushing her body into submission. I want to tell you how the TV turned snowy in the corner of the room, its blue glow coloring their skin. I want to tell you how silent tears taste on lips pressed closed, fighting sound and salt, in a bedroom, inside a house filled with people. I want to tell you how it felt to be alone with someone else's flesh thrust inside me, how the ceiling turned porthole and I dreamt of floating through it. I want to tell you how I got married at twenty-one and divorced at twenty-three and how a rape had nothing to do with why.

I want you to know how a couple of years later, I found myself with a new boyfriend who forced love from my throat, held my head in his hands and took my voice with his cock until I was crying and could hardly breathe. I want you to know that the same man once woke up in the night and forced himself into a part of me I didn't allow him to touch. I want you to know how both times he laughed before asking if I was *seriously that upset about this*. I want you to know I didn't leave him then. Instead, I stayed with him and continued to laugh, and play, and be his friend, until one day I was gone, and on the phone apologizing for leaving.

I want to tell you how a year later, an older man saw all my hurt and cried with me in a parking lot. I want to tell you how he made me feel temporarily safe, how he never had to use the power of his body when he forced me to have sex with other men while he watched, and watched, and urged them on. I want to tell you how he made me believe that there were things I owed him with my body if I wanted to experience being loved by him. I want to tell you how the future of our relationship dangled in front of me anytime I tried to refuse, and when he watched one man fuck me and I cried, told him *no more of this, I don't want any more*, he then invited another man to do the same. I want to tell you how I hated myself for enjoying it.

Reading *College Girl* was a profound experience that cracked open a part of me I didn't yet recognize. I had only started referring to the incident on my twenty-third birthday as rape two years earlier. This revelation was extremely hard for me because I felt that without providing the context and the minute-to-minute breakdown of what had happened with that man, no one else would believe it was rape. Though studies have found that "women who voiced non-consent endorsed labels of rape and sexual assault at significantly higher levels than women who did not voice non-consent" (Cook and Messman-Moore 2017, 519), internal narratives of self-blame, dismissal of pain, and cultural normalization of sexual violence all contribute to a person's "willful decision to dissociate oneself from rape" (Johnstone 2016, 281). But despite all of my own doubts and insecurities associated with naming my rape, Shane believed that I had been and showed compassion when I talked about it. The validation that came with that was profound.

So when I read *College Girl* and the heart-wrenching opening chapter in which the rape is detailed, I felt deeply guilty for using the word "rape" to refer to my own experiences. My rape did not look at all like that one did. Mine was not as violent or as ugly. She had done nothing to provoke or cause it, like I believed I had. She had not invited the man into her home, or chosen to lay on her bed and kiss him, like I had. All I could think as I read and read, consumed by the narrative, was how fucking audacious I was to refer to what happened to me as rape when there were women out there every day who had suffered what it was like to be *truly* raped. Caught up in a game of comparison so many women play, I couldn't stop measuring my own experiences against those I saw as more valid. In *Not That Bad*, Roxane Gay tells us that "for years, I fostered wildly unrealistic expectations of the kinds of experiences worthy of suffering, until very little was worthy of suffering" (Gay 2018, x). In my case, I felt that though it had happened and had been horrible, I had mostly moved on and was doing okay. "Everything was terrible but none of it was that bad" (Gay 2018, x). If it was real rape, that wouldn't be the case. *Real* rape doesn't leave room for that. *Real* rape ruins your whole life, I thought, and you are never again okay.

And yet, I was reeling. I was reeling not just because of how the language of rape felt somehow out of my grasp. I was also reeling because, while I wasn't destroyed by the rape on my twenty-third birthday, I felt completely ruined by my relationship with Shane, and the many sexual violations that had been regular components of it.

Shane was the first person I chose to tell about my rape and, when I did, he kissed my wet cheeks and promised tenderness to me with a sincerity I trusted almost immediately. In the early weeks of our relationship, we were snowed-in in my apartment for four days, and we spent that entire time talking and having sex. He learned about the dark parts of my childhood, my abusive marriage to Carl when I was only twenty-one, and my ex-boyfriend Jack who came before him a year earlier, whose sexual domination of me had left me feeling used and humiliated on more than one occasion. He opened up to me as well, the wounds of his former marriages bared, still raw beneath all the scarring. But his focus was mostly on me, who I was and how I loved. In my loneliness and desperation to be protected from the accumulation of several years' damage swelling within me, my heart was open to any intimacy I could find. So my love for him came quickly, with an all-consuming intensity I couldn't believe.

There are some men who, when they hear you have been raped, when they find out your body once existed as the site of another man's violence, start imagining the ways they might participate in your history of violation. Such men want to plant the flag of their hard-pricked desire to make you remember them forever, long after you've lost your relevance to one another, in the threads of your sexual history. It is important to me that I remember Shane as he was—silent gunfire, a slow leak of poison, a violence threaded through everything. It is important that I remember his shift away from gentleness into something like ownership, when he first proposed that true vulnerability was handing yourself over to someone else and trusting them with the pieces.

Reflecting on my relationship with Shane, in light of reading *College Girl*, was enormously confusing. How was it that a memoir about an explicit experience of rape was triggering within me pain from a relationship in which I *hadn't* been raped? I had said "yes" verbally, if not in some other way, to almost everything that had happened with Shane, and those things I hadn't said yes to felt so reminiscent of my previous relationships. There was no real way I could possibly recognize them as sexually violent without calling my entire relationship history into question. And how could I do that without also interrogating the entirety of who I was and what had led me to these experiences? Further, if I was this disturbed by the things I had said yes to, while normalizing the things I hadn't said yes to as a regular part of loving and dating men, what did it even mean to give consent? And how the fuck would I ever begin to understand it?

Aside from marital rape, which only began to be criminalized in the 1970s, cultural conversations about sexual violence do not spend near enough energy on the widespread prevalence of rape and sexual violation that occurs in romantic relationships between men and women. Studies have found that 50 percent of college women "reported having unwanted coitus over a 2-week data collection period" (Bay-Cheng and Eliseo-Arras 2016, 386). The research, which cites gender norms and expectations as the "cultural scaffolding of rape," specifically notes the pressure put on women, most especially young women, to conform to the expectation that their sexual role within a relationship is to please their male partners, resulting in the belief that doing so is a necessary component to maintaining a relationship (387). While sexual violence scholars might recognize pressure to have sex as a red flag for sexual coercion, leading to sexual assault, cultural rhetoric surrounding heterosexual relationships reinforces the notion that boys and men are out-of-control sexual creatures, whose sexuality must be maintained and managed by girls and women as a normal part of the relational model. This suggests that coercive behavior is par for the course if a man is behaving like your average straight male with a healthy sexual appetite, as "the view of male sex drive as stronger than the female and indeed 'uncontrollable' is held by both girls and boys from an early age" (Hakvåg 2009, 123). bell hooks explores this rhetoric of the "male sexual being," looking at how the culture sexualizes men and women in oppositional ways. She explains:

> The belief that if men are not sexually active, they will "act out or go crazy," directly contributes to the acceptance of male sexual violence . . . this is why rape—whether date rape, marital rape, or stranger rape—is not deemed a serious crime . . . the assumption that he's "gotta have it" underlies much of our culture's acceptance of male sexual violence. (hooks 2004, 77)

The result of this is the normalization of a certain amount of unwanted sex as something to be expected in a relationship between a man and a woman, with

Hakvåg suggesting that "the prevalence of sexual coercion within normative heterosexuality occasionally makes sex and sexual assault look awfully similar" (121). Still, with unwanted sex normalized, "marked by hesitation, reluctance, or an ambivalent kind of unwillingness," rather than happening *explicitly* against a woman's will (Cahill 2016, 753), recognizing coercion as sexually violent can be difficult. Therefore, the responsibility of consent is placed on women to communicate, loudly and clearly with a "yes" or a "no," whether or not they wish to consent to sex. However, problems come with the assumption that *yes* always means *yes* and does not account for the fact that there are many reasons, beyond those involving her own sexual desire, for why a woman might say yes. These can involve coercion, emotional manipulation, or social rules that suggest women are not allowed to say yes without being a slut, and not allowed to say no without being a prude.

A 2017 study of college students' consent communication styles found that responsibility was placed at women's feet across gender lines, emphasizing a "no-win" reality for women who are on the one hand expected not to have sex, while on the other also expected to give in to male sexual desire. As gender norms "seem to influence students' perceptions of consent and consent communication," this can in fact lead women to say *no* when they mean *yes* and to say *yes* when they mean *no* (Jozkowski, Marcantonio, and Hunt 2017, 241). This results in an even grayer understanding of how consent communication functions in real-world sexual scenarios. As the authors explain:

> Affirmative consent policies promote the sex-positive ideal of "enthusiastic consent" . . . unfortunately our findings suggest that it may not be realistic to expect women to be direct when communicating their sexual desires, especially their enthusiastic consent, because of concern about developing a negative reputation. (Jozkowski, Marcantonio, and Hunt 2017, 243)

While communications scholars recognize that all of these factors influence how a person communicates, some feminist efforts regarding sex education have embraced the oversimplification of consent as a simple yes/no binary "because the ambiguity and complexity of language routinely gets used to justify rape," leaving room for women to be blamed for not consenting, or resisting, clearly enough (Harris 2018, 8). Given the fact that in a research study about women's sexual refusal tactics, "77 percent of all participants in the study 'responded in the affirmative when asked if they had an interest in learning more effective refusal skills'" (Kitzinger and Frith 1999, 295), while young men admit that they typically seek consent in women's body language, facial expressions, and emotions more so than in verbal affirmation (O'Byrne, Rapley, and Hansen 2006), there is no question that consent communication as we currently define it and teach it doesn't work. It in fact clouds women's perceptions of whether or not non-consensual sex is rape, or simply another day in a straight relationship. In fact, the belief that whether or not a woman gave verbal consent is the *only* factor in determining whether or not she had been raped is so prevalent in our cultural discourse around sexual violence that studies show some women who have experienced sexual violence have, in a moment of violation, chosen *not* to say no in order to "label her experience as something more benign than rape, such as miscommunication" (Cook and Messman-Moore 2017, 510). This reminds us that rape acknowledgement, or recognition, is anything but simple, and that perhaps a yes/no binary for understanding it is simply not enough.

When you begin to question what you have always been told about consent, it is impossible not to measure your own sexual experiences against what is culturally inscribed as consensual or nonconsensual sex. The reality was that throughout my relationship with Shane, I felt routinely violated and frequently pressured into sexual situations with which I was not at all comfortable. I engaged in them because I truly believed I owed him anything he wanted sexually if I was ever to get what I wanted from him emotionally. Ellisa Bassist confronts this complication in her essay "Why I Didn't Say No," citing the notions that "love and sex were supposed to hurt," and that the "cost of something is often mistaken for its value" (Bassist 2018, 323, 331), making the line between consent and violence in her own relationship history blurry. As her essay highlights, the idea that there is nobility in female sacrifice and suffering is nothing new. But the more that I researched and wrote through the pain of realizing that I had somehow misunderstood what healthy, consensual sex looked like for my entire adult life, the more that I questioned who I was as a woman, and worse yet, as a feminist. I couldn't stop asking how I could consider myself a feminist if I wasn't comfortable calling a rape a rape, or abuse abuse, or holding the men I loved accountable for the pain that they had caused me.

When I was twenty-five, a half a year before I met Shane, I moved a thousand miles, in part, to end a relationship I wanted out of, but didn't know how to end. This was not the first time I responded to heartbreak by moving from Pennsylvania to Tennessee, believing somehow that the thick air and heat would sweat the pain out of me. When I was twenty-two I had moved to Tennessee in an effort to escape a marriage that had failed before it even had time to start.

On our honeymoon it was clear that Carl had a problem with drinking. We had dated for three years while I was in college and, though there had been incidents that told me he was a man who couldn't handle his alcohol without turning belligerent and angry, I had no sense of how serious the problem actually was. He snuck liquor onto our cruise ship in a thin plastic bag. The alcohol was like an IV drip that he buried in his swimming trunks and polo shirts. One night, after he screamed at me, called me names, and kicked me out of our suite, I sat on the tropical print carpet in the hallway, my eyes red with tears and cheeks pink from the Bermuda sun, and took a picture of myself on the digital camera I received as a wedding present only a few days earlier. In the picture it was clear I had been crying. The skin around my eyes was translucent and puffy with sadness. My hair was pulled back in a messy ponytail, unbrushed and knotted from chlorine. I'm not sure why I took the picture. But as I sat there in the hallway, staring at the close-up picture I had just taken of my face, with its sad frown formed from quivering lips, I remember thinking about how incredibly long a human life could be, and how terribly young I still was.

Five months into our marriage, Christmas came and we traveled to my mother's house to spend Christmas Eve with my family. At this point, no one in my life knew Carl had a drinking problem. No one knew he was unemployed, that I was going broke paying his bills and mine, and that I spent most nights locked in the bathroom hiding from his mounting violence, or on the kitchen floor, cleaning up his mess and praying he'd stop hurting me. Besides, there was still some good between us. On nights he wasn't drinking, I was too grateful to see him sober to fight about all the times he wasn't. So we would watch movies together, cuddled on the couch and kissing like we were happy. We'd go to open mics and I'd watch him do stand-up, proud of how everyone in the audience always seemed to love him. We picked out a Christmas tree together and made up silly songs, singing back and forth in the car when we drove around in the ice and slush of the city where we lived. Somehow, in all my faith and hopefulness, I still believed it was going to get better, and there was no reason to tell anyone otherwise.

It was nearly midnight on Christmas Eve and my family had all gone to bed. I was still just as excited for Christmas morning as I was when I was a child. Carl and I lay close on an old futon mattress in my old bedroom, watching a VHS tape of *A Christmas Story* for the second time that year. About halfway through the movie I started to fall asleep and he whispered for me to keep sleeping; he was just moving to the chair on the other side of the bedroom to get more comfortable. When I woke a couple of hours later, stirred by the snowy sound of the TV still on after the movie had ended, it appeared that he had fallen asleep there. Kicking at him playfully, I told him to join me on the mattress. His eyes lifted slowly, hazy and hard.

"What?" he said, loudly, his tongue slumped over the curve of his bottom lip, the slight glint of drool on his chin reflecting in the TV light.

My stomach shifted and settled into panic with the realization that he was drunk, on Christmas Eve, in my parents' house and no one even knew he was an alcoholic. Instantly, the pieces of my life I had tried so hard to compartmentalize were coming together, and the narrative of my marriage I had run myself ragged trying to control was slipping from my grasp, soon to unravel in a humiliating, public display of drunkenness and abuse I could no longer deny. My body flooded with fear.

"What?" he said again, louder.

I tried to quiet him, but he grew belligerent in his volume and aggression, pushing himself up to stand and lumbering over to the mattress. He fell on top of me, vibrating the floorboards of the old wooden house and sending a tremble of sound through the entire upstairs. Terror grew thick in my chest—what would happen if they woke up? What if they all found out that this man they loved, who *I* loved, must have snuck alcohol in his overnight bag and waited for me to fall asleep before guzzling it down? In all of my excitement about Christmas, and spending time in the safety of my mother's home surrounded by my family, it had never occurred to me that this might happen. Why hadn't it occurred to me? Why hadn't I prepared for this, checked his bag before we left, or broken the tradition of spending the night on Christmas Eve in case of something like this? How could I have let this happen?

His body shifted on top of mine, the weight of his form crushing me into place. The sickly sweet scent of cheap vodka spilled from his mouth as he told me he was going to fuck me. Though I was furious, shaking with worry that any moment my mother would fling open the door and discover the truth about my life, I tried to be gentle with Carl. I giggled something like *not right now, babe*, or, maybe, *not in my parent's house*, and I smiled somehow, as if strategic flirtation could save me from the situation, or expedite its ending. But the more I resisted, the more impatient he grew. His fingers fumbled with the elastic waist of my bed shorts, slipped beneath my underwear, and thrust inside of me. I can't remember if it hurt, or if I told him to stop. I was assessing the situation—the danger of pushing his heavy body away from me and how he would no doubt react, screaming, thumping, punching his fists into plaster. It would terrify my family. It would ruin Christmas. It would reveal him to everyone as the abusive alcoholic husband he was, and me as the weak-willed woman who stood by him.

I don't remember how much he really kissed me, just that there was slobber and wet that tasted toxic. Maybe I kissed him back, or maybe I just turned my head to the side and stared at the snowy television. I only know when I cried it was soft like the suffering I somehow learned to take pride in as a woman, keeping my shit together while a man hurt me, not letting on how much, or in how many different ways. I only know I was crying and he was inside of me; I couldn't move and there was nothing I could do to stop him.

The next morning, I greeted my family with all the glee appropriate to Christmas morning. I went through my day opening presents, laughing, smiling, taking pictures, eating too many pancakes and cookies, and never addressed what happened—not with Carl, not with anyone. My shame surrounding this violation and my lack of vocabulary to actually understand it still overwhelm me when I revisit it. Talking about it, I reasoned, would make my entire family uncomfortable. As Bassist contends, for women in our culture "stifling trauma is just good manners" (Bassist 2018, 334). The reality is that even if Carl remembered what happened Christmas Eve 2009, it is unlikely he would remember it as it happened, or at least in the same way that I remember it happening to me. Despite everything I know about sexual violence that tells me I did not give consent, that I actively did what I could to prevent it, that the physical threat of his body on top of mine, that I was trapped with no option to refuse sex, I still don't feel comfortable calling it "rape." Instead, I call it a "violation"—a word that feels right, but doesn't carry the weight or the imbedded cultural knowledge of what such a thing really looks like, or even means.

Three years later, I met Jack. Our relationship started as a rebound from an emotionally devastating breakup with a man who I had loved desperately, but who did not have any interest in sex. Despite an intense love for one another, after a year-and-a-half of trying, he could not change who he was and I could not change what I needed from him. When we broke up, he told me that I was a sick woman for valuing sex more than I valued love, and this made me feel ashamed. But when Jack came along, with his attraction to me so blatant it bordered on objectification, I couldn't resist the feelings of validation this sprouted within me.

Jack was unlike anyone else I had ever met. He was the product of a violent, broken upbringing, in and out of foster care, juvenile detention, and eventually jail. His pain was bred from a combination of childhood abuse and neglect, melded with struggles with mental illness, and an association with poverty he wore as a badge of honor. Like so many men who came before, he triggered within me the deep desire to transform him and his life with the power of my warmth, care, and love. Jack was many things, most especially a bold, outgoing, intelligent, hilarious, goofy person, whose sheer mass in height and weight and propensity toward violence with other men made him the kind of man destined to go through life as the one phone call someone would make whenever in trouble and in need of someone ready to fight. But, as so many women do, or at least as I have so often done with men who were clearly wrong for me, I searched for the depth in Jack and found a goodness, a lightness shining through the black hole of pain that so often swallowed him and informed the decisions he made for how he lived his life. As strong as Jack presented himself to the world, I could see how lost he was and I wanted to help him find his way.

Early into our relationship, Jack moved in with me. He did this not because our relationship called for it, but because he had nowhere else to go and exercising boundaries for myself was not something with which I had any experience or reason to believe I deserved. We never talked about it, or made the decision directly. It just happened when his belongings began to accumulate in piles around the two-hundred-fifty square feet of my studio apartment, suffocating me out of my own space. I wasn't happy with this, but I also didn't fight it because the incredible loneliness inside of me bubbled up as failure, and the sexual validation I received from Jack in contrast to the regular rejection that peppered my previous relationship influenced my every decision. I invited him into my life because at the time I believed attention was a valid substitute for love and respect, and that my capacity for love was best spent on the people who had no idea how to return it, but were in desperate need of experiencing it.

When I tell people about my relationship with Jack, which in total lasted about nine months, I emphasize the good parts—the hours spent belly-laughing together like children unable to catch their breath, cooking together in an apartment kitchen that was in no way up to code, playing my ukulele and singing songs together, screaming at him for bringing a gun into my apartment without realizing it was a broken BB gun from his childhood. In so many ways Jack made me extremely happy, distracting me from the parts of myself I didn't want to face yet, and teaching me to embrace the pockets of joy I could find in anything if I looked hard enough.

But there was a darkness about our relationship that even now I am uncomfortable acknowledging, mostly because I still can't bring myself to hold him accountable for it. As much as I cared for Jack, I didn't love him in the way I had loved other men. I always knew in my heart our relationship was temporary, even when he told me he'd love to marry me some day, even when he talked about having children with me. I told him I wasn't ready, that I didn't want that kind of commitment and I didn't see things going there.

But, saying "no" to his love was not acceptable. So often he begged me to say it, ridiculed me for not wanting to, and told me someday I would utter those words, *I love you, I want to be with you longer than just right now*. But, as months passed and I refused to say it, wanting to hold on to some degree of autonomy, Jack grew angrier and more frustrated with me, determined to get what he wanted.

One evening, in the lamplight of my apartment I slid to the floor and knelt before him. I put my mouth around him and looked in his eyes. He followed my gaze, smiling, his hands in my hair directing my movement. Sexually, I loved to relinquish my control to him, and he loved taking it. But as he grew closer, he began to ask for something.

"I want you to tell me you love me."

This was not the first time Jack had demanded I tell him how I felt about him, but it was the first time he held my head in his hands, my voice muffled by his flesh pressing the back of my throat. A dread filled my chest, but I chuckled, trying to be playful and offset how uncomfortable he was making me.

He persisted.

"I need you to say it."

I pressed my hands on his thighs and pushed myself away from him. "You know how I feel about that," I said, more serious in my tone. "I've told you, I can't say that until I'm ready."

But Jack had spent his life believing brute force was the only reliable way to get what he wanted, and if my *I love you* was not to be freely given, it was something he felt entitled to take when and how he wanted. Clutching my hair, he forced my head down and his penis back into my mouth.

"Say it," he said. "Say you love me."

Panic struck through my center as I realized I couldn't breathe. I slapped his thighs, the sign I had given other times we got rough together, a sign that told him to slow down and let me go. But he didn't let go and instead urged me further.

"Say it now and this will all be over," he told me. He was smirking, enjoying himself with a sadistic grin. I shook my head, determined not to give into him. But with my nose pressed into his flesh and my eyes filling with tears, my body started to shake. My fingers dug into his skin, and I tried to pull myself off of him.

But he held my head still.

"Say it," he said, slowly. With our eyes locked, I watched his face turn dark. He was not going to let me go. He was going to force me to say it. I blinked back tears and tried to speak, but only a gurgle came out. He asked me again, and I tried, again, to say it. I said it over and over until the urgency of my fear and anger came through the muffled sound and I articulated, as clearly as physically possible, "I love you."

He laughed, letting me go, and I pushed myself off of him.

"I knew it," he said smirking.

My body convulsed, breaking into sobs. I don't remember what I said to him, just that I screamed. My voice rang through the tiny apartment. I stood up, trembling as I rushed to the bathroom, pulling the door closed and locking myself inside. The mirror above the sink was speckled with water marks from shower condensation. I stared at my reflection. My eyes were red and blinking. I knew in that moment something had been taken from me, but it took me years to figure out what that was.

I ended my relationship with Jack, officially, by moving to Tennessee for a job with AmeriCorps. Shortly after, in an effort to avoid love while at the same time seeking it with a drive and desperation so intense I can hardly believe it now, years later, I met Shane. It is hard for me to write about my relationship with Shane without admitting there are parts of myself I am ashamed to say still exist inside of me. But at the time I was twenty-six and Shane was fifty-two, and all I was seeking from any man I met was love and protection. Under his gentle authority, I gave myself over to him, believing he would heal me as he promised he could, if only I trusted his guidance. Though Shane was much more than his age, a broken man surviving mountains of childhood trauma at the hands of an abusive father, two failed marriages, and the lost custody of his son, the context of our relationship that I want to emphasize is how I came to love him and why I verbally consented to experiences that left me damaged enough to identify them with narratives of rape.

When I first met Shane his kindness toward me was unmatched by any man I had ever encountered. His unrelenting interest in me manifested in hours sitting and talking, asking me questions about my life, wanting to know my greatest joys and most devastating heartbreaks. He was determined to understand every single thing about me, probing for more details about my family, my relationship history, my thoughts on books and music, and every step of my writing process. I spent hours talking and sharing, afraid to be too vulnerable but being told as he kissed my forehead and held my hand that everything I felt was valid, every dream I had, achievable. I had never before felt so seen by a man. Sometime during the first month we knew each other, he spent five hours reading the novel I was writing out loud to me, asking questions about the characters, commenting on the poignant moments, and the parts that made him laugh. When I told him how much I loved Joni Mitchell, he showed up at my apartment, unannounced with an Appalachian Mountain dulcimer and told me I should learn to play, that my voice was too beautiful to not be heard. Shane intoxicated my life, throwing me off-balance at every turn, while insisting that this instability was the best part about being alive, the source energy needed to truly understand what it meant to be human.

Shane's obsession with me and my life resulted in my obsession with pleasing him and making myself available to his ever-growing list of demands which were increasingly impossible to meet. Shane had sexual fantasies he had never before been able to fulfill. He had fantasies that involved his female partner, driven by uncontrollable lust, having sex with other men in front of him, while he watched, pleasuring himself to all of the unbridled passion. But for me, romantic love did not involve multiple people, and sex with other men was not something I wanted at all, especially when I was still seeking verbal confirmation of Shane's love for me—something he held over my head and told me I might eventually earn. For as many times as Shane told me he didn't want me to do anything with which I wasn't comfortable, there were so many more times when he made his expectations clear with his anger, or his silence, his unwillingness to respond to me when I talked to him, or his insistence that I was not a woman he could ever be with long-term if I wasn't willing to do the things he wanted. This behavior of abuse is consistent with Nicola Gavey's explorations of coercion in heterosexual relationships. In Cahill's review of Gavey's work we learn that coercive sexual pressure can result in "unjust sex," or sex that requires a woman to concede to sexual acts she doesn't want in order to avoid emotional or physical punishment, with her "agency employed only so that it can be used against her," thus making her feel complicit in her own victimization (Cahill 2016, 755). So often I found myself agreeing to things I didn't feel comfortable with, things I didn't feel safe doing, because I believed it was all a part of the exchange, a price a woman like me needed to pay to continue experiencing the exhilarating force of his attention. After I did what he asked, Shane would talk to me about my "performance," wanting me to recollect all of the thoughts and feelings I had during the experiences, and I would try my best to talk about it in the ways he wanted me to. Any hesitancy to share, any withholding on my part, any wrong word choice I made in describing the physical and emotional sensations I was experiencing, could jeopardize Shane's happiness with me. Yet, with Shane, the more I tried to please him, the more I seemed to let him down, and I was quickly drowning in the undertow of his growing obsession with my sexuality, and his desire to control it.

Though perhaps the specifics of the convoluted relationship I had with Shane are not necessarily things with which most people would identify, I will say that the way Shane anchored his entire being to me, and the way I responded to it by never venturing too far away from the dead weight of his control, is an experience familiar to anyone who has ever been stuck in an abusive relationship. But rather than physical violence, or verbal abuse, Shane used my weakness around sex and knowledge of my past trauma, including the rape on my twenty-third birthday, my relationship with Jack, and the many instances of violence I experienced with Carl, to inform how he would control me, and urge me to do what he asked. To rationally explain how he achieved this is still impossible for me, but I now recognize it fully for what it was.

Despite fulfilling many of my own sexual fantasies with Shane, exploring my own propensity toward kink and sex positivity that I stand behind today as valid components of a healthy adult sexuality, Shane's psychological control over me manifested in his complete control over my body. But as hooks writes, "Love will not prevail in any situation where one party wants to maintain control," no matter how normal it might begin to feel (2000, 152). He made it clear both directly and indirectly that his love and commitment were prizes to be earned if I could make and keep him happy. But broken people are not made happy by the love of another person coursing through them. This I know, not just from Shane, but from myself. We can search for love in all of the most beautiful and dangerous places, but love that comes at a cost will never heal us. A love that asks us to give ourselves away will never result in our restoration. In the case of this kind of love, we can only hope for survival.

Survivor stories aren't just the recollections of things that happen to us. They are the product of collective narrative—the trampling whisper of our own inner voices questioning, affirming, and reconsidering what happened to us and why. They often also echo a culture that is working hard against us, imbedded jagged and violent in the soft tissue of our brains, telling us in words and wounds that our lives didn't happen the way that we think they did, that our memories can't be trusted, that our quickness to feel or shut down in response to a trigger word, insensitive joke, or the narrative arc of a popular television show stems from weakness rather than recognition.

Though when I first starting writing about rape I was inspired to do so because of my relationship with Shane, the incident with Jack was one of the first from my entire relationship history I was able to recognize as sexually violent—a violation that came with no ready name and seemed to defy description when stripped of its context. This was not the only time Jack used force in our relationship. Sometime after the forced *I love you*, he entered me while I was sleeping, waking me up by anally penetrating me. I reacted to this the same way I did the time before. I saw my own red eyes staring back at me in the bathroom mirror. Shortly after these memories began to resonate as violent, I started to reflect on my marriage to Carl, and the incident on Christmas Eve—a secret I had not discussed with anyone, choosing instead to focus all conversations about my marriage on the tragedy of addiction and what it does to families.

I still don't know exactly how to write about these experiences, just that they have stayed with me, for years, coloring how I connect with new people as well as how I feel about myself and the "kind of woman I am." Somehow the pain I carry with me from all of these events has never felt valid because I have never had a way of understanding them, or naming them. This is why I, and more established scholars of sexual violence, believe more time and attention must be given to research that asks women to name their own experiences, still recognizing that naming is not the "final moment of truth recognition" (Harris 2011, 45). And one of my truths is that I never once ended a relationship after or because of sexual violence.

Though some part of me believes I am a weak woman, a bad feminist, a stupid girl willing to trade her bodily autonomy for a shred of love, a greater part of me now knows that the primary reason I continued my relationships with these men was that I did not believe these experiences were abnormal, or worthy of the rage they ignited within me. I believed that for one reason or another, these men didn't understand that they hurt me, didn't know what they had done was wrong, and that it was unfair to hold something against them that they didn't intentionally do. I believed the sacrifice of my body was part of what came with inviting men into my life and agreeing in action, if not words, to love them.

In so many ways, this is at the root of what has formed American rape culture—the belief that rape is an inevitable consequence of men and women co-existing in the world. This belief places all responsibility on women to avoid, prevent, and report rape when it happens. However, the idea that rape is inevitable, even normal, lessens the likelihood of it being appropriately punished, and thus challenges women who have been raped to take one of two options: either participate in the legal system and culture that delegitimizes their trauma by reporting it, or pretend it never happened in the first place and try to move on. Still, despite normalization, most women who have been raped, assaulted, or violated know that what happened to them was not okay. The disconnect comes with believing that the only thing that could have prevented it was a change in women's own behavior, rather than a change in the behavior of the men who have hurt them.

Of course I know that if I had asked Jack to leave after the first incident, the second would never have happened. Of course I know if I had not believed myself a monster for "valuing sex over love," I would not have believed I deserved what happened when I had sex *without* love. Of course if my relationship with Jack was not built on the foundation of a failed marriage in which I had blamed an incident of sexual violence on my husband's alcoholism, never addressing the damage it had caused me, maybe I wouldn't have stayed with either of them as long as I did. Of course, if none of these things had happened, I wouldn't have turned myself into a cliché and sought love with a man twice my age, who learned to weaponize my pain, and swell the damage within me to an unmanageable volume. Of course if I hadn't, despite all of my feminist education, believed in my bones that the men in my life had a certain right to my body as an exchange for emotional intimacy, none of this would have happened.

Herein lies the complex and conflicting neoliberal narrative that exists within me, and so many women with a history of sexual violence. Bay-Cheng and Eliseo-Arras explain the two opposing narratives of a modern, empowered woman: "The Pleasing Woman" and the "Together Woman" (Bay-Cheng and Eliseo-Arras 2008, 387). The former they describe as "actively selfless" in the meeting of male sexual needs, while the latter is seen as self-actualized and empowered—a binary that they explain "promotes the notion that since women are presumed to exert complete control over their own life circumstances, women who are victimized are somehow weak, inept, or lacking in self-respect" (387).

Despite the majority of women not blaming their partners for coercing or forcing sexual situations they did not want, and instead blaming themselves for not knowing better or communicating more clearly (Bay-Cheng and Eliseo-Arras 2008, 393), I recognize that my actions did not light the fire of violence under the men that I loved and cared for. My actions simply reinforce how cultural narratives that normalize male entitlement to female bodies, especially within relationships, embed themselves in the marrow of women, challenging them to fight hard if they want to be seen as rightful owners of their own bodies. Still, I need it to be known that even as I write this, so many years later, with a much greater understanding of the cultural implications of rape culture, I question whether or not I have the right to do so. But we all have a right to our stories—even when they don't make sense, even when they make us question who we are. So I ask myself again, for the millionth time, "Is my pain worthy of all the space it's taking up? Did it really hurt as badly as I remember or am I only exaggerating it?" I sometimes wonder if I remember the stories right—if he really did that, really said it that way, really didn't know he did something wrong—and if my experiences even matter, especially when they are not unique.

In a culture that has historically defined women as the property of their fathers and husbands, experiences of sexual violence within relationships do not exist in a vacuum. The explanations for why they happen, why they go unreported, and why women stay with, forgive, and love the men who sexually violate them cannot be understood solely from recounting the moments of violence themselves. They must also be understood within the larger contexts of the love and intimacy between the two people in the relationship. And the trouble is, American rhetoric about relationships creates a double-bind for women that reinforces the notion that any objection to partnered sex is consistent with failing as a partner, while reminding them that their sexual desire must be kept secret, locked away for husband's-eyes-only, or else they deserve whatever is coming to them. Asserting bodily autonomy within a relationship model that continually inscribes that men "gotta have it" and women "gotta fake a headache or be on their period" for a refusal of sex to be recognized as valid is an impossible task. And the more a woman or girl experiences violations of her autonomy, the more normal such ideas become to her, and the harder it is to fight against them. The challenge, then, of writing my stories as if they are only about sexual violence is that the contexts are necessary components to the narrative.

The contexts *are* the violence.

As I continue to develop as a writer, scholar, and person, I find that my life continues to be shaped by the things that have happened to me and how I have struggled to understand them. Reading *College Girl* triggered in me a formidable urge to interrogate the meaning of consent and reconcile disconnects within my own sexual history. With the support of my professors and advisors I began writing about sexual violence by blending memoir and research, leaving my MFA program with plans to continue this exploration in my PhD program. Now, my desire to connect the rhetoric of rape culture with the reality of lived experiences has led me to a dissertation project that will focus on amplifying the voices and stories of women who have experienced sexual violence at the hands of the men they have known and loved. This has led me to form partnerships with community organizations in my area, present at multiple conferences a year to discuss my work and personal struggles with sexual violence, and connect with women both within my institution and elsewhere who, like me, continue to question the validity of their own experiences, even when they know better. And despite everything, I really *do* know better.

But the struggle continues.

So the purpose of this essay is not to convey what happened on my twenty-third birthday, or in my past relationships, or to justify why I have always related to *College Girl* despite the continual struggle to see my experiences as valid in light of someone else's. The purpose of this essay is to relay the contexts that shape these things. It is about my journey exploring the sexual violence I am not comfortable naming rape, but feel forced to if I want to participate in conversations about rape culture. It's about the guilt I feel using that word. It's about the shame I still feel for standing by men who hurt me, even now changing their names when I write about them, both for their protection and mine. It's about the secrecy shrouding casual conversation with friends and colleagues about relationships that makes it hard to know which stories are appropriate to share and which I must keep locked inside, a tight fist in my chest awaiting revolt. The purpose of this essay is to bring new narrative to stories I once wrote my own voice out of in an effort to convince myself that my history with men was somehow better than what I actually experienced.

But a history is just a series of stories.

I am the author of my own.

These are my revisions. I'm now trying to tell it all as it really happened.

REFERENCES

Bassist, Elissa. 2018. "Why I Didn't Say No." In *Not That Bad: Dispatches from Rape Culture*, edited by Roxane Gay, 324–39. New York: Harper Collins.

Bay-Cheng, Laina Y., and Rebecca K. Eliseo-Arras. 2016. "The Making of Unwanted Sex: Gendered and Neoliberal Norms in College Women's Unwanted Sexual Experiences." *The Journal of Sex Research* 45 (4): 386–97.

Cahill, Ann J. 2016. "Unjust Sex vs. Rape." *Hypatia* 31 (4): 746–61.

Cook, Natalie K., and Terri L. Messman-Moore. 2017. "I Said No: The Impact of Voicing Non-Consent on Women's Perceptions of and Responses to Rape." *Violence Against Women* 25 (5): 507–27.

Gay, Roxane. 2018. "Introduction." In *Not That Bad: Dispatches from Rape Culture*, edited by Roxane Gay, x–xii. New York: Harper Collins.

Gray-Rosendale, Laura. 2014. *College Girl: A Memoir*. Albany: SUNY Press.

Hakvåg, Hedda. 2009. "Does Yes Mean Yes? Exploring Sexual Coercion in Normative Sexuality." *Canadian Woman Studies* 28 (1): 121–28.

Harris, Kate L. 2018. "Yes Means Yes, No Means No, But Both These Mantras Need to Go: Communication Myths in Consent Education and Anti-rape Activism." *Journal of Applied Communication Research* 46 (2): 155–78.

———. 2011. "The Next Problem with No Name: The Politics and Pragmatics of the Word *Rape*." *Women's Studies in Communication* 34 (1): 42–63.

hooks, bell. 2004. *All About Love*. New York: Harper Collins.

———. 2004. *The Will to Change: Men, Masculinity, and Love*. New York: Simon and Schuster, Inc.

Johnstone, Dusty J. 2016. "A Listening Guide Analysis of Women's Experiences of Unacknowledged Rape." *Psychology of Women Quarterly* 40 (2): 275–89.

Jozkowski, Kristen N., Tiffany L. Marcantonio, and Mary E. Hunt. 2017. "College Students' Sexual Consent Communication and Perceptions of Sexual Double Standards." *Perspectives on Sexual and Reproductive Health* 49 (4): 237–44.

Kitzinger, Celia, and Hannah Frith. 1999. "Just Say No? The Use of Conversation Analysis in Developing a Feminist Perspective on Sexual Refusal." *Discourse & Society* 10(3): 293–316.

O'Byrne, Rachel, Mark Rapley, and Susan Hansen. 2006. "'You Couldn't Say "No" Could You?': Young Men's Understandings of Sexual Refusal." *Feminism and Psychology* 16 (2): 133–54.

Chapter Four

"I Don't Know What's Real and What's Not"

How Journaling Helped Me Cope with Trauma

Hélène Bigras-Dutrisac

In the final entry of the journal[1] I kept as an undergraduate university student, I write: "I needed this [journal] to keep me sane and grounded when I went through that hellish phase and once I was done with it I guess I felt like I could manage my feelings without journal writing." Though I had written regularly in this journal for three years prior to this last, reflective entry (written a year after the traumatic events I testify to throughout my journal), I stopped writing just days later and never wrote another entry again. I have spent a great deal of time wondering what motivated me to keep a regular journal for those three years and what prompted me to stop so suddenly. I often attempted to keep journals as a child because, at the time, I found the idea of keeping a diary in which unique chapters of my life would be forever recorded exciting. As a child, however, it was always only a matter of days before I got bored with the process. The journal I kept regularly in adulthood as an undergraduate student was different. This was not a journal I had wanted to keep; it was a journal I had *needed* to keep in order to cope with one of the most difficult and traumatic periods of my life.

Harriet Blodgett argues that diaries are important tools of survival and subversion for the women who keep them. Keeping a diary, she writes, provides the diarist with the opportunity "to record what is important to her, and by the daily time that it claims for itself, counters the patriarchal attack on female identity and self-worth" (Blodgett 1988, 5). The diary allows one to speak for oneself and therefore "sustains one's sense of being a self, with an autonomous and significant identity" (Blodgett 1988, 5). I agree with

71

Blodgett's claims that the diary form can be understood as a powerful and subversive survival tool for women, especially considering that the diary has been conventionally understood as a woman's form (Gannett 1992, 125). Still, despite this gendered history, I believe the diary's potential as a survival tool or coping mechanism can be extended to include any/all individuals and communities that experience forms of systemic oppression. Furthermore, my experience with journaling trauma has convinced me that the diary's potential as a tool for survival and coping may be particularly important for survivors of trauma, since such survivors may experience a loss of autonomy and/or have their sense of self taken from them by abusive individuals, institutions, or systems of power.

As I note in my last journal entry, I kept a diary because "I needed to document everything I was feeling in order to understand my emotions." For me, the act of keeping a diary did not *sustain* a sense of self I felt I had but could not safely express. Rather, journaling was both a self-reflective process in which I attempted to uncover "truths" about a self I felt I had long lost and a way through which to produce this self through a narrative that I felt I had some control over; diary writing was my attempt to witness the trauma and loss of self that I was experiencing. In this chapter, I explore the diary's potential as a tool of survival, demonstrating both the possible benefits and limitations of diary writing for survivors of sexual trauma and intimate partner abuse. By presenting and reflecting on excerpts from my own diary, I hope to reveal how the diary can act as an outlet through which survivors can attempt to express unspeakable events. Keeping a diary helped me counter the gaslighting[2] tactics of my abuser, allowing me to return to—and reflect on—experiences, emotions, and responses that I no longer trusted myself to remember or understand.

SO I GUESS I'M USING THIS WORD DOCUMENT AS A JOURNAL NOW . . .

I was twenty when I met my abuser, and in the middle of my second year of university. He was twenty-four and extremely charming, confident, and outgoing. It seemed like everybody knew and loved him and I felt incredibly lucky whenever he expressed interest in me. When we first met, I was still recovering from a devastatingly difficult first heartbreak and I felt particularly vulnerable. At the beginning, spending time with Brian[3] felt like an adventure. He was always in a good mood, made everyone around him laugh, and always wanted to have fun. Brian agreed with me on everything at first, even expressing interest in feminism and gender-related political issues. He seemed too good to be true.

Brian always got whatever he wanted; usually his charm and confidence did the trick, but when that failed to work, he resorted to intimidation and fear to make sure everything go his way. The first time I witnessed this tactic, I remember thinking it was like a switch had been thrown off and on. Though the intimidating tone was harsh and kind of scary, I usually figured the person on the receiving end deserved it and Brian always confirmed this theory with me afterwards. Over the course of our relationship, I saw Brian use this tactic many times: at a club that charged a cover fee he refused to pay, for example, or to scare a friend into apologizing to him for implying that he was abusive towards me.

Brian became increasingly jealous over time, reading my text messages over my shoulder, constantly asking me who I was talking to, and making strange and often mean "jokes" at my expense to shame me for speaking to other men. In time I became aware that he was seeing other women, but he had a list of reasons why this was only acceptable for him to do and not for me. Whenever I was uncomfortable with anything, Brian made it clear that the discomfort was my own fault. After all, he would argue, I was just a close-minded, immature, jealous, and highly insecure young girl and that was no one's fault but my own.

The anger followed soon after the jealousy, and Brian's anger was unlike anything I had ever seen. Every word he said in anger seemed to target my deepest insecurities and his insults were so deeply personal and so profound-ly hurtful that they almost always left me unable to speak. No matter what the argument was about, I always ended up in tears, begging for forgiveness. His words made me feel I was so deeply broken, so flawed, so repulsive that no one could ever love me. I was desperate for his forgiveness and approval because I could not bear to be the person he had convinced me I must be.

Soon enough, my entire self-image was dependent on him; I could only see myself through his eyes. This power dynamic made taking advantage of me incredibly easy, but I never stopped the sexual assaults, never left him, and never turned him down when he wanted me to do something I did not want to do because when I was with him, I felt like I was a person. The pain I felt was real and I could name it and manage it. The pain I felt when Brian wasn't interested in me, however, was much worse. All I knew then was that I hated myself but could not get away from my own body.

The confusion and disgust I felt in relation to my sense of self led me to my diary, a password-protected Word document that I would regularly write in for the next three years. If I could write down what was happening to me, I thought, maybe I would be able to objectively assess my actions and feelings, and either confirm or challenge Brian's version of events. I did not think of this document as a "real" diary. Rather, the Word document was an emergen-cy resource, an efficient and readily accessible method that allowed me to jot down my thoughts and feelings without delay. The diaries I envisioned and fantasized about keeping as a child looked nothing like the cold, blank computer screen I ended up using as a journal. "Real" diaries were carefully hand-written using beautiful and neat cursive calligraphy. They were physical objects that you could hold and keep forever, and they were limited by a finite number of pages that I imagined provided the writer with a sense of closure—or at least a way by which to organize and compartmentalize different periods of one's life.

I now understand that the diary form is much more fluid, elusive, and complex than what I once envisioned. According to Philippe Lejeune, the diary has "no set form, no required content" (2009, 168). It is simply a *"series of dated traces* [série de traces datées] . . . [that] attempt to capture the movement of time" (Lejeune 2009, 61) and that can take the form of written texts, images, objects, or relics (Smith and Watson 2010, 191). While journaling therefore does not always include writing, Sidonie Smith and Julia Watson provide a useful definition for its written form that helps locate the diary genre in relation to subjectivity. As they explain, the written diary is a form of life writing (Smith and Watson 2010, 226) that, like other forms of life writing (including memoir and autobiography), therefore "takes a life . . . as its subject" (Smith and Watson 2010, 4). Indeed, diary writing—like autobiography and other forms of life writing[4]—does involve a process by which the self is examined.

Still, while the definition of life writing quoted above makes it clear that this process may include a reflection by which one writes *about* oneself, Leigh Gilmore emphasizes the emergence of "a self-representational practice through which a subject-in-process is *constructed*" (my emphasis) (2001, 97). I understand the process of life writing as both producing *and* reflecting the self. In my view, when we write about ourselves, we create a particular "self" informed by our understanding of who we are at the moment and place of writing that is based on our experiences in/with the world(s) in which we exist. This is especially important in relation to trauma, which, as Laub explains (in the context of the Holocaust), destroys the possibility of addressing both others and oneself since, "when one cannot turn to a 'you' one cannot say 'thou' even to oneself" (1992, 82). Writing (about) the self through life writing forms such as autobiography and journaling can help work through this loss of identity, however. As Kim Verwaayen puts it, "We write ourselves (fractured, fabricated, piecemeal as we may be) in the personal, public, and private histories we recollect, re-create, and revise in aggregated memory. We inhabit many bodies/memories as a kind of collective resistance and self-discovery" (2013, 129). As I write this chapter, I reflect on my experiences of trauma and on the diary entries that outline selected bits and pieces of some of these experiences. The ways in which and the extent to which I remember these experiences, as well as the tools I employ to theorize and understand them, are sure to shape the writing I produce and the self that emerges from/in my writing. Relatedly, the diary entries I wrote years ago, and the writing of this chapter today, will surely shape how I understand and remember my experiences of trauma into the future.

At the same time, the process of writing oneself does not necessarily preclude the possibility of writing *about* oneself. As Smith and Watson explain, "Radical challenges to the notion of a unified selfhood in the early decades of the twentieth century eroded certainty in both a coherent 'self' and the 'truth' of self-narrating" (2010, 200). This shift in how the "self" was understood and theorized rightfully problematized notions of a Western, universal subject telling the "Truth" of her/his story through autobiography (Smith and Watson 2010, 201). While I agree that this approach to autobiography and the "self" is problematic, I argue that feminist contributions to such discussions allow us to theorize a different "self" that can be both produced and reflected in life writings about the self. Feminist philosopher Mariana Ortega, for example, conceptualizes the self as fluid, embodied, situated, and in process (2016, 77), therefore creating space for a self-reflective process (in autobiographical and other forms of life writing) that is neither universalizing nor reductive. As I explain in more depth below, these sorts of approaches to the "self" complicate simplistic distinctions between fact and fiction and challenge definitions of an autonomous "self" unaffected by one's historical, geographical, or social contexts. By linking selfhood to one's embodied location(s) and experiences, and by acknowledging the fluidity and multiplicity of one's "self" (Ortega 2016, 66), we create the possibility of writing authentically about our truths rather than about the "Truth."

The task of defining the diary genre becomes even more difficult when we consider not only the "self" who is written through/into the journal, but also how the meaning of diary-writing itself changes across time and space. As Smith and Watson explain, for example, the Western canonical definitions of life writing that emerged in the Enlightenment era have historically excluded, ignored, and overlooked the life writings produced within/by marginalized or Othered communities and individuals (unfortunately, these types of dismissals are still common) (2010, 3). While Alexandra Johnson organizes diaries according to type (such as travel diaries, creative diaries, war diaries, etc.) and historical period (for example, eighteenth-century, twentieth-century, or twenty-first-century diaries) (2011, "Contents"), sorting journals in this way can place limits on the genre and exclude diaries that are refused access to—or that themselves reject—these narrowly constructed categories. When we begin to consider the complexities and multiplicities of the "self," it becomes increasingly difficult to justify compartmentalizing lives and stories based on these sorts of simplistic categories.

The politics of these methods of classification are particularly important in relation to the history of diary-writing and life writing more generally. If diary-writing is a form of life writing that takes a life "as its subject" (Smith and Watson 2010, 4), then it is essential that we acknowledge and address how definitions of what constitutes a deserving, important, interesting, or legitimate life affect the types of journals (and life writing more generally) considered worthy of study and recognition in the Western canonical tradition. Smith and Watson argue that the interpretations made by the scholars who studied and contributed to the canon in the 1960s were fraught with assumptions. As they write, these scholars "assumed the autobiographer to be an autonomous and enlightened 'individual' who understood his [*sic*] relationship to others and the world as one of separateness in which he exercised the agency of free will. . . . They assumed a concluding point at which some kind of self-understanding through reflection upon past achievement takes place. And . . . they assumed the representative status of the narrator . . ." (Smith and Watson 2010, 199).

I JUST WANT TO KNOW WHO I AM AGAIN

There are many perspectives by which one could unpack and problematize the assumptions challenged by Smith and Watson, but for the context of this chapter, I would like to linger on the effects of such assumptions for individuals and communities that could not or did not fit the definitions of the "self" laid out by conventional autobiography scholars. In *Rhetoric and Resistance in Black Women's Autobiography*, Johnnie Stover argues that the (white male) authors most often cited as pioneers of the autobiography genre "did not have to prove their worthiness as human beings, writers, or citizens" in the ways that black women autobiographers have (2003, 22). This is exemplified in Stover's work on nineteenth-century African American autobiographers, whose narratives "had to be authenticated by white voices at the time of [their] publication through attached letters or introductory statements" (Stover 2003, 23). Gilmore adds to this critique of the canon, asking how "the logic of representativeness" at the core of autobiography might affect the writing and reading of trauma narratives. In *The Limits of Autobiography: Trauma and Testimony*, she therefore asks us to consider how the testimonies of women trauma survivors are received and understood in patriarchal contexts. As she explains, such narratives "are likely to be doubted, not only when they bring forward accounts of sexual trauma but also because their self-representation *already* is at odds with the account the representative man would produce" (my emphasis) (2001, 23). For those of us with testimonies and self-representations that are received with suspicion, distrust, or even contempt, writing about the "self" as it has been historically understood in the Western tradition outlined above is complicated. But this suspicion does not only come from outside oneself; it can also be internalized.

This internalizing process is exemplified in many of the journal entries I wrote following violent or otherwise dangerous encounters with my abuser. On November 1, 2013, for example, I wrote the following journal entry:

> I'm so confused. I feel like I don't know who I am and can't control myself and it really scares me. I'm hurting myself and I'm hurting the friends that I am so lucky to have and I don't know why or how to stop. It's not a big deal and I don't want to overdramatize. I just want to know who I am again. My self-esteem is lower than ever and I wish I could get away from myself for a while but obviously I can't. I don't understand anything and I'm scared. I feel very alone and I'm tired of struggling to feel okay. I don't know what to do now.

I hardly remember the night before I wrote this entry thanks to a cocktail of drugs and alcohol I had consumed in secret so that my friends would not find out. Drinking enough to black out before meeting up with my abuser was common for me. And, as my diary entries show, these encounters almost always ended painfully. Still, I returned to him again and again. The morning of the November 1 entry, a close friend of mine sat me down with tears in her eyes to talk about how worried I was making her and our other friends. Moments earlier, before leaving my abuser's apartment, he had told me that I was fine and that my friends should stop treating me like a child. While it was clear to my friends, family, and community that I was struggling, my abuser's gaslighting tactics and his habits of minimizing the concerns of those closest to me made me feel like I no longer had a firm grasp on reality. Furthermore, my inability to stop caring about him and my desire to return to him—no matter how horrible my encounters with him—made me highly suspicious of myself. At the time, I often found myself wondering why I—a proud feminist with a strong support system and the financial (and other) means to leave him—kept making decisions that I knew were hurting me and everyone I loved.

Throughout my diary, I frame my experiences of trauma as confusing, self-destructive events caused—at least in part—by my own inability to control myself. The feelings of suspicion, distrust, and even repulsion I felt towards myself are indicative of what Gilmore calls "a neoliberal distortion of reality" (2017, 10) in which individual choice and responsibility is emphasized while political, social, and historical contexts are dismissed (2017, 93). In my journal entries, I place the blame on myself, framing my inability to end an abusive relationship as a "choice," *and* I place the burden of responsibility to end the abuse on myself, as is exemplified by the numerous lists in my diary outlining the actions *I* must take to avoid making what I understood as "snowballs of bad decisions."

The neoliberal framework that guided my understanding of myself and of my experiences of trauma contributed to an overwhelming sense of alienation from both myself (through the internalized self-blame outlined above) and a world that did not understand my experiences of trauma and responses to abuse as "normal" or "appropriate" thanks to oppressive ideologies and norms (rape culture,[5] for example) that would not recognize someone like me as an "authentic" survivor. As Gilmore argues, neoliberalism destroys the possibility of understanding the systemic forces at play in trauma survivors' experiences and responses. This is especially true when the narratives of trauma survivors don't match up with the expectations of dominant groups. As she explains, "A radical decontextualization of testimony occurs when an audience is prevented from grasping an individual in context" (Gilmore 2017, 17). When it is the individual who is unable to contextualize (and grasp) her/his/their own experiences, guilt and self-blame can set in and make it increasingly difficult to feel justified in sharing such experiences with others.

I'M GOING TO TRY MY BEST TO GET IT RIGHT, BUT I MIGHT MAKE MISTAKES . . .

I have always known that my experience of trauma was likely to draw skepticism and unlikely to receive sympathy from the dominant members of a neoliberal and patriarchal society. This is not only true because of the internalized self-blame and shame that I mentioned earlier; it is also due to the feminist consciousness I already identified with during my relationship with an abusive man. I knew then that my experience did not meet the expectations of a neoliberal narrative in which the individual alone "transforms disadvantage into value" (Gilmore 2017, 89) since I was unable to leave my abuser and "rise above" the abuse. Furthermore, as explained above, my location as a woman already positioned me and my autobiographical account as untrustworthy and suspicious. Though I understood this as unjust during my journal-writing days, the gaslighting tactics of my abuser and the trauma-, drug-, and alcohol-induced gaps in my memory prevented me from extending this political consciousness to the skepticism and self-blame I had so deeply internalized. I had the theoretical knowledge necessary to identify the victim-blaming tactics of a rape culture, yet this theoretical knowledge did not translate into embodied knowledge.

This loss of confidence in my sense of "self" evokes Gilmore's conceptualization of "the limit of representativeness" (2001, 5). As renowned trauma scholars such as Cathy Caruth and Dori Laub have argued, trauma exceeds language and is therefore incredibly difficult to articulate (Caruth 1995; Laub 1992). Trauma also affects memory, and its belated return (through flashbacks and nightmares, for example) (American Psychiatric Association 2013,

275) defies linear conceptions of time and challenges conventional under-standings of what is "real" (Morrigan 2017, 56). This makes the process of testimony and self-representation extremely difficult in any setting, but the conventions of autobiography, which demand a "truthful" and "coherent" account given by a narrator with a "representative status" (Smith and Watson 2010, 199) make the task feel almost impossible. This is perhaps especially true in relation to testimonies of trauma. As Gilmore argues, "By bringing predominantly legalistic models of testimony to bear on life narrative, and thereby importing the universalizing tendencies of law, we foreclose the alternative knowledge that emerges in dissonant narratives" (2017, 80). When minute details are missing, forgotten, or even misremembered by sur-vivors testifying to trauma, their entire story becomes suspect and, too often, it is entirely dismissed. This is why "the fantasy of autobiography . . . never quite fulfills its promise in local terms. It is considerably more partial and exclusive as a practice, though as a fantasy it seems 'free' and available to all" (Gilmore 2001, 13). While many authors (including the ones Gilmore discusses in *The Limits of Autobiography*) have written about trauma and the "self" in ways that challenge and/or expand the conventions of the "fantasy of autobiography" (often because of the legalistic frameworks on which auto-biography relies) (Gilmore 2001, 23), the attempts I made in my diary entries to produce, articulate, and represent my "self" and my experiences of trauma through autobiography were ultimately limited by the politics, norms, and confines embedded in conventional understandings of trauma and autobiog-raphy that I had internalized.

This is perhaps best illustrated in a diary entry I wrote in January 2013. While most (if not all) of my other diary entries seem to be written *to* and *for* myself, this particular entry contains none of the reflections, self-deprecating jokes, or extensive commentary on my emotions and responses that the ma-jority of the other entries contain. Instead, the entry reads like a legal docu-ment written by a witness about to stand trial. In it, I recall my experience of sexual assault in chronological order, including as many details as I could remember at the time of writing. Though few individual diary entries stand out in my mind, I do remember envisioning this entry, at the moment of writing, as a piece of evidence—an *eyewitness* to what I had experienced.

This entry's typography also distinguishes it from my other entries; while the font in my regular journal entries remains relatively constant, I use bolded and italicized font to highlight and delineate particular sec-tions of my January 2013 entry. My use of boldface serves to foreground what I believed to be the key issues at stake. The italicized sections clear-ly indicate flashbacks that interrupt the temporal chronology of my testi-mony in order to provide explanations or contextual information to the reader. In the entry, I write:

I asked him if he was trying to say he liked me and he said yeah, he really liked me. . . . Then I told him I'd miss him a lot too.

The rest of the night is a bit vague and I'm going to try my best to get it right but I might make mistakes in the order that things happened in. They will not be intentional. [emphasis in original]

He started touching me and everything was fine but [then] I stopped him. . . . He asked me why and I said I just didn't want to. He insisted and I repeated "just because. . . " I'm not sure why I didn't want to tell him I was on my period; probably because I was worried he'd be upset or disappointed . . .

I had been upset earlier in the day because I felt really used. I usually end up feeling that way after we have sex . . . I think I feel this way because he rarely talks about me in a positive way unless it's to thank me for doing something for him, to compliment me on my appearance, or for listening or understanding him. It doesn't feel like it's often about me as a person and sometimes I wonder if he even cares about how I feel or how I'm doing. Maybe I'm wrong or being sensitive though it's just how I feel. . . . He's also told me that I couldn't make him fall in love with me. It makes me feel like I'm not good enough for him and makes me question what I'm doing wrong. . . .

As is the case with the italicized sections of the text, the boldface font signals an interruption in the chronological sequence of events outlined in the rest of the journal entry. Yet my choice to use boldface rather than italics for the section in which I apologetically acknowledge that my testimony may include gaps and minor errors illustrates how important these two specific sentences must have felt to me as I wrote the entry.

The significance of this section can be better understood by turning to Gilmore and her application of Foucault's example of the Panopticon to describe the symbiotic relationship between self-representation and self-surveillance at the heart of autobiography. As Gilmore argues:

Along with the dutiful and truthful accounting of a life one might find in autobiography, the self is not only responsible but always potentially culpable, given autobiography's rhetorical proximity to testimony and the quasi-legalistic framework for judging its authenticity and authority that is so easily mobilized. . . . The prevalence of surveillance not only characterizes a relation between the self and others but becomes, as it is internalized, a property of the self as self-reflexivity or conscience. (Gilmore 2001, 20)

The bolded excerpt of my January journal entry thus exemplifies the self-surveillance Gilmore outlines, imploring an imagined or implied reader to withhold judgment and look beyond the facts of the events in order to witness the "truth" of my experience despite an acute awareness of my position as an unreliable subject, imperfect victim, or, to use Gilmore's language, a *tainted witness* (Gilmore 2017). This panoptic phenomenon also points to the limits of diary writing and its potential for healing and subversion. While expressing this experience of trauma through writing helped me cope with the effects of the assault, and though the diary was a useful—even necessary—outlet that enabled me to survive a very difficult period, it did not address the structural changes nor collective action needed to address the pervasiveness and systemic nature of sexual violence.

The italicized sections perform a similar function. In the italicized section quoted above, for example, I interrupt my retelling of an exchange between myself and my abuser, in which I describe hesitating for a moment after being asked for sex. The section attempts to justify this hesitation by contextualizing it in relation to what I describe as feeling "used." The rest of the entry (which I have not included here) describes my experience of a particularly violent sexual assault that felt severe enough for me to want to document it in detail the next day. In the entry, I explain how my abuser framed my refusal to have sex with him as irrational and selfish, and I describe the feelings of insecurity and guilt that led me to give up and passively accept the assault until an anxiety attack became disruptive enough to make my abuser stop and fall asleep. Despite these events, and despite my body's aggressive responses to the assault (I cried, had an anxiety attack, and vomited during the course of the night), I continued to doubt and blame myself for the experience in my journal entry.

As the italicized section demonstrates, even as I attempted to testify to my experience of sexual assault to *myself*, in my own diary (a diary I presumed no one would read), the properties of self-surveillance I had internalized made me feel that to testify to my lived experience of abuse as I had experienced it was not enough. The ways in which I frame my response to sexual acts that I did not want to partake in as wrong, irrational—or *sensitive*—and even as not worthy of being taken seriously (they're "just" my feelings after all) points to the limits of autobiography as a "free" practice of self-expression and urges us to reflect on the forms that witnessing and testimony can or must take depending on context.

My use of boldface and italics to convey the truthfulness of my account (in spite of the missing details) and to articulate my experience of trauma also illustrates the failure of language in relation to trauma. As Caruth suggests, "the phenomenon of trauma . . . brings us to the limits of our understanding" (1995, 4). When we attempt to articulate traumatic experiences, it is therefore sometimes helpful (or even necessary) to look beyond language. If we apply this theory to the boldface and italicized fonts in my January 2013 diary entry, it becomes evident that my use of these different fonts functioned as a visual means through which to express myself and convey elements of my experience that exceeded language. These articulations of trauma seem to mirror the involuntary and instinctive physical responses I experienced the night of the January entry. While I was unable to recognize the experience as a sexual assault at the time of writing, my embodied physical responses signal that a part of me must have known that something was badly wrong with the ways in which my body was being treated. Though this knowledge may have been buried too deeply to be articulated through language, it emerges in the emphasized sections of the January journal entry.

> I just wanted him to like me and I gave up on trying to make him see my point of view . . .

In "An Event Without a Witness," Laub recounts an interview with a Holocaust survivor whose parents helped him escape the Plashow labor camp in which they were detained when he was just a child. According to Laub's interpretation, the young boy created an "internal witness" from an old photograph of his mother, and this first witness enabled his survival for the duration of the war. For Laub, establishing an internal witness helps trauma survivors create and integrate cohesive narratives to counter the chaotic and incomprehensible nature of trauma. As he explains, the Holocaust survivor's "testimony to himself came to be the story of the hidden truth of his life, with which he has to struggle incessantly in order to remain authentic to himself" (Laub 1992, 87). Although diaries such as the one I kept in my early twenties may appear, at first glance, to fit Laub's account of an internal witness, there is a fundamental difference between the internal witness Laub describes and the journal I used to cope with sexual violence and emotional abuse; while I used my diary to process events and emotions that I felt I could neither understand nor integrate, my attempts at testimony were stunted by the patriarchal mindset I had internalized. In other words, while the young boy's photograph of his mother reminded him of a self with a loving mother and, for a time, allowed him to "reconstitute the internal 'thou'" (Laub 1992, 85), my journal writing confirmed and reproduced the dehumanizing narratives I was being fed by both my abuser and larger patriarchal structures and, therefore, destroyed any possibility of reclaiming my "position as a witness" (Laub 1992, 85).

The spread of this panoptic self-surveillance into my diary entries prevented me from remaining authentic to myself and attests to the importance of collective action and structural change to the processes of responsible witnessing and testimony. The differences between the kinds of witnessing described by Laub and the attempts at witnessing found in my diary can be compared to the concepts of "eyewitness testimony" and "bearing witness" presented in Kelly Oliver's *Witnessing: Beyond Recognition*. Oliver suggests that:

> The double meaning of witnessing—*eyewitness* testimony based on first-hand knowledge, on the one hand, and *bearing witness* to something beyond recognition that can't be seen, on the other—is at the heart of subjectivity. The tension between eyewitness testimony and bearing witness both positions the subject in finite history and necessitates the infinite response-ability of subjectivity. (Oliver 2001, 16)

When it comes to eyewitness testimony, the contextual information surrounding the events neither matters nor exists. Instead, what matters is what can be physically seen in the moment of the event. If a young woman returns to her abusive partner, for example, people may assume that she either lied about the abuse or is deserving of it. When we bear witness, however, we go beyond what our own eyes can see and consider the contexts (or subject positions) of the witnesses (the people listening to the testimony as well as those testifying). In the case of the young woman returning to her abuser, for example, bearing witness might entail considering the survivor's financial (in)stability, the cultural contexts in which she was socialized, or the complexities of her relationship with her abuser.

Unlike with eyewitness testimony, bearing witness allows the witness to work through "the trauma of objectification by reinstituting subjective agency as the ability to respond or address oneself" (Oliver 2001, 105). By allowing trauma survivors to recount the truth(s) of their experience and by recognizing the complexities, contexts, and irrepresentability of trauma and subjectivity, we can move beyond the coping tools provided by journaling and create space for healing and lasting structural change. This can only happen, however, when we recognize and address trauma survivors as subjects with agency. As Oliver argues:

> When testimony is put on trial and personal experience is judged as credible or not by public institutions, then the speaker is in the paradoxical position of justifying her status as subject. Once again, the performance of speaking proves subjectivity even while the social context calls it into question. This kind of questioning and the continual call to legitimate yourself as a self, to legitimate your right, or ability, to speak, make witnessing your own oppression even more painful and problematic. The right or ability to speak is accorded to those who have been accepted as legitimate subjects. (Oliver 2001, 158–59)

As I have already demonstrated with excerpts from my diary, I spent much of my journal-writing days trying to justify my status as a subject while simultaneously putting myself, my memories, and my interpretations of events on trial.

In a July 2013 entry, for example, I recount a visit to the city in which my abuser was living at the time. While we had established that he would pick me up in the morning and drop me off again in the afternoon, when I asked to be taken home, he told me that he had been drinking alcohol and could no longer drive me home. Since I was in an unfamiliar city and had no access to a car (my abuser knew that I did not have a driver's license), I agreed to stay over. I recall these events in my entry, writing: "He *kinda* tricked me into staying over at his place because he would be drinking and couldn't drive me home but he insisted it would be a non-romantic sleepover. . . . I started to feel iffy and lose some of my cool from early on." In this passage, I acknowledge the problematic way in which my abuser robbed me of my subjectivity by *tricking me* into staying over despite my clear reluctance to do so. I also acknowledge my feelings of discomfort and fear at the prospects of a potentially dangerous encounter with someone I did not trust. Still, my distrust of myself and the credibility of my account is evidenced by my attempt to diminish—even entirely dismiss—the violence of the encounter by using (and emphasizing with italics) the word "kinda."

I MADE ZERO PROGRESS FROM SEPTEMBER TO NOW, BUT THERE IS ALWAYS A SILVER LINING!

The limitations of the diary as a means through which to bear witness to one's trauma do not truncate its potential as an outlet for diarists, particularly when survival is at stake. Still, it is essential that we address the discourses surrounding diary-writing and trauma (particularly in relation to diary-writing as a therapeutic tool for "healing") if we want to stop the violence that these discourses can do and give survivors the opportunity to authentically bear witness to themselves and their trauma. In *A Brief History of Diaries*, Johnson describes journal-writing as "universal" and "primal" to all human beings (2001, 98). She turns to science to support her arguments about its inherent benefits for trauma survivors, citing family practitioner Neil Neimark's self-help book *The Write Way to Manage Your Stress: Writing Tools & Inspirational Stories for Hope, Healing & Personal Growth* (2015) to make the case "for diary as support group, erasing shame or trauma" (Johnson 2011, 98). In the excerpt Johnson selects from Neimark's book, he writes that "when we journal about traumatic life events and reconstruct the painful thoughts and images associated with those events, we are, in fact, changing the very structure and pattern of brain activity" (quoted in Johnson 2011, 98). The belief that diary-writing has inherent benefits (especially for trauma healing) is, as Johnson suggests, commonly held within the medical/therapeutic fields and within the general population (2011, 98). As I point out in one of my journal entries, this sentiment was echoed by the therapist I started seeing over the course of my relationship with Brian. As I write: "Tonight I'm just going to briefly go over the past couple days because [my therapist] thinks it might help me come to terms with my feelings and maybe give me closure."

The problem with this approach to healing is that its reliance on the universal and natural effects of both trauma and journaling ignores the contexts in which they are experienced. As I have already demonstrated, trauma survivors may be unable to reconcile their own experiences with normative conceptions of subjectivity and trauma narratives. This conflicting information can make the process of reconstructing painful events difficult and, as my journal illustrates, can lead to journal entries that increase feelings of shame rather than erase them. Furthermore, the belatedness and indefinability of trauma makes it very difficult to relay in writing. When subjects and their experiences of trauma must be read as intelligible, writing one's trauma is even more challenging. As Berlant suggests in *Trauma and Ineloquence*, however, existing outside the realm of intelligibility is no easy feat. She writes:

> We track the contemporary story of "our" intelligibility as Enlightenment subjects who feel that the self exists because it has internalized those genres of discipline and fantasy or faith that originate in the law and in religious confession since Augustine. . . . We become available as a subject to the extent that we enter into the bargain of intelligibility. (Berlant 2001, 49–50)

This often unacknowledged "bargain of intelligibility" can be particularly harmful for trauma survivors who may not always feel safe exploring the complexities and messiness of trauma, even in private diaries. As Morrigan argues, authoritative discourses about trauma in the West (including legal, medical, and psychiatric discourses) can often be accompanied "by consequences such as criminalization, deportation, non-consensual psychiatrization, incarceration, re-victimization and invalidation . . . whether we as survivors engage with or consent to these systems or not" (2016, 121–22). While diary-writing may appear to exist outside of these dominant discourses when no external readers are involved, the prevalence of these discourses makes internalization almost impossible to escape. Moreover, fears of being "discovered" as an unintelligible subject can deter survivors from articulating experiences, responses, or emotions that do not align with normative trauma narratives. This is especially true for marginalized populations whose narratives may already sometimes be marked as unintelligible (and therefore suspect) by institutions and systems of power.

I began this chapter with a quote from Harriet Blodgett in which she describes the subversive potential of diary writing. While her claims address women specifically, the more general idea that taking time to journal can counter the oppressive systems of power that aim to silence us resonates with me. At a time in my life where my self-worth had dwindled to almost nothing, I was compelled to document my experiences of abuse and sexual violence. The journal I kept during this difficult period may not have allowed me to "bear witness" according to Kelly Oliver's definition of the term, but it did give me space and time for myself and, in so doing, reminded me that I deserved to survive. My diary gave me an opportunity to make sense of chaotic events I felt I could not control; it allowed me to create coherent narratives from the scattered bits and pieces I managed to recover.

Still, my attempts to make sense of what was happening to me did not bring me the closure or healing I was looking for. According to Laub, losing one's internal witness and learning one's "real truth" can be very costly (1992, 88). For the Holocaust survivor from the Plashow labor camp, the inevitable loss of the internal witness he had created from his mother's photograph upon meeting his "real" mother after the war led him "to fall apart" (Laub 1992, 88). Finding my way to an authentic and "truthful" way to bear witness to my trauma also required me to "fall apart." By unlearning the normative ideologies I had internalized (with the help of feminist texts, professors, and classes), and by turning towards loving friends and family who allowed me to rebuild my sense of subjectivity, however, I managed to find hope in the knowledge that I was not alone. As expressed in my final journal entry, "Things have been hard and I know my relationship with [my abuser] will affect my future relationships, but at the same time seeing that I'm capable of loving and being loved in a healthy way despite what happened two years ago gives me a lot of hope and pride."

There is no way to predict exactly how or when trauma will bubble up to the surface. Though I rarely think back about my years as an undergraduate university student, I continue to struggle with the effects of the trauma I experience in often unexpected and surprising ways. I now understand that surviving and bearing witness to trauma is much more complicated than simply writing it down in a diary. Still, returning to the diary I kept during my abusive relationship reminds me of its significance as an urgent call for collective action and structural change. The patriarchal belief systems entrenched in my being convinced me that the abuse I was experiencing was justified and that my pain was insignificant and exaggerated. In order to authentically witness my trauma, I had to learn how to see myself as a person who experienced something painful and unjust that she neither wanted nor deserved. I came to this knowledge thanks to the work of feminist scholars and activists who helped me unlearn the oppressive mechanisms that protect abusers at the expense of victims and survivors. I may not have been able to witness my trauma during my diary-writing days, but I am now fortunate enough to have the tools, the language, and the supportive community necessary to recognize my experience as legitimate and myself as a subject worthy of address.

NOTES

1. Alexandra Johnson explains that the words "diary" and "journal" share the same Latin root for "day" and argues that the words have been used interchangeably since Samuel Johnson defined diary in his Dictionary in the mid-eighteenth century (2011, 13). The two words are also used interchangeably by autobiography and diary studies scholars Philippe Lejeune (2009, 61) as well as Sidonie Smith and Julia Watson (2010, 266). Since my definition of the journal/diary is grounded in the work of these theorists, I also use "journal" and "diary" interchangeably throughout this text.

2. According to Cynthia A. Stark, gaslighting can be understood in two ways: (1) as a form of "testimonial injustice" that occurs "when someone denies, on the basis of another's social identity, her testimony about a harm or wrong done to her," or (2) as a form of abusive emotional manipulation aiming "to get another to see her own plausible perceptions, beliefs, or memories as groundless" (2019, 221). The gaslighting I reference in this chapter encompasses both definitions since my abuser dismissed my experiences, emotions, and responses as groundless based on my social identity as a young(er) woman.

3. Names have been changed.

4. While Lejeune does not consider diary-writing to be a form of autobiography (2009, 93; 201), I approach autobiography more broadly and, like Gayle Letherby, propose that "all writing is in some ways auto/biography and that all texts bear traces of the author and are to some extent personal statements" (2014, 2).

5. Anniken Laake, Lucia Willumsen, and Cynthia Calkins define "rape culture" as "a term broadly used to describe the normalization and pervasiveness of rape-supportive attitudes and sexual violence in a society" (2017).

REFERENCES

American Psychiatric Association. 2013. *Diagnostic and Statistical Manual of Mental Disorders*: DSM-V. 5th ed. Arlington: American Psychiatric Association.

Berlant, Lauren. 2001. "Trauma and Ineloquence." *The Journal for Cultural Research* 5 (1): 41–58. https://doi: 10.1080/14797580109367220.

Blodgett, Harriet. 1988. *Centuries of Female Days: Englishwomen's Private Diaries*. New Brunswick: Rutgers University Press.

Caruth, Cathy, ed. 1995. *Trauma: Explorations in Memory*. Baltimore: Johns Hopkins University Press.

Gannett, Cinthia. 1992. *Gender and the Journal: Diaries and Academic Discourse*. Albany: SUNY Press.

Gilmore, Leigh. 2017. *Tainted Witness: Why We Doubt What Women Say About Their Lives*. New York: Columbia University Press.

———. 2001. *The Limits of Autobiography: Trauma and Testimony*. Ithaca: Cornell University Press.

Johnson, Alexandra. 2011. *A Brief History of Diaries: From Pepys to Blogs*. London: Hesperus Press Limited.

Laake, Anniken, Lucia Willumsen, and Cynthia Calkins. 2017. "Rape Culture." In *The SAGE Encyclopedia of Psychology and Gender*, edited by Kevin L. Nadal, 1403–5. California: SAGE Publications. http://dx.doi.org/10.4135/9781483384269.n470.

Laub, Dori. 1992. "An Event Without a Witness: Truth, Testimony and Survival." In *Testimony: Crises of Witnessing in Literature, Psychoanalysis and History*, edited by Shoshana Felman and Dori Laub, 75–92. New York: Routledge.

Lejeune, Philippe. 2016. *On Diary*, edited by Jeremy D. Popkin and Julie Rak. Translated by Katherine Durnin. Honolulu: University of Hawaii Press.

Letherby, Gayle. 2014. "Feminist Auto/Biography." In *The SAGE Handbook of Feminist Theory*, 45–60. London: SAGE Publications Ltd.

Morrigan, Clementine. 2017. "Trauma Time: The Queer Temporalities of the Traumatized Mind." *Somatechnics* 7 (1): 50–58. https://doi:10.3366/soma.2017.0205.

———. 2016. "Making Space for Complexity: The Arts and Counter-Narratives of Trauma." *Knots: An Undergraduate Journal of Disability Studies* 2: 120–29. https://jps.library. utoronto.ca/index.php/knots/article/view/27030.

Oliver, Kelly. 2001. *Witnessing: Beyond Recognition.* Minneapolis: University of Minnesota Press.

Ortega, Mariana. 2016. *In-Between: Latina Feminist Phenomenology, Multiplicity, and the Self.* Albany, NY: SUNY Press.

Smith, Sidonie, and Julia Watson. 2010. *Reading Autobiography: A Guide for Interpreting Life Narratives.* 2nd ed. Minneapolis: University of Minnesota Press.

Stark, Cynthia A. 2019. "Gaslighting, Misogyny, and Psychological Oppression." *The Monist* 102 (2): 221–35. https://doi.org/10.1093/monist/onz007.

Stover, Johnnie. 2003. *Rhetoric and Resistance in Black Women's Autobiography.* Gainesville: University Press of Florida.

Verwaayen, Kim. 2013. "Folding Back The Skin of Text: Anne Michaels's *Fugitive Pieces* of Trauma, Testimony, and Auto/Biographical Form(s)." *A/B: Auto/Biography Studies* 28 (1): 126–49. https://doi:10.1080/08989575.2013.10846821.

Chapter Five

Jailbait

At the Intersection of Teenage Desire and Statutory Rape

Marissa Korbel

We talked on the phone sometimes. But mostly we used Instant Messages (IMs was what I called them) sent via our America Online accounts. My screen name was Rissabelle; his screen name is lost to me, except for the pseudonymous one I gave him when I wrote about him: Lear42. He called me Rissabelle at school, in person, when we were making out in cars. He hummed it along my clavicle, sang it like it was my secret name, my Lolita name. Rissabelle. Rissabelle.

Unlike Lolita, Rissabelle was a name I gave myself. I never had many nicknames. My name wasn't suited to them. When I first had an AOL account, I didn't even use a cutesy pun or nickname; I used the French words for things I liked: sunflowers, spotlights, butterflies. I was fourteen years old.

It was a strange, generationally-defining experience to be granted the internet in my early teens. The internet, at least the internet most people could access from their desktop computers, was America Online, a dial-up internet portal and email service, that also hosted chat rooms and allowed instant messages to be sent between users. It also had this feature where you could "unsend" an email before someone opened it, and you could see when it had been opened. There wasn't really a way of engaging with people *en masse* then; you either knew someone well enough to have their screen name, or anonymously you interacted with people in chat rooms. The chat rooms were full of people you would never see in real life, or probably even online, ever again. This made chat rooms ripe for role-play and sexual experimentation; nobody knew who Rissabelle really was. I could be anyone. I could be any age. I spent years lingering in different chat rooms, reading what people said and did publicly and fielding IM requests from strangers who wanted to "cyber." That was what we called sexting; it was short for cyber sex, a new form of dirty talk which required no talking, only typing. Cybering with someone was far less intimate than phone sex because your voice wasn't involved, and you could disappear by closing the IM box on your screen. Unless the person had written your screen name down, it would be impossible to find you again. This meant that when the men I was cybering with went down roads that I didn't want to pursue, I would simply leave. They didn't even feel like men so much as robotic boxes full of sick ideas. I never felt like I owed them my time or attention, or even an explanation. I wasn't a girl. I was Rissabelle.

If only I was as good at protecting myself in real life.

It was novel then to email someone, especially teachers. I remember the first teacher I emailed, Ms. Pannone, and how she wrote back to me like they were letters. We saw each other two to three days a week in class, but I loved her and started writing emails to her. It was like having a more equal relationship with her. The screen made me sophisticated. Words could be arranged and edited to sound adult, serious. Unlike real letters, my handwriting didn't tip me off as childish, bubbly.

By the time I met the teacher who would be the focus of this story, I was fifteen and had already spent years online with strangers and known adults. I had emailed other teachers. There was nothing transgressive about emailing him.

Until the emails themselves became transgressive. At fifteen years old, here is what I knew: grown men were after me, and I was quite curious about them and their desire. Lawrence[1] (Lear42) was only the most recent in a string of adult men who pursued me. He wasn't even the first teacher who pursued me, but he was the first that I pursued back. That mutuality (my wanting and his wanting) made what we shared feel different from the "pervs" I had dismissed for years before him.

There was Terry, the dance teacher who kept me after class one day and kissed me on the mouth without warning. I was fourteen years old, and hadn't seen it coming. When I failed to respond to his kiss because I was frozen in place, he lectured me about the mixed "vibe" I'd been sending him and spent the next year and a half berating me and ignoring me in class. It was humiliating.

There was also Michael, a teacher who would follow me to the train after school, chatting easily while he leaned against the wall next to me, pinning me, making me a literal captive audience. There was a driver's ed teacher who leered at me when I stayed after to inquire about a test grade. A grown man followed me to the bathroom at my aunt's wedding, pressed me against the wall when I came out, and felt me up. Friends' fathers made comments about my developing body, and their daughters' bodies. Some of these took place in front of my own parents, who were silent, perhaps out of politeness, fears of confrontation, or their own internalized misogyny. By the time I met Lawrence, I had been primed to allow him into my life.

I was also very attracted to him. In some ways, that is the difference between Lawrence and all the men who tried before him: Lawrence was someone I fantasized about. I wanted him back. I was excited to have his attention. The others had been overwhelming, scary sometimes, occasionally intriguing. But I was really only curious about their attraction, and the leverage it gave me. I was interested in their power, and wanted a proxy to it. With Lawrence, it was easy. He was my teacher, an accomplished actor, and someone I wanted to approve of me. But he was also someone I legitimately and with my whole body desired. Sixteen-year-old me would tell you confidently that she had been a knowing and willing participant in the affair and that she was at least as responsible as he was for it happening. And although I am still, twenty-two years later, younger than he was when he kissed me, I remember exactly what it was like to fall in love with my teacher and to capsize myself in that desire.

What do we know about adolescent girls' desire? In the abstract, this question has been studied by feminist researchers beginning in the 1990s. From Deborah Tolman to Peggy Orenstein, Mary Pipher to Jessica Valenti, adult women have studied hundreds of teenage girls' experiences of sexuality and embodied desire. The research is written from an adult's perspective. That is, the researcher and her own adolescent desire are removed, invisible. The young women interviewees are quoted, and their experiences are relayed, but their words come through the mouthpiece of the supposedly neutral, adult woman researcher, with her editorial lens.

Because of my history, I cannot write about adolescent desire and mandatory reporting in a neutral way. I have a point of view, even if it remains tangled and circular, a swinging pendulum of rage and sadness and frustration. As a lawyer now, I work for an organization that represents survivors of gender-based violence, and provides training and legal research to those who are also federally-funded to work for survivors. My focus is training and research on minor and campus survivors. I mainly research federal and state laws, like Title IX, and the privacy issues survivors on campus struggle with uniquely. I think about mandatory reporting, either in the abstract as an issue, or the specifics of it for a trainee, every single week of my life. I still don't know what I feel about it. On the one hand, mandatory reporting ruined my life, and set a far greater trauma into motion than just the fallout of the affair with my teacher. On the other hand, mandatory reporting saved me, although I never would have said that at the time.

When I was an adolescent, my desire formed in response to being perceived as desirable. Young women and girls forge their sexual selves in a world that constantly objectifies, polices, and dictates what is sexy. These girls grow into women whose desire is dominated not by their own sense of longing or lust, but "by the wish to be the object of the erotic admiration and sexual need" (Bergner 2009).

Many feminists have studied how controlling female sexuality reinforces and strengthens patriarchy (Tolman 2005, 16). Adrienne Rich, the poet and feminist scholar, named one of these invisible systems *compulsory hetero-sexuality* in 1980 (Rich 1980, 631–60). Rich pointed to a variety of social phenomena that form the tapestry of compulsory heterosexuality, a complex system where women's desires are manipulated to control them and make them dependent on men for their needs. In current discourse, we refer to much of this as *rape culture*: objectification of women's bodies; elevation of the male sex drive to a right; idealization of heterosexual romance; erasure of female sexual agency and desire; rape, sexual violence, and pornography; and lesbian erasure. By naming and formulating the contours of the *institu-tion* of compulsory heterosexuality (as opposed to just the sexual orientation of heterosexual), Rich laid the foundation of understanding how and why female sexuality and desires are shaped the way they are; that is, as respon-sive to, and dependent on, their desirability to men.

My adolescence brought the system of compulsory heterosexuality out of the theoretical and into my body and psyche. I have memories of my body, and my pleasure including masturbation to orgasm that predate my visibility as a woman or sexualized body. Those experiences were exploratory, and primarily queer, taking place between me and other pre-pubescent girls at sleepovers, in bathrooms, or hiding in literal closets for privacy. Once I became visible to the male gaze, however, those experiences, desires, and knowledge seemed to disappear. In its place, I was no longer an agent of my own want. Instead, I was beginning to look outward, at others, but particular-ly at men, to see what was desirable about me. Author and psychologist Kerry Cohen, a psychotherapist and author of the nonfiction book *Dirty Little Secrets: Breaking the Silence on Teenage Girls and Promiscuity*, describes it thusly:

> Teenage girls' experience of desire is subverted and redirected into narratives about male attention. Genuine sexual desire is lost inside the power of getting that attention. The influence of this, the heady control of getting a boy or a man to look our way, to desire us, is perhaps the easiest way for girls to feel any kind of influence when it comes to their sexuality. In a culture where girls' genuine desire is shrouded in silence, where there is no language of ownership for a girl's sexual feelings, it is easy to see how girls gravitate toward this kind of power. (Cohen 2011, 39)

Lacking a language for myself, my own feelings, or my desires (particularly because of their queerness, but also because the culture at large does not legitimize pre-pubescent pleasure, or give us a narrative structure for it) I focused instead on the things I could name: male attention and its attendant power dynamics.

Like most women, I have a story about the first time I remember being perceived as womanly, or as the legitimate target of male sexual desire. I was eleven. I had begun menstruating the year before. My body was rapidly changing: I had small breasts and soft hips and had obtained what would become my adult height (five foot three). My mother's friend was visiting us, and had taken to wearing a fall, or a half-wig. This hairpiece clipped into the crown of her head, transforming her jaw-length, thin, unremarkable hair into something out of a music video. I asked to try it on, and was shocked at how much my appearance was also transformed, particularly from the back. I looked like a woman. Delighted, I asked for permission to wear it to my friend's house down the street. On my walk down the block, a pickup truck passed by on the road, and out of the cab flew a wolf whistle and comment on my body.

I felt real.

I also felt scared, vulnerable, in danger. I remember running to my friend's house with an eye over my shoulder. I was too afraid to wear the fall on my walk back home, but in her room before I left, we both marveled at its ability to make us appear older, available, like women and not children.

Situating this experience within Rich's framework, this was my induction to compulsory heterosexual desire. I would be pursued whether I wanted it or not, so I'd better learn to handle it. My desirability came from being seen by men. I was birthed from their wanting, subject to their construction, only real if they believed in me. Naomi Wolf observed in 1997 that girls are "expected to be sexually available, but not sexually in charge of themselves" (Wolf, 1997). So it was with me. I had a body that was becoming objectified and commodified by the world around me, regardless of my needs. I was not going to be the captain of my own body; I would need a man for that.

Mary Pipher analogized the seismic shift of when girls become women as a catastrophe, a wreckage. "Just as planes and ships disappear mysteriously into the Bermuda Triangle, so do the selves of girls go down in droves" (Pipher 2005, 8). Later, quoting Simone de Beauvoir, Pipher explains that during adolescence, "girls stop being and start seeming" (Pipher 2005, 11). Certainly my own adolescence felt catastrophic. Not only did I lose my child body, the one I had called home for all of the life that I could remember, I lost my child identity, too. Things that were permissible in a child body, even admired, were suddenly not allowed. I felt this most distinctly in my physical relationships. Adult women like my mother, aunts, and female teachers remained accessible as sources of comfort; it was alright to hug them, to lay my head in their lap, to sit close to them (even the ones I had little crushes on). In contrast, physical contact with adult men (including my father, uncles, and male teachers) became fraught with messaging, expectations, and a gendered performance that I had to learn how to deliver. It was no longer innocent to hug them, or even to sit close to them. In becoming a lightning rod for male desire, my body became a liability.

At the same time, my body was being policed. My clothes were constantly subject to scrutiny, both from individual family members and well-meaning adult friends, and from my schools and other institutions (like summer camp). My own high school was an arts magnet; if we had a formal dress code, I don't recall what it said. But when I attended social functions like dances or plays at other schools, I had to navigate those campuses' rules about how I could dress. I was asked to leave a school dance because I was wearing a top that showed my shoulder, required to put on jeans at camp by a counselor who felt my dress was too short, and constantly made aware that my body was a problem, not just for me, but for the men and boys around me who couldn't be expected to control themselves.

Both before and after adolescence, I was told by well-meaning adults that I was precocious, or "wise beyond your years." I took it as a compliment: I read a lot. But when I actually looked up the meaning of the word, I found entries like this one from Dictionary.com: "Precocious: 1640s, 'developed before the usual time' (of plants), with -ous + Latin praecos (genitive praecocis) 'maturing early,' from prae 'before' (see pre-) + coquere 'to ripen,' literally 'to cook' (from PIE root *pekw- 'to cook, ripen'). Originally of flowers or fruits" (Dictionary.com 2019). Even the idea of precocity in young women is gendered. Developed before the usual time according to who? Maturing early according to what timeline? If a flower or fruit is ripe earlier than expected, isn't it probably because it was precisely its time? What a strange imposition of time on the mystery of becoming.

I became used to being mistaken for older. I had breasts and hips before the end of elementary school, which mortified me. I wanted to be friends with the boys, same as ever. I wanted to fit in with them (I was the only girl). I wanted to pick scabs and catch footballs, ride skateboards and fart and laugh. I wanted to be the same as before, when we were all just children. But puberty was irreversibly cruel.

At the same time everything about me was going soft, the boys I'd palled around with for the previous decade (literally since we were babies in playgroups) were metamorphosing too. They thought differently. All of a sudden, I was valuable not only as the girl, the only girl. Or their friend, Marissa. But as a body to be touched, to be coveted, to be kissed. I was a prize to be won in a recess pickup game instead of a player. I was a trophy.

I was twelve the first time a man (or very nearly; he was seventeen) told me I was jailbait. I called him my "boyfriend," but really, he was a high school junior lighting tech who would find secret places to make out with me when he wasn't needed. We were both working on a community theater production of *Annie*. He never took me on a date, never bought me dinner, never spent any social time with me at all (though my diaries from that time are filled with fantasies and longing for him to do those things). Instead, he would pull me into the lighting booth or wrap me in the legs (those narrow black curtains at the sides of the stage that block the audience's view of the wings). Alone, briefly, he would whisper in my ear about all the things he wanted to do to me, including take my virginity, and how he had to do it before he turned eighteen. He'd tell me that I couldn't be twelve because "you *feel* at least fifteen," while running his hands over my breasts and hips. He was the first man who tied the desire I felt to the illicitness of our age gap. He made jailbait sound aspirational.

The term "jailbait" was coined in the 1930s, a slang term used to describe the significance of a girl's age both to her sexual consent, and to a male partner's criminal liability ("Children and Youth in History" 2019). When I think about jailbait, here is what I see: an old-timey jailhouse with bars around cells, and one teeny tiny worm tied in the middle of the room. Hooked on a line, maybe. I can't see the detail. I think of fish bait, and a cartoon jail, and the word falls apart like nonsense. But it wasn't nonsense when men whispered it to me in the middle of my attempts at saying no, at having boundaries, at making my way out of bathrooms and backrooms. These were the quiet places where men took me, caught me, found me, pinned me. There were abandoned kitchens, guest rooms, pool houses, and backyards. It wasn't nonsense at all. It was dangled in front of me as a kind of superpower: the ability to make grown men risk jail for my body.

In that context, of course, it felt like power to be wanted, desired so much that men would transgress the law to be with me. It came out of the mouths of older boyfriends as they approached their eighteenth birthdays. It came out of the mouths of the adult men who flirted with me. It came out of the mouths of my male teachers. I kept hearing it, over and over again until the word itself became a sort of erotic compliment, until I tied my desire to its dynamics. So when I was sixteen and my very attractive Shakespeare teacher began to flirt with me, offer me private coaching, and hire me to babysit his toddler at his house, I felt certain that I was the one with the power. I believed, and he reinforced, that I was making him take crazy risks: kissing me in the driveway of his house with his wife inside; inviting me over when she was out; claiming he'd forgotten the tickets so he could run home and be with me while on a date with her; making out in his car on the drive home. I felt like a magnetic field, impossible to resist, drawing him to me over and over again. I felt like the force that brought us together. I thought I had all the control. How innocent and wrong I was.

I told my best friend about the affair casually, about six weeks after it started, in front of her mother, a licensed therapist. I didn't think twice about saying something because Beth was a cool mom, and I was convinced that I held all the cards. When Beth told me that she'd have to report my teacher to the school, I felt surprised before I felt betrayed. Over and over, I tried to convince her that this was consensual, that I wanted to be with him, that my desire was at least as responsible for our relationship as his was. Yes, of course, he'd told me not to tell anyone, that he could lose his job and his marriage, that I could ruin his life. But I was sure that my precocity, womanly physicality, and intelligence made me fair game, an equal. Yes, I knew that other girls my age weren't mature enough to handle a relationship like ours, and I thought those laws (like mandatory reporting and statutory rape) were made to protect *them*. They were not made to protect girls like me. We knew what we were doing. We were jailbait.

My intuition that statutory rape laws were made for *some* girls, some innocent, sweet, taken-advantage-of girls, didn't come from nowhere. It's actually an ideology that was drafted into the laws themselves. Up until the late 1990s, in some states, defendants in statutory rape cases could claim a "promiscuity defense" (Oberman 1994, 32–36). The essence of the defense was that the girl had already been ravished, was worldly, knowledgeable, a promiscuous girl who didn't need protection because she was already not a virgin (35). Statutory rape was meant to protect some girls, the good ones, from the men who would prey upon their innocence. If the girl was not innocent when he met her, what was the harm?

Of course, this ideology makes sense in the original context of statutory rape laws. Originally a property crime, the king of England prohibited "ravishment" of maidens under twelve (Cocca 2004, 10). In 1576, the age was lowered to ten (11). The animating ideology, of course, was that girls and women were chattel, passed from their fathers to their husbands. A girl's chastity significantly impacted her "value" in that market. Colonial America basically imported the language from England, with some states setting the age of consent at ten, and some at twelve (11). In America, these laws only applied to white girls. Most Black girls were slaves, and post emancipation, they were seen as former slaves. Black women and girls were commodified as property regardless of their chastity (11). The problematic American social construct of Black female sexuality was in opposition to white female sexuality. White women and girls were often defined by their purity and chastity, and contrasted with the Black women and girls' "licentious temptress" stereotype (11).

At first, statutory rape was a strict liability crime, allowing no defenses if the prosecution could prove that the girl was underage and "of previously chaste character," and that the perpetrator had sex with her (Cocca 2004, 11). By protecting the chastity of white virgin girls, "early statutory rape law became a tool to preserve morality" (Oberman 1994, 26). The first major reforms came in the Victorian period, toward the end of the nineteenth century. A coalition of white feminists, working-class men's groups, and religious conservatives lobbied to raise the age of consent. One of the feminist objections was the "double standard that demanded female chastity before marriage, yet allowed men access" to girls as young as eleven without repercussions (Cocca 2004, 12). The image of the passive, white, poor, innocent, young girl "drew the support of more religious elements" (13). All around the United States and in England, the age of consent was raised to sixteen, or in some places, eighteen (Larson 1997, 44). Confusingly, teenage girls were now too young to consent to sex, but not too young to consent to marriage.

While the early feminists had been successful in advocating for a change in the laws, they had little control over their implementation. Male judges and prosecutors often still viewed teenage girls as temptresses, particularly if they were immigrants. They "would often sentence the male defendant to probation while sentencing the female on delinquency charges" (Cocca 2004, 16). In other words, while the feminist ideal that animated these reforms was to protect and uplift young women, the implementation of the laws in a patriarchal, racist judicial system often had the opposite effect. Adolescent girls *were* harmed by the state, using the very laws that were meant to protect them from harm by individual men: a classic double-bind.

Moreover, statutory rape laws (and rape laws generally) were used to justify violence and lynchings of Black men. Society viewed Black men similarly to Black women (licentious, overly sexual), with the added sexist assumptions that men were stronger than delicate white women, and therefore the likely perpetrators of sex crimes. Rape and statutory rape were treated much more seriously when they were perpretrated (or thought to be perpetrated) by Black men against white women (Wriggins 1983, 105). My Shakespeare teacher was Black, and I am the only girl I know whose statutory rapist was actually charged with a crime.

However, I was not the only one of my friends to ever be involved with an adult man. I had more than one friend (both boys and girls) who dated men in their twenties and thirties while we were in high school. And there were rumors about other student and teacher relationships that circulated every year (most involving a particular math teacher, and none of them ever "proven" like mine was). Teenage girls have been linked to adult male sexual partners since at least the 1990s (Ponton 2000, 214) with estimates as high as 60–80 percent of teenage pregnancies being caused by adult men (Zavodny 2001, 192). Further, data suggests that as the age of the victim goes down, the age of the perpetrator goes up (192). It isn't possible to link girls' desire to these outcomes; we don't know what percentage of teens felt coerced or forced into these experiences, and what percentage of them felt subjectively consenting, like I did. But it is true that both dynamics certainly exist. I have known women and girls who have had both kinds of relationships, and our culture is full of examples, both of teenage girls who are raped, sexually abused, coerced, trafficked, or otherwise non-consenting to their older partners. The Jeffrey Epstein case was a prominent recent example of this dynamic. On the other hand, there are many teenage girls who maintain, even as grown women, that they weren't victims, but were empowered, such as Lori Lightning and Sable Starr, who have maintained well into their middle ages that their sexual relationships with 1970s rock stars, including David Bowie, Iggy Pop, Jimmy Page, Mick Jagger, Steven Tyler, and others, were entirely consensual. Starr and Lightning claim they were willing participants, even lucky, although they admit that these sexual relationships were inherently coercive, with the men being famous rock stars, and the girls being barely into high school. There are drugs and alcohol involved in every encounter they describe, and in some cases, girls are physically kept from leaving by bodyguards, locked doors, or other methods (Mattix 2015).

We know that teenage girls do feel sexual desire, even if it is inherently constructed by the patriarchal culture in which they grow up. Teenage girls experience embodied desire, have sexual fantasies and yearnings (Tolman 1994, 325). I was not an exception. And yet, research suggests that many girls don't know how to express or own their desire in their sexual experiences. Without a clear cultural script for what female-driven desire looks and sounds like, girls follow the lines they are given by the patriarchy: namely that their role in sexual encounters is passive, submissive, and dissociated. Girls consent to sex or sexual encounters that bring them no pleasure (325). I did this more times than I can count between the ages of eleven and twenty-five. I was curious about sexual experiences: making out, perhaps. I found older boys attractive for many reasons, but one of the primary ones for me during this span of my life was that they would have "experience" and "know what to do with me." As a child, my precocity, intelligence, and physical maturity led the adults around me, including my own mother, to categorize me as "intimidating" or "too much" for boys my own age. I think that they meant to assuage my hurt feelings, as most of the boys my own age that I liked didn't show interest in me. But the unintended other meaning of their words was that I should look for someone older and wiser who could "handle me."

As Deborah Tolman writes, "What remains clear is that women's sexuality holds a fundamental contradiction under current gender arrangements: It involves both pleasure and danger" (Tolman 1994, 80). As a high school girl in the late 1990s, I was incredibly aware of the danger of my own sexuality. I could get pregnant; I could get HIV or any number of other STIs that might or might not become permanent health issues. I carried my anxiety about these outcomes next to my curiosity about sexuality, and my desire to experience pleasure. Researchers have suggested that in adolescence, girls develop a "dual consciousness" of anxiety and desire (80). Girls navigate this duality with the narrative of romantic love, which gives them a template for appropriate "good girl" behavior, as well as an idea of masculinity that is in opposition to her femininity. So, in exchange for her passivity, receptivity, submission, and naiveté, and within the bounds of a romantic relationship, a teenage girl can allow sex or sexual encounters to "just happen" to her (3), relying on her male partner's assertiveness, dominance, and experience. She can still be a good girl, as long as her partner is willing to take control, and as long as she remains in her place as a "good" sexual object and not a subjective participant with her own yearning. I certainly hoped, from very early adolescence, to find partners who would be "experienced," which was my way of saying partners who would initiate and take responsibility for our sexual dynamic. I had so many desires, but I didn't know how to ask for them; instead I hoped that the older, more experienced romantic partners I chose would know how to unlock my pleasure, and would encourage my desire.

When I was sixteen and dating a teacher I thought was thirty-six (but who was actually forty-two), I justified our relationship's obvious age gap and uneven power dynamics with the same lines and ideas I had been hearing all of my adolescence: I was mature for my age, I could handle an adult man. And I was responsible for keeping us both safe, by keeping the secret of our affair to myself. I failed to do that in telling my best friend, and I felt guilty about it for at least a decade after. I had known there were consequences for talking about our relationship. I shouldn't have said anything at all, let alone in the earshot of an adult. It took me a long time and many sessions of therapy as an adult to separate out my responsibilities and desires from his. I was in my thirties, and a mother, when I finally realized that my desire was not to blame. Instead, it was his irresponsibility with me as a student, a girl, and his narcissism that put us both in harm's way. He failed both his adult and educational duties, and then narrated his failure as an inability to resist me. It was a strange sort of cultural gaslighting: on the one hand, I was the most desired, most powerful I would ever be; on the other hand, I was not allowed to use my body, even when I desired back. Thus, when my teacher was fired and prosecuted for statutory rape, over and despite my objection that I had consented to everything we did, and that I didn't want him to get in trouble, I was left with a troubling silent void. There was no language for the experience that I had, and the labels that other people applied to it were incorrect, or sounded wrong. This is how I came to call the relationship an affair, a word that suggests the socially illicit construct of our relationship, but not the violence of rape, sexual abuse, or molestation. As a grown woman, I have come to identify myself as a survivor, generally, because what I experienced was certainly a kind of gender-based violence. But the word "rape" feels too strong. Instead, I think of it as coercive and slippery, a gray area where I have some terminology, but none of it fits right.

I am not the only woman or survivor to struggle with the language and label for my not-rape experiences. In an essay called "The Not-Rape Epidemic," author Latoya Peterson explains "rape was something we could identify, an act with a strict definition and two distinct scenarios" (Friedman and Valenti 2008). These two scenarios were, of course, stranger rape and date rape, with intercourse accomplished either by force or by drugging. In both scenarios, the violence or intoxication are perceived as markers of coercion. But, up until recently, girls haven't had the language to identify experiences that involved subtler coercion without physical force or drugging.

I came of age in the late 1990s, the same decade as Peterson, and I remember also feeling like rape was a clear enough concept: I knew how to hold my keys between my fingers in a parking garage; I'd taken self-defense classes before I went to college; I knew not to leave my drink unattended. But I did not know how to talk about the strange, coercive, overwhelming physical experiences I had with my teacher, and with so many before (and after) him. I didn't know how to talk about the feeling of wanting *something* with my body, but leaving my body behind when sex happened between us. What was I after? How would I know if I ever found it? It was impossible, really, to name these things. The only words we have for a girl who wants, sexually, are judgmental: jailbait, slut, vixen. Maybe it's because of that linguistic gap that I landed on, and clung so tightly to, Lolita. Within her (or at least what I perceived to be her), I found the tension between sexual precocity and dissociation, between abuse and seduction.

The idea that girls don't want sex without marriage has sounded antiquated all of my life. Sex education that covered STIs and pregnancy, the biology of the reproductive system, and the way penises can penetrate a vagina was the best I could have gotten. Many teenagers get abstinence-only sex education, or live in states with laws that prevent discussion of homosexuality in the classroom. But even in schools where we teach sex education, and in states like California, which recently decided to teach consent, we still don't teach pleasure (The California Healthy Youth Act, California Education Code 51930–51939 [2016]). According to sex educator Dr. Chris Donaghue, "the bulk of sex ed curricula fail to even recognize that most sex is for pleasure. Few people that are having sex are actually doing it for procreative reasons. We need to be talking straight sex and gay sex and trans sex and non-gender sex. Right now, most of it is procreation centric, which then also covertly is heterocentric" (Holmes 2019). Teaching pleasure means teaching agency means saying that sometimes, the adolescent body desires. It means saying that they have skin and nerves that thrum, spaces where the whole electric molten world of pleasure and yes comes together. What we say with statutory rape is: *under a certain age, your yes doesn't matter*. What we say is: *yes or no is the same*. But it's not the same. One part of the trauma of my teenage affair happened between me and my teacher, in my body. I've learned the word for floating out of my body and "letting him have it" is dissociation. I've learned it is a trauma response. I've learned that the violent shaking that would sometimes happen after I left his house was also a trauma response. But, beyond that, the trauma for me came when my teacher was fired and prosecuted against my wishes. Trauma was my best friend's mother calling my school, regardless of what I wanted. Trauma was losing my voice in a relationship where I once felt agency. Trauma was nonconsent, both because I didn't agree to the reporting or its repercussions, and because the legislature had removed my ability to give consent, legally.

I wasn't innocent or chaste when I first met Lawrence, but that wasn't an issue. Second- and third-wave feminists pushed for reforms to statutory rape laws, alongside laws prohibiting sexual harassment, spousal rape, child sexual abuse, and more. The definition of rape expanded to include more than an unknown man forcing himself on a woman using physical violence. Statutory rape became a gender-neutral crime; instead of a man "ravishing" a chaste girl under sixteen, it was any person over a certain age having sex with any person under a certain age. For felony statutory rape, the age span between the young person and the older one had to exceed a certain number of years. Many second-wave feminists saw the old statutory rape laws as "less as protective and more as punitive, less as empowering and more as infantalizing." Their solution was to formally equalize girls and boys in the law, removing the gendered language and the promiscuity defense, as well as the chastity requirement for the victim. Radical feminists and liberal feminists, who still come down on opposing sides of today's gender and sexuality questions, disagreed on removing the gendered language from the statute.

Liberal feminists were in favor of removing the gendered language, believing the "gender specific laws undermined female agency and equal rights" (Cocca 2004, 17). It also meant that young men would never be recognized as statutory rape victims. Their theory was that equalizing the language of the law would lead to greater social equality, and society would think about vulnerable young people, not just victimized young girls. Radical feminists agreed that boys could be victims, but argued that girls were fundamentally in need of distinct protection (65). Gender-neutral language would imply that girls and boys were similarly situated, when they were not, considering the majority of sexual assaults were committed on females by males. It's clear now, with the benefit of more than twenty years of data, that simply writing gender-neutral laws did not, in fact, usher in a renaissance of gender equality. Just as with the Victorian reformers of the late nineteenth century, twentieth-century feminists had little control over how the laws they advocated to change would be implemented. And with implementation, we have seen that the laws are used to reinforce racist and patriarchal ideas about femininity, victimhood, and predatory behavior.

Certainly, this is manifest in my own experience. I was given far too much leeway and not enough sway. Every conflicted social and legal narrative lives in my politicized body. From pre-adolescence to puberty to womanhood to motherhood, my body forms palimpsests of desire and regulation, consent and disempowerment. All of these stories are my stories, and all of these voices harmonize inside my electric body. A whole legal history resides between my thighs: what I can do, when and how, with whom, and under what circumstances. But, at each stage, one thing remains: what I want is buried. My desire, all feminine desire, remains absent from the conversations.

How can we both acknowledge that a female adolescent's desire exists and is valid for her to experience and talk about, and refuse adult perpetrators who would use that desire in their own defense? How do we rescue teenage girls from the double-bind they're in: they cannot legally consent to sex, and they still live in desiring, culturally sexualized bodies. We cast teenage girls as the objects of cultural lust, and disempower them by taking their consent away, placing it up on a shelf for later, when they're old enough, in the legislature's opinion, to make adult decisions. For my part, I wish that statutory rape was discussed less in terms of valid consent, and more in terms of desire and appropriate response. Rather than speaking of the law as invalidating a young person's consent, I would like to hear people talking about whose desire and impulses should be protected. Adults (particularly those over the age of twenty-five, with fully developed judgment) should not return an adolescent's desire. In my own situation, I think about what might have been different, how everything could have been prevented, if my teacher had been willing to say no. Rather than pretending that teenage girls don't know what they want, or can't ask for it, we could begin acknowledging that they do have desire, and don't have the necessary judgment to determine appropriate targets. Rather than calling them jailbait, we could call them what they are: young and beautiful in their early exploration. And we could protect that by expecting adults to set appropriate physical and emotional boundaries, and holding those accountable who do not.

NOTE

1. Note that the names in this chapter are not pseudonyms except for Lawrence, the teacher.

REFERENCES

Bergner, Daniel. 2009. "What Do Women Want?" *New York Times*, January 22, 2009. https://www.nytimes.com/2009/01/25/magazine/25desire-t.html.
Brick, Peggy. 2000. *The Sex Lives of Teenagers: Revealing the Secret World of Adolescent Boys and Girls.* New York: Dutton.
"Children and Youth in History." 2019. Accessed October 18, 2019. http://chnm.gmu.edu/cyh/primary-sources/46.
Cocca, Carolyn. 2004. *Jailbait: The Politics of Statutory Rape Laws in the United States.* Albany: State University of New York Press.

Cohen, Kerry. 2011. *Dirty Little Secrets: Breaking the Silence on Teenage Girls and Promiscuity*. Naperville: Sourcebooks.

Friedman, Jaclyn, and Jessica Valenti. 2008. *Yes Means Yes!: Visions of Female Sexual Power and a World without Rape*. New York: Seal Press.

Holmes, Dave. 2019. "The Case for Inclusive, Comprehensive Sex Ed." *Esquire*, June 28, 2019. https://www.esquire.com/lifestyle/sex/a27569998/comprehensive-sex-education-america. Accessed October 18, 2019.

Larson, Jane. 1997. "Even a Worm Will Turn at Last: Rape Reform in Late Nineteenth Century America." *Yale Journal of Law and the Humanities* 9 (1): 44.

Mattix, Lori, and Michael Kaplan. 2015. "I Lost My Virginity to David Bowie." *Thrillist*, November 3, 2015. https://www.thrillist.com/entertainment/nation/i-lost-my-virginity-to-david-bowie.

Oberman, Michelle. 1994. "Turning Girls into Women: Re-Evaluating Modern Statutory Rape Law." *The Journal of Criminal Law and Criminology* 85 (1): 15–79.

Orenstein, Peggy. 2016. *Girls and Sex*. Harper Collins: New York.

Pipher, Mary. 2005. *Reviving Ophelia*. New York: Riverhead.

Ponton, Lynn. 2000. *The Sex Lives of Teenagers*. Plume: New York.

"Precocious." Dictionary.com. Accessed October 19, 2019. https://www.dictionary.com/browse/precocious.

Rich, Adrienne Cecile. 1980. "Compulsory Heterosexuality and Lesbian Existence." *Journal of Women's History* 15 (3): 11–48.

Tolman, Deborah L. 2005. *Dilemmas of Desire: Teenage Girls Talk About Sexuality*. Cambridge: Harvard University Press.

———. 1994. "Doing Desire: Adolescent Girls' Struggles for/with Sexuality." *Journal of Gender and Society* 8 (3): 324–42.

Wolf, Naomi. 1997. *Promiscuities: A Secret History of Female Desire*. New York: Fawcett Books.

Wriggins, Jennifer. 1984. "Rape, Racism, and the Law." *Harvard Women's Law Journal* 6 (103): 103–141.

Zavodny, Madeline. 2001. "The Effect of Partners' Characteristics on Teenage Pregnancy and Its Resolution." *Family Planning Perspectives* 33 (5): 192–99.

Chapter Six

Does Any Woman Have Just One Survivor Story? One Vagina's Monologue

Sally J. Kenney

Trump's election rattled me. How could bragging about grabbing women by the pussy not disqualify him in the minds of a majority of white women voters? How could the so clearly better qualified candidate lose? The president has not only sexually assaulted individual women, but it feels as if he is expressing his profound misogyny every day. We are governed by a gas-lighter-in-chief: "Pay no attention to my fraud/treason/sexual misconduct, shift your attention instead to the Mexican border, or Baltimore, or China. What you attest to did not happen, you are a liar; it happened, but it is not a big deal, and you deserved it" (Stern 2007). For the Women's March in 2016, I donned a giant vagina costume to march with the New Orleans Abortion Fund and pinned a sign to myself that said "no grabbing." The march felt a little like going to a funeral of a beloved person who has led a long and full life. You are so happy to reconnect with other loved ones but, in the end, your loved one is still dead. The march was fun, the days since excruciating. My brother pronounced my costume undignified for a dean. (I am a director, not a dean; despite my email signature containing my job title the last ten years, my family struggles with nomenclature.)

I have many secrets that I share reluctantly; and some, for the first time in this essay. I am a survivor of sex discrimination, sexual harassment, domestic violence, sexual assault, abandonment, and bullying—in short, given the statistics, I am a typical 60-year-old woman living in the United States (Pereda et al. 2009). I am a political scientist whose field is public law. I study sex discrimination and most recently have written about gender and judging. Studying trauma that I, too, have endured has its rewards but also produces its own distinctive form of suffering (Campbell 2002; Kenney 1995, 1999; Schauben and Frazier 1995). I am compelled to do the work I do, teaching courses on rape, reading widely, connecting scholars, and advocating for policy change, in part, because of my personal experiences. Yet as I sit in a faculty meeting and fight for tenure for a woman against misogynistic colleagues or seek to dissuade the sole woman dean or my provost from promoting a serial sexual harasser to full professor or watch the Kavanaugh hearings as a judicial selection scholar, I am overwhelmed. "Triggered" does not even begin to capture the spiral of rage and despair I feel in response to these events. As one of my favorite greeting cards with a cat in the ass-licking position, back paw in the air, on a yoga mat says, "I meditate, I do yoga, and I still want to kill someone." At times, that someone has been me. Reading the *New York Times* during the last two years of Donald Trump and #MeToo feels like ripping a scab off my wounds every day. The air force pilot now senator who exploits her power to discredit another survivor (Cooper 2019). The Mennonite women in South America (Toews 2018). The students of Horace Mann (Kamil and Elder 2015). The gymnasts at Michigan State. The Gambian beauty queen. The many victims of our rapist-in-chief. My colleagues. My friends. My students. Children. I am learning to "lean in" to the suffering (my therapist would say, in her Buddhist way, "sit with") rather than chase the elusive healing or closure. I refuse to avert my gaze.

Muriel Rukeyser wrote in 1968, "What would happen if one woman told the truth about her life? The world would split open." Philosopher Kate Manne's analysis of misogyny in *Down Girl* (2018) describes how we exonerate men and engage in what she labels himpathy.

> I came to doubt my initial reflexive instinct to turn away, as opposed to subsequently varying my lens and widening my focus. And I came to worry that such instincts were having a bad effect on my thinking, or reflected a kind of intellectual cowardice . . . not to look too hard at the residual patriarchal forces operating in our culture, as the patriarchal forces themselves gather in the backroom to laugh at our expense and grow stronger in our absence. In my grimmer moods, I picture party hats and hooters . . . I . . . let myself look long, hard, and awkwardly, sometimes from uncomfortable angles, and quite often painfully, in what felt like all the wrong places, in the wrong ways, at the wrong times, in the wrong order. (xxii–xxiii)

Judith Herman wrote in *Trauma and Recovery*, the bible for all subsequent work:

> It is very tempting to take the side of the perpetrator. All the perpetrator asks is that the bystander do nothing. He appeals to the universal desire to see, hear, and speak no evil. The victim, on the contrary, asks the bystander to share the burden of pain. The victim demands action, engagement, and remembering. (1997, 7–8)

I will remember. I will share the burden of pain. I will name the world as unjust. I will not use the passive voice—women are sexually assaulted. Like so many brave others, I will say who assaulted me when and how.

Despite growing up with Phil Donahue and then Oprah, living in the era of reality TV and Judge Judy, participating in the consciousness-raising of second-wave feminism, briefly sucked down the rabbit hole of EST in the 1980s, reading rape narratives and feminist memoirs, undergoing therapy, sharing details of my family circumstances and my experiences of sexual assault, sexual harassment, and even sex discrimination induces terror. The mere receipt of this invitation to write about my secrets generates a voice in my head that waves its robot arms and shouts, "danger danger!" I worry about those whom my telling will hurt. I cringe at the idea that colleagues will think that they now understand why I behave as I do, or people who dislike me will have even more ammunition with which to criticize me, or worse yet, laugh.[1] I fear I will be diminished in the eyes of my students, my credibility as a scholar compromised. I imagine the shock of in-laws and relatives who will be reinforced in their view that I am emotionally unstable, politically wacko, and have no boundaries or sense of decorum. I dread the idea that my family will deny what happened, ignore it, or minimize it ("yes, but were you *raped*?"),[2] using it as further evidence that I am damaged, inferior, attention-seeking, self-absorbed. These are not unfounded fears, but reactions I have already experienced as I test the waters by sharing my experiences with others.

Remarkable therapists taught me many things. My current therapist has helped me to understand that being triggered, for want of a better word, means that when I experience a traumatic event, my brain reverts to the age I was when a similar thing happened and I react as if I were still that age (Fisher 2017). So when a colleague squeezes my bottom at a holiday party and I freeze, I have been transported back to when I was molested at age seven. I have to reassure myself that I am no longer that child but a (then) fifty-year-old full professor with an endowed chair and member of the senior leadership team of my university. I have power, knowledge, emotional self-awareness, and the capacity to diagnose, analyze, react, cope, survive, respond, and defend myself. The likelihood of responding to assaults with tonic immobility (freezing) is high (70 percent). The earlier in life the trauma, the higher the likelihood of responding by freezing (Möller et al. 2017). I have also learned that subsequent events are traumatic because they trigger the memory of the earlier (usually repressed and unprocessed) memory (Hauslohner 2014). Subsequent events make it no longer possible to ignore earlier events, leading one to react far more strongly to the recent event than one ordinarily would have. This phenomenon may be the gender-based violence equivalent of *ontogeny recapitulates phylogeny*. Those who theorize about violence against women urge us not to disaggregate the effects of multiple incidents of sexual harassment (Schultz 1997) or separate women's experience of domestic violence from their experience of street harassment and violence perpetrated by paramilitaries (Menjivar 2011). We need to contextualize such events as neither individualized nor private but mutually constitutive—more than cumulative but synergistic.

When I was twenty-three years old, I voraciously read feminist fiction, canonical feminist tracts, and feminist legal theory with little guidance and no roadmap. I read Catharine MacKinnon's profound analysis of how rape law incorporates the male point of view while I was sitting alone in a dark carrel in the basement of the Princeton library while pursuing a PhD in Politics (MacKinnon 1983). Assuming the somewhat implausible hypothetical that a rapist is genuinely mistaken about whether a woman consents (Harding 2015), he conceivably could lack *mens rea*. Yet a woman could still have experienced rape. In adjudicating, however, the law privileges his experience in determining whether he is guilty. Susan Estrich (1988) provided yet another example of the male standard as she explained how the law expects victims to fight back, demanding the response we demand of manly boys facing a schoolyard bully rather than a girl facing unequal gender power.[3] Those facing sexual violence are not supposed to be a pussy, by pleading or crying, but instead "man up." Fight or flight, however, is not the full range of responses: reactions to an amygdala highjack in the face of danger are fight, flight, freeze, or fawn, all of which are evolutionarily adaptive. (Though I remain wary of evolutionary psychology, particularly its biologism and gender essentialism, I find biological understandings of how our brains work to help reduce shame—the human brain is simply wired a certain way. Many animals respond similarly.) Freezing, fainting, and disassociating are ways the mind protects us and helps us to survive. Nobody likes to be a victim and American culture particularly stigmatizes this position (Cole 2007; Mardorossian 2014). Ironically, the more sophisticated the feminist and agentic the woman, the more shame she may feel when her response is to freeze rather than to, as the armless knight in Monty Python's *Holy Grail* commands, "fight on 'tis only a flesh wound." Survivors like me may be drawn to this work because tending and befriending (Taylor 2000), as well as fighting, fleeing, freezing, or fainting, are evolutionarily adaptive responses to extreme stress. But just as I do not want to ignore or minimize my experience, nor do I want it to define me. I am more than my wounds; victimhood does not exhaust my story.

While writing this essay, I saw Heidi Schreck's transformational show, *What the Constitution Means to Me*, which not only touched me deeply but shifted my thinking. She profoundly observes that resistance does not always mean fighting back but may mean simply surviving. Telling her family's stories of sexual violence and betrayal as well as revealing the circumstances of her abortion was so intense for her that she walked off the stage during the first show, unable to continue to perform (Fierberg 2019). Nevertheless, she persisted, stating: "Stories connect us, and I needed my story to be heard." Recounting how she continued to love her grandmother who had betrayed her mother touched me deeply. Heidi's mother charged her stepfather with sexual abuse, which the grandmother denied. I also admire Schreck's ability to find humor and joy, to laugh at herself and not take herself too seriously. Historian Vanessa Holden challenges her audience (and soon readers, with the release of her book) to reject a narrow-minded masculine standard of courage. She reframes the narrative of the Nat Turner slave revolt from one simply of men's heroism to one focusing instead on the bravery of black women in keeping themselves and their children safe, choosing to survive, rather than lacking the courage of the men who used violence and died, leaving their families unprotected.

Survivors from Susan Brison (2003, 2014) to Jessica Valenti (2016) have demonstrated that most women survivors have more than one story to tell. Christine Gidycz's research (2011) reveals that young women who have been assaulted in high school are twice as likely to be raped while attending college than other women. Hannah Gadsby's powerful recent "comedy" dialogue *Nanette* explores how we curate certain parts of our experiences and leave out others, just as Roxane Gay, in her essay "What We Hunger For," in *Bad Feminist*, left out that she continued to see her "boyfriend" after he orchestrated her gang rape. Women experience a spectrum of sexism, sexual harassment, and sexual violence over the life course. To paraphrase the introduction from *Law and Order*, "these are five of my stories." I tell them not in chronological order, but in the order of the ease with which I can tell them. More people know the first story, so that perhaps makes it easier to tell. It involves sex and shame, but no physical violation of my bodily integrity, just threats. I feel less culpable. I have processed it the most in therapy. My argument, however, is that I cannot understand my feelings and reactions to the first four episodes until I began to metabolize the fifth, which I have only just begun to do.

EPISODE ONE: DIRTY JOHN AND THE AWAKENING

The hope that telling my story would humanize me thereby making me a more effective leader and generate staff buy-in for a new project motivated me to begin to tell the first story. For the last ten years, I have paid the school fees of several children in Kenya whose lives are affected by HIV (either they are orphans or have one or both parents living with HIV [Friends of Ngong Road]). I invested many hours to develop a service project with Tulane students to work with these children at a summer camp and served on the organization's board of directors. The staff at the Newcomb Institute found it hard to see how it fit in our mission of educating undergraduates to achieve gender equity. One member of my leadership team observed me tear up when I talked about how meaningful my work with AIDS orphans in Kenya was during a speech to the local Rotary Club. She urged me to tell my story to staff so that they might discover "that I had feelings, too." This characterization shocked me to the core. I think of myself as overly sensitive, soft-hearted, and empathetic—a bleeding heart. I experience my inner life as a tsunami of emotional currents. I cry at AT&T ads and those Mastercard ads about what is priceless. No feelings?[4] I also began to tell my story to inspire and encourage those who were survivors or orphans to believe that they could still achieve their dreams, that they were not so wounded that they could not lead good lives. During my second trip to Kenya with a group of women sponsors, staff arranged for us to meet with the class of high school graduates and staff, 20 or so, who had carefully prepared to tell their stories. When two broke down in tears, saying they had let the program down by getting pregnant and having a child out of wedlock before graduating from high school, I was compelled to share my story, although doing so left me shaken. I wanted them to both know that their lives were not over, that they were not shameful disappointments to their American sponsors. I later helped craft a program of youth peer providers on sexual and reproductive health. As the Newcomb Institute geared up our work on sexual assault on campus, I began telling more of my story when invited to be the keynote speaker at our student sexual assault conference, and a bit more at a conference for young women political scientists. Yet I cannot help feeling that those I work with are uncomfortable, not wanting me to burden them with my issues or make them confront their own.

My father died in a car accident in June of 1972 when I was thirteen. He was a commodity broker. We believe a con man and sexual predator read the obituary in the newspaper and phoned my mother, pretended to have been a customer of my Dad's, and asked if he might stop by to express his condolences. He took my mother out that night and they started a relationship. Like a batterer, his pattern as a controlling man was to methodically isolate my mother from her family and friends while sponging off of her financially. I was relatively safe from him for a year until my brother left home for college. After that, he moved in. Like the con man made famous by the podcast *Dirty John*, he sought to turn my mother against my sister and me. Our Mom, who had been the conscientious 1950s housewife, seamstress, cook, choir accompanist, Camp Fire and Cub Scout leader, suddenly stopped attending my sporting events, fixing meals, or transporting me to school, activities, and jobs as she devoted all her attention to him. My sister and I began to feel like interlopers in our home and my mother's life. Eventually, he and my sister had a confrontation over the television, and she left home at sixteen, getting her own apartment.

Instead of three against two (and most importantly, the three including my brother, the firstborn son), it was now two against one. *Dirty John* would be standing naked in the bathroom with the door open looking out the window when I got up in the morning. One night, when my mother was away, he hammered on my bedroom door that had no lock when I was in my bathrobe having just gotten out of the shower. Opening the flimsy door, I was terrified, blubbering an apology for whatever he was shouting I had done. My mother later claimed that she knew better than to leave him alone with my sister and me (although she did), which speaks volumes about her capacity to do what Jennifer Freyd describes as knowing and not knowing—a form of double-think (Freyd 2013).

One Friday night early in my sophomore year of high school, I arrived home shortly after 10 p.m. Having never experienced the classic Freudian moment of walking in on or even hearing my parents having sex, as I ascended the stairs, I could not make sense of the sounds I was hearing. I thought to myself, *why is the TV on upstairs this late and this loud*? Slowly my brain processed his loud exclamations of sexual pleasure. Like the character Daniel in the show *Rectify*, who was gang-raped on death row and is transported back to the rape by the breathing and grunting of his roommate masturbating, I cannot hear the words he used without thinking of that night. (Sadly, the endearment he shouted at my mother, "punkin," is a term she used for my brother, my sister, and me.) My 60-year-old self does not believe children, especially teenagers, need to be shielded from the fact of their parents' sexuality, but even now it feels as if my mother placed her (or more likely his) sexual pleasure above my well-being by forcing me to hear them. Or was it that my mother, as had I, had simply ingested the cultural standard that her status depended on being attached to a man (Voss 1983)?

The timing of this incident now leads me to suspect it was no accident. Between school, sports, and my job, I was rarely at home to limit their activities. But I would have been expected to be at home at that time of night. I cannot help wondering if it were an orchestrated event to cement his control over my mother by driving me, too, from our home? And it worked. Like Dr. Christine Blasey Ford, I cannot remember how I got from my house late at night (before cell phones or Uber) to my high school nurse's house, a woman I knew had helped my sister. I must have called a taxi on our landline downstairs in the kitchen. I packed only my waitress uniform for work the next day. To the extent that I had a plan, I think it must have been to get my mother's attention or to enlist the aid of my sister. But I had severely miscalculated—I got neither. I was on my own at fifteen.

With the help of our high school nurse, I got my own modest apartment in a building she owned, but it was outside of the school district. Like my sister before me, I convinced the Social Security and Veterans Administrations to pay the survivors' benefits from the death of my father directly to me rather than to my mother. My sister was on probation for getting arrested for shoplifting a Bic Banana pen at Sears while having a marijuana joint in her purse. I had learned from my more economically marginal friends at the roller rink and boys who worked with me at Country Kitchen who lived in a juvenile detention facility nearby. They told me that having two juvenile offenders in the family—both runaways—would mean if I were caught or got in further trouble that I would be set to Mitchellville, the juvenile detention hall for girls. The deep belief that "there but for the grace of God go I" informs my work teaching women in prison.

Dirty John's arrival marked a sexual awakening, the kind Jessica Valenti so beautifully describes in her memoir *Sex Object* (2016). Like the girls in the film *The Magdalene Sisters* (2002), I was abruptly marked as a bad girl for hitting puberty and attracting the attention of men. My biggest challenge was not money—I got by with my waitress earnings and social security (not that I managed either particularly well, often avoiding the school nurse at rent time or bouncing checks)—but transportation. Like many cities, Des Moines's bus routes went to and from the city center, not across suburbs. After spending an hour trying to get to school, changing buses downtown and arriving late, I concluded hitchhiking was the better option. My homeroom teacher saw me hitchhiking and, rather than picking me up and offering to help, tried to get me kicked out of school for living outside of the district. I may have been in the top 2 percent of my graduating class and the state champion of extemporaneous speech the following year as only a junior, but to her I was a bad girl, deserving comeuppance for my bad attitude, reflected by my refusal to stare at the loudspeaker during morning announcements with a Nancy Reagan–like look of rapture.

I played on the sophomore girls' basketball team and, because we were sophomores and more importantly girls, we had the worst practice time in the gym—6 a.m., which meant I was hitchhiking in the dark of winter when few cars were on the road. Invariably late, I always had extra wind sprints to run off as punishment. One day, I was picked up by a trucker who asked if I minded if he "beat his meat." After my brain refused to process his words and my contorted face said, "What?" twice, he rephrased: "you know, jack off." My middle-class Presbyterian self who had never touched a penis (not counting changing the diapers of many infants as a babysitter) responded with outrage and informed him that if he did not stop immediately, I would jump out of the cab. Shamed or perhaps just startled by my authoritative tone, he dropped me at the front door of school without further incident. What I feared more than climbing into those high cabs of truckers were automatic locks controlled by the driver. I always checked the door before I got in to see if it had handles, as if the ability to dive out of a car at high speeds could keep me safe (Senn et al. 2015).

A not-very-worldly fifteen-year-old in her own apartment was easy prey, and I had my share of ugly experiences.[5] It is tempting to conclude with what Roxane Gay chastises her contributors for in *Not That Bad* (2018): it was not that bad and it could have been worse. When I see fourteen-year-olds now, I am reminded that when I was barely wearing a bra, I had a fake ID and went to bars, hanging out with adult men. I feel sad when I see how dangerous the situations I was in were and I see my young self as I study the range of horrible things that many men do to girls. Many runaways, treated as juvenile delinquents and bad girls, are fleeing sexual abuse and, desperate for affection, make easy targets for sex traffickers.[6] But I did attract many kind and loving people for which I am forever grateful, including many men who reminded me not all men were predators and not all men saw me as a sexual object. The nephew of the school nurse and brother of a classmate in the apartment next to me was kind and watched out for me, as did the elderly couple downstairs. My debate coach, the assistant manager at Country Kitchen, or older workmates would often drive me home. Volunteer empty nesters (we called them "choir parents") who had known me all my life took me to and from choir practice and church each week for two years, treating me to dinner each time and driving me to work afterwards on Sundays. The substitute teacher for our debate coach asked me to move in with her and her husband, who traveled for several days each week for work, and their one-year-old baby. Until I graduated a year early from high school, I was once again under the protection of adults, loved, and supported. I consider them my foster family. I was in contact with my mother about once every month or two—she attended my high school graduation and visited me in Iowa City right before I started college.

EPISODE TWO: FLEEING FIRST FIANCÉ

I do not remember telling anyone the full details of the events that led me back into *Dirty John*'s territory for a second time.[7] Despite all the advertising of Viagra and Cialis, our society treats men's sexual dysfunction as taboo and particularly fails to discuss its prevalence in sexual assault.[8] There's something particularly demeaning about describing a death threat issued while lying legs spread with a penis inside me in a puddle of cum. Not really the image of myself I want to share with my spouse, on Facebook, or Instagram, or invite my detractors to enjoy.[9] The image and memory seared indelibly in my mind is the precariousness of being in a single top dorm bunk bed watching the ceiling as I froze in terror and shame.

I headed off to the University of Iowa a year early at seventeen having chosen that school because my boyfriend (*First Fiancé*), two years older, attended it.[10] We had traveled back and forth over the previous eighteen months in our on-again, off-again relationship. I met him working at Country Kitchen, but he had also gone to my high school, shared some of my sister's circle of friends (she was his age), and, like me, was academically gifted, graduated a year early, and came from a troubled family. His controlling and abusive father was unemployed. *First Fiancé* was trying to extricate himself from his father's control, a task made more difficult because he lived with his older brother who acted as his father's agent. The brother intensely disliked me as a bad influence, as if *First Fiancé* were a boxer and the brother was the coach in *Rocky* shouting "women weaken the legs." What *was* rocky was our relationship. He drank, used drugs (including acid), pulled all-nighters working night shifts or studying, and struggled financially, wasting money on parking tickets and bank overdraft fees. He often stood me up. Despite my intelligence, strength, and feminism, my family and culture taught me that without a man, I was nothing. We were both sexually inexperienced, fumbling around without much education or communication skills. I endured the pain and humiliation of his poor treatment to act out the charade of coupledom. We became engaged my first semester of college when I was seventeen. I still have the $400 diamond ring.

When I think back to that time, I am stunned by my utter lack of feminist or even gender consciousness, but perhaps more so by my total lack of preparation for being a woman in a man's world or my lack of any kind of reflection on how to negotiate and explore my own sexuality with the world's many dangers. Only one woman professor taught me as an undergraduate; neither Political Science nor Philosophy had any women faculty nor courses on women's studies. A fellow waitress told me about Betty Friedan's *The Feminine Mystique* while we stood at the milkshake machine between waiting on tables. If only I had read Lisa Wade (2017), Laura Hamilton and Elizabeth Armstrong (2013), Jessica Valenti (2016), or Leslie Morgan (2009). As one small step, the Newcomb Institute has started a summer school for high school girls called "Dismantling Rape Culture," but most of our attendees are already survivors.

My disposition toward friendliness and interest in people from other countries precipitated my breakup with *First Fiancé*. I have always been sensitive, big-hearted, and drawn to helping others, particularly those oppressed. If I had lived at an earlier time when life choices for women were even more restricted, I might have been a missionary as was my great-aunt in Lahore, Pakistan, rather than a feminist professor. The governor of Iowa, Bob Ray, committed the state to welcome at least one thousand Vietnamese boat people (eventually ten thousand came [Leys 2018]), and some of these young men and women were studying on campus trying to pass their TOEFL exam to gain admission to the University of Iowa. I struck up a conversation with one man while working in the dining service, scraping uneaten food from plates on their way to the dishwasher. He invited me to a social gathering. I arrived to discover a group of men in the sitting room and a few women hovering in the kitchen. The men ignored the Vietnamese women and leapt to light my cigarette, competing for my attention. I do not know if they were simply lonely, wanting an easier path to citizenship, or trying to raise their status by garnering American friends or an American girlfriend, but after that night, they hounded me, knocking on the door of the dorm room I shared with two other women at all hours of the day and night. It would not be the only time my friendliness especially toward non-Americans would get me into trouble.

First Fiancé and I had lived together the summer before college and I intended to stay with him over the Christmas break and work at where else?—the Iowa City Country Kitchen, my home away from home. I had waitressed many Christmases and Thanksgivings since I left home, but nothing is more depressing and eerie than staying in a college dorm over a holiday. (Whether it was from being home during a break-in, or from my sister showing me the "rape cords" the University of Pennsylvania had in the women's bathroom stalls when she was in graduate school, I fear being cornered and trapped when I am working late in an empty office. I am afraid that someone will follow me into the restroom, turn off the lights, and assault me—just as Dr. Christine Blasey Ford has felt since she was assaulted that she always needed two doors to feel safe.) The dorm was abandoned. I do not know why we were there and not at his apartment. We had sex and he came almost the moment he entered me. I will remember to this day the feeling of lying under him on the top bunk under the patchwork quilt my grandmother had made of garish double-knit remnants of the fabrics we used to make our clothes in the 1970s. Seventeen years old, I was not a sophisticated or critical sexual partner. If something went amiss, I would attribute it to my own inadequacy or simply remain bewildered. I had not yet discovered *Our Bodies, Ourselves* and Google had not yet been imagined. Rather than attributing what had just happened to his own arousal or the fact that he rarely slept, had an unhealthy diet and did not exercise, smoked, abused alcohol and drugs regularly—or simply something that happens and nothing that is wrong or shameful—he blamed me. For "fucking all those Vietnamese men." (While I had dated others in high school, I had been completely faithful that fall and especially once I was engaged.) While still inside me, he said, "I should just kill you now." I did what I always seem to do in such situations: I froze, saying nothing, lying still. Eventually, he got up, dressed, and left without a word. I locked the door. Alone in the dorm and shaking, I called my Mom.

To her credit, when I told her we had broken up, without question or criticism she drove the 120 miles from Des Moines to Iowa City to pick me up. We had to stop at his apartment to collect my belongings. He went in his bedroom and closed the door and I could not bring myself to ask for the linens. I cried all the way from Iowa City to Des Moines. I think I cried first for how sorry I felt for him, the damaged person I hoped to rescue. Then I cried for my diminished status, a seventeen-year-old without a fiancé, let alone a boyfriend. I was nothing. He was supposed to heal my wounds of abandonment as a fellow damaged person, not deepen them. Only very late in life did I fully appreciate that only I can do that for myself. Despite my shame and suffering, for the second time, I discovered my strength and dignity were more important than an unhealthy connection. I could walk away if I had to, no matter what the cost.

It was a grim holiday break: no tree, presents, or dinner, or holiday treats—we had all but given up on Christmas after my Dad died. My solace was waitressing at Country Kitchen, the graveyard shift ten to six. When I have been lonely, working with people on the night shift or on holidays comforted me, like sharing a spaceship in the dark. A fling with an assistant manager of another store kept me out of the house most of the time I was not working. Yet when I tentatively began to confide in him about my situation at home, he joked that I was getting "that little lost lamb look," as if describing my situation was an attention-seeking performance or narcissistic indulgence. His indifference might have been a red flag had our relationship extended beyond the winter break. (I do, however, continue to puzzle over my attraction to people who lack empathy.) His physical attraction flattered me and bolstered my confidence that I might be desirable. *Dirty John* mostly menaced in the background since I was almost never home. I took taxis to and from work. When I did return home from work at 6 a.m., the house was freezing (they turned down the thermostat at night to fifty-five). I managed to survive the break without incident. My most acute memories were of being freezing cold in my bed and trying to get warm, the smell of grease that stuck to my body and clothes, and the sorrow I felt as *First Fiancé* dispatched his sister (badly treated by her current boyfriend) with a belated Christmas gift— a leather coat—to try to win me back. Hers was one young woman's attempt to get another woman to continue a bad relationship thereby validating her own bad choices as the best we can hope for.

EPISODE THREE: FIANCÉ NUMBER TWO
AND DIRTY JOHN TAKE THREE

Rather than continue paying tuition for a fourth year of college, because I had tested out of so many classes, taken a heavy load, and taken summer classes, I was admitted to the graduate program in Political Science with a full-tuition scholarship and a generous stipend. I was now living with a different fiancé and became pregnant. *Fiancé Number Two* was working to pay for his undergraduate degree himself and had no interest in getting married, becoming a father, or supporting a child. I was ambivalent at the time, less so in retrospect. His utter lack of indecision, concern for what I might want, or empathy for me clarified the profound limitations of our relationship, and I was crushingly disappointed, although not necessarily surprised. (I still did not believe that I was really worthy of love and affection.) I returned from the abortion clinic and he went off to study in the library, leaving me alone contrary to medical advice (you are supposed to have someone with you in case you start bleeding, so you do not bleed to death). Nor did my sister, one of the few other people who knew, volunteer to stay with me. I dropped out of graduate school shortly thereafter, fleeing to work on a Senate campaign in Des Moines. My foster family, the substitute teacher who now had three children, did not have room after all, despite initially telling me I could live with them when I was deciding whether or not to accept the job. Wanting to get away from *Fiancé Number Two* and begin my new job, I ended up back in my mother's home.

Being at home again at twenty-one, six years after I had left embarrassed me, although it is hard to explain why to twenty-one-year-olds today. For several weeks after the abortion I was not supposed to take a bath because of the risk of infection. *Dirty John* yelled at me for using the shower (something about water leaks) and my mother, who did not want to explain my situation to him, did not intervene. Soon after I moved back, when my mother was away taking care of her mother, he cornered me into having lunch and offered himself as my sexual guru, spinning the preposterous yarn that he had been an apprentice of Kinsey. As I declined, curling my lip with disgust, I felt the room-spinning vertigo I had after hearing his cries of sexual ecstasy on the stairs. In retrospect, I suspect he was yet again simply just trying to drive me from the house. Always outmaneuvering me, he managed to stick me with the bill and then pocketed the change. When I appealed to my brother for emotional support, he coldly told me that I should stop relying on family. A new friend who worked in the same building introduced me to a man who rented the apartment below him and I rented a room from him.

Later that summer my brother (four years older) had a nervous breakdown and my mother, my sister, my brother's girlfriend, and I all dropped everything to try to keep the most valued man of the family out of a psychiatric ward. My sister had held people down for electric shocks in her job as a nurse in Omaha, and without much deliberation, we all thought we were somehow better equipped to deal with the crisis than any trained professional. In retrospect, it was the typical response of our family to deny problems and to attempt to discreetly muddle through rather than acknowledge them and seek help. In the midst of this bizarre round-the-clock vigil, my mother kicked *Dirty John* out of the house. I enjoyed one magnificently empowering moment of standing up to him as he came to the back door and telling him to "fuck off." Was it that I was older? Or, was I a little more practiced in self-assertion? Or, was it that I was part of a family block again? As my mother described her tipping point, she sobbed that *Dirty John* had laughed at my brother's wild rantings, making fun of "her pride and joy."[11] I told her what had happened at lunch, but that revelation generated not one word of response. I wonder now if my mother had her own form of tonic immobility; at the time, it felt like a rejection and an erasure, not being the pride and joy and all. As it happened, like many abused women, my mother did not make a clean break. Once my brother had moved back home, as she was leaving the house, she even asked if I cared to join her and *Dirty John* on their date.

Much later, when I went into therapy and worked through things with my mother, I discovered how she figured out he was a pathological liar. Her first inkling was when she had gone to pick him up from the hospital after he had broken his wrist and discovered he had been admitted under a different name. She learned that he used several aliases, had a wife, daughter, and a granddaughter who lived in town, had served time in jail, and was a kleptomaniac (full tool boxes and clock radios everywhere) as well as a pathological liar. Her discovery of a letter from the next victim he was grooming was the last straw. He would go on to sue my mother for palimony claiming a common law marriage and received temporary alimony, something that was very hard for women to obtain at that time.

While I was studying abroad at Oxford, unbeknownst to us, my mother did a front-page interview with the *Des Moines Register* (Voss 1983). Under her picture the caption read, "a colossal mistake." After years of covering for my mother, I felt horribly exposed and ashamed that my Dad's side of the family would read all about *Dirty John* in the paper. Some teachers, extended family, neighbors, and members of our church thought I was a sullen adolescent, simply unwilling to accept my mother's new partner, and continually urged me to reconcile with her. We pretended that I lived at home and all was well. My paternal grandmother had taken me aside and told me how nasty I was to my mother and that I was a bad person. I offered not one word in my own defense, one of my first introductions to the phenomenon of gaslighting, a term regretfully I only recently learned (Stern 2007). Many people like my homeroom teacher simply thought I was a juvenile delinquent, a wild and bad girl, despite all the ways I was continuing to thrive, despite the obstacles.

Two convictions shape my current work with incarcerated persons teaching at the Louisiana Correctional Institute for Women and work for clemency for survivors of intimate partner violence. I share a secular version of "there but for the grace of God go I" and believe we are not defined by our worst acts (a value I struggle to apply to all). When I judge my mother, or others, my therapist reminds me that I know little about what anyone else was going through. With each year, I feel more generous towards others' shortcomings. I am open to the literature of restorative justice. Yet, despite this, I do not know how to find my way to compassion for *Dirty John* and still feel a keen sense of betrayal as a result of my mother, sister, and brother's behavior, even though I can now appreciate that they were all doing the best they could. I still struggle with feelings that I am unworthy of love because of the way my family treated me. *Dirty John* had a very high-pitched distinctive laugh, and hearing anyone laughing like him really—there is no other way to describe it—gives me the willies, makes me freeze in my tracks and transports me back in time. I cannot abide the pet word he was shouting at my mother in the throes of sexual gratification. Any pet word he used still makes my skin crawl. Once I thought I saw him on the running track of the YWCA in Minneapolis, and I thought about pushing him over the rail to the gym below. (It was not him.) You would think that time would produce distance, crowding out these memories with others more important, but that is not how the brain works. Instead, every new remembering strengthens the neuropathways to that memory. The grooves of the channels are strengthened, no matter how much I will them to no longer matter.

EPISODE FOUR: COACH LACTOSE INTOLERANT

Five years later, I had a second B.A. from Magdalen College, Oxford. I had met a wonderful, smart, funny, kind, empathetic, devoted, and constant, feminist man who turned out to be the best thing in my life for the next thirty-seven years. I had passed my comprehensive exams for a PhD at Princeton. I was writing my dissertation in Oxford while he finished his degree. A friend helped me secure what I thought of as a dream job as a European tour guide of high-school students when I was twenty-four. I guided a bus, six countries in fourteen days, to countries I had never been to before the days of GPS with an Austrian bus driver who did not speak English (I spoke no German). We had a short two-day orientation and I was briefed by a company representative, but I was too inexperienced to know what I did not know and was overconfident. I was more stressed than I have ever been—and on my own—remember, no mobile phones or emails; international phone calls were expensive. Another guide offered to swap drivers, but I did not trust that she had my best interests in mind and my snap judgment was that he would push me around (a mistake, in retrospect, as he not only spoke English, but was more experienced navigating places like Rome where my driver repeatedly got lost). In times of extreme stress, I often find it hard to discern who is trying to be kind and who is trying to manipulate me.

I did my best to prepare, learning a little of each language and buying guides and maps. I made many novice mistakes but was getting the hang of things, even though lots of things went badly wrong: we got lost, one of the adults broke her wrist, bags were lost, and so on. The planning, worry, anxiety, pace, and desperation to please kept me sleeping poorly. If only I had had any sleep aid, I probably could have kept my equilibrium. Also, if I had been to these places before, I would have opted out of many activities. We went from morning until night with no breaks. I dropped more than ten pounds in the first week. By the time we hit Florence, I was in a bad way.

Through a series of acts I now understand as grooming, one of the teachers, a wrestling coach (*Coach Lactose Intolerant*), offered emotional support and advice. He was one of those furtive small men who had bulked up, shortening his pectoral muscles so he had a primate-like, arm-forward quality. In retrospect, I observed how his hypervigilant wife kept him on a short leash and clearly knew he was untrustworthy. He suggested we go for a walk in a park since it was a beautiful sunny day and the others were at museums. *Coach Lactose Intolerant* had told his wife he did not feel well enough to go. His lie should have been my first clue. He told me I needed to relax, which was true: I had had no breaks, no exercise, and very little sleep for over a week while under tremendous stress. He suggested he give me a neck and shoulder massage like the ones he would give his wrestlers, anxious before a match. Once I finally relaxed for the first time in days in a sleepy trance, he slipped his hand down my pants. I froze but managed to tell him to stop. His response was, "Why not? It will make you feel good and help you relax." He eventually did stop after I repeatedly said no (I did not leap up, push his hand away, or strike out). Acting as if nothing were amiss, I said it was time to get back. We chatted amicably on the way back while inside I was breaking apart. I was a sleep-deprived, stressed, twenty-four-year-old a long way from home with an opportunistic predatory creep. (And a high school teacher! Did he do this to students?) I felt like I had cheated on my husband, exercised poor judgment, and been gullible. I was more upset than ever, feeling like a failure on every front. I told the other guide, and she kindly minimized it, saying, "You did nothing wrong. Think of it as a free massage."

Later that night, posing as the savvy tour guide rather than a person hopelessly out of her depth, I hopped in the front seat of the taxi. The fat, white-haired taxi driver started chatting with me, taking my hand and placing it on his balls. I could feel throbbing beneath his thin pants. Why did I not pull my left hand back like it had been scorched by fire and punch him with the right? Why did I respond to the schoolyard bully, as Estrich describes it, like a sissy rather than a real man? As I cried, I haltingly told him I had been assaulted earlier that day. Astonishingly, he took pity on me, given the fact that he was happy to abuse me for his own gratification up until that point. I blamed myself for being stupid enough to get in the front seat with him. To this day, I recall his leer and remember the throbbing every time I might have to get in the front seat of a taxi. I hate talking to drivers and wish I could enter a "do not converse" code on my Lyft profile. I sometimes want to scream, "Is there anything in my demeanor or response that suggests I am inviting a conversation?" I make my husband do all the talking, telling him to think of me as deaf and mute. Better to be a standoffish bitch than a victim. I worry that any attempt at friendliness could seem to invite sexual contact. Thirty years later, I would watch one of my staff members, a twenty-something African American, in Kenya practicing her Swahili chatting with drivers, men opening the gates, and security guards, wanting not to be the *mzungu* (Swahili for foreigner or white person). I feared for her, remembering the price I paid for not wanting to be the Ugly American.

As the bus made its way from Rome to Switzerland, I unraveled. The company was making a marketing film using an experienced guide who wanted to film on my bus. I now believe that these events affected me so much because they triggered a reaction from earlier childhood events. But after about ten days without sleep and under tremendous stress, I was no longer thinking straight. We had been taught that we had to make the driver obey us, or we would have no authority. We needed to insist on it at all times. We were in charge. When we stopped for lunch, the filmmaker came to where I was waiting and told me to come with her to get back on this bus. I imagined that this was some sort of company test I was determined to pass. I told her that I had told the driver to pick me up here not there and I was going to insist that he do so. So they drove off without me, with all my belongings other than my fanny pack, leaving me alone in rural Switzerland. I sat on the bench for a while bewildered that they did not come back and congratulate me for passing the test. Then I remembered from the briefing that they had said there was a hotel up the hill that they sometimes used. I walked up there, told them which company I was with, and asked to check in. The London office wanted to talk with me, and the receptionist transferred the call to a little booth, as they did in those days for international calls. I screamed at the person on the phone, "What are you going to do next to test me? Stab me to see how I react?"

Although I was completely unglued and paranoid about the company, I was right, I only now see, about their extreme incompetence, letting a twenty-four-year-old novice out directing thirty people on a bus to places she had never been with no support or training. I later learned from my "friend" who had gotten me the job that at least one person each summer would have a nervous breakdown and quit the tour midway. I guess I was that summer's "cost of doing business." The company had not engineered the many things that had gone wrong, but nor had they done anything to prepare me for them or minimize their likelihood. I told them I did not want to talk to anyone in the company again and slammed down the phone.

My feet were blistered from the sandals I had impetuously bought at the shop in Florence with my tour guide discount. I asked the woman behind the desk to call me a doctor. She put two pills on a tray, told me to take them, and I did. I then went up and took a hot bath. As the room started to spin, I stumbled out of the bath in a towel, fell face down on the bed, and woke up fourteen hours later. What drug had she given me? Why did I take it? She told me that the doctor had come in while I was unconscious and then examined and bandaged my feet. Who else had come in and done what? I will never know.

The company called my husband, told him that I had flipped out somewhere in Switzerland and was refusing to talk to them. They said they would fly him there, and he could pay them back later (paying exorbitant same-day rates, of course). He arrived and I was manic, still thinking I was under some test or hazing and about to be vindicated. My Mom sent my sister over to Oxford to stay with me. I love my sister, but she is not the person you want taking care of you when you are hurt. When I told her about the incident in the park, her response was, "That just shows what a bad way you were in because you would have never done that normally." I was so ashamed. I felt like a complete failure. Not only had I not earned the money I needed to earn for the summer, but I had plunged us into debt. How many thousands of pounds would the company try to extract from us? (I later learned they intended to write off those costs but could not or would not tell me that.) I remember the wisdom of two friends vividly. One, when I described the situation to him, said, "Sounds like you are better off out of it." Another, who worked with me running an abortion counseling hotline chastised me for blaming myself, saying, "You are a feminist! You know better!"

Still fragile, we moved to East London. I sat in an apartment alone, a long way from friends and family, and tried to write a dissertation. My husband worked for Shell. I severed all ties with my friends in Oxford so the company could not trace me. I felt I did not deserve to spend money on myself, so I often skipped meals, bought no clothes or books. We did not eat out or go to movies. I would go to the grocery store and be frozen with indecision and come home empty-handed. I was completely blocked on the dissertation, sometimes calling and telling my husband he had to come home from work as I could not make it until five o'clock. He would patiently calm me down. I felt like I had let him down—he had married this strong, intelligent, independent feminist leader and here was I, a sniveling mess. I went to the doctor and had lost so much weight she tested me for parasites. She said I was a classic case for antidepressants and prescribed them. My Mom and sister talked me out of taking them—we still likened any kind of mental health treatment to *One Flew Over the Cuckoo's Nest*, thinking we knew better how to care for ourselves. It was hard to socialize because London was so big. But when we would meet friends, I could hardly hear the conversation over the screaming in my head of what a loser I was, a disappointment to everyone. I think that experience was the worst thing that ever happened to me. Only in the last few years have I begun to understand the event as so immobilizing because it unleashed feelings and memories about what happened to me when I was seven.

EPISODE FIVE: THE EARLIEST AND MOST CONFUSING

I have procrastinated writing this section for at least six months, if not forty years. Reading *A Woman in Berlin*,[12] Alice Sebold, Jessica Stern, Mac McClelland, Ray Douglas, Joanna Connors, Chanel Miller, Lara Naughton, Laura Gray-Rosedale, Liz Securo, Thordas Elva, Patricia Weaver Francisco, and Kiese Laymon has given me enormous insight. As I watch #MeToo break all around me, I am emboldened to speak out. When I experienced sex discrimination during the tenure process, I threatened legal action but quietly wondered whether I had the stomach for litigation. I had attended Jean Jew's defamation suit against the university (Chamallas 1993) and I studied sex discrimination plaintiffs (Kenney 2008) and knew well the toll it took on their health, their relationships, their careers, and their personal safety. I had read and quoted the litigants in the Foreign Service who sued for sex discrimination saying, "I felt that if I didn't proceed, my only reason for not going was this fear, and for the rest of my life, whenever I thought about this (which would be a thousand times a day, depending) I would have known myself to have been a coward" (McGlen and Sarkees 1995, 117). But secretly, I felt like a coward.

Employed at the University of Minnesota, I was paid $46,000 less than my closest male comparator. Our salaries were public information and that number stuck in my craw. Like the other women full professors on the University's Women's Faculty Cabinet, I doubted that raising a stink would make a difference; instead, it might just bring to the surface others' low opinion of me and my contributions. But as I taught my graduate course in women and public policy, I read and taught *Women Don't Ask* (Babcock and Laschever 2003), *Getting Even* (Murphy and Graff 2006), and Lilly Ledbetter's case and subsequent legislation (Ledbetter and Isom 2012). I began to think that I could no longer respect myself if I took the position with my students that it is better to bury your head in the sand, not dwell on the negative, and get on with the work you love, knowing you are well remunerated in the scheme of women globally, than to try to earn equal pay. Dahlia Lithwick's powerful piece about her silence about sexual harassment on the Ninth Circuit Court of Appeals (2017), Martha Nussbaum's speaking out (2016), and Susan Brison's essay (2014), along with so many others, have had a powerful effect on me and given me courage.

Alison Bechdel spoke at Tulane about her creative process and her powerful graphic memoir, *Are You My Mother?* In the book, Bechdel asks her mother what the most important lesson was that she learned from *her* mother? Alison's mother responds, "that girls matter more than boys." Her first graphic novel, *Fun Home*, is about her father, a funeral director and a closeted gay man who had been arrested for stutory rape of underage boys, including his students. He committed suicide as Bechdel came out. She had also drawn intimate portrayals of second-wave feminists in her comic strip *Dykes to Watch Out For*, so she had had many years to reflect on the risks and benefits of personal disclosure and revealing family and relationship secrets. I confided to her my ambivalence over being unable to forgive the writer Louise Erdrich after learning that she had failed to protect her children from sexual abuse by their adoptive father Michael Dorris, the darlings of the Native American literary scene (Covert 1997). I found Erdrich's novel *Shadow Tag* (2010) to be self-serving revisionist history and asked Minnesota feminist friends to stop giving her books as representative Minnesota gifts to visitors. Why could I forgive my own mother for failing to protect me from her abusive partner but not Erdrich for failing to protect her children? Bechdel urged me to write about my experiences.

As my deadline loomed and I had a blank entry for this section, I dreamed that I was an adult at the funeral or memorial service for my father. Relatives were about to disclose his extramarital affairs (my father had no affairs, to my knowledge, and has never been part of a whiff of scandal—the honorable man who, as a child, did his siblings' neglected chores so they would not get in trouble). In a fury, I cited Matthew 7:1, King James version: "Judge not that ye be not judged." (I am a lapsed Presbyterian. Perhaps all those years of Sunday and Bible School were not wasted after all?) I then said if anyone said anything bad about my father, I would walk out. I fled, in the pouring rain, only to be trapped in quicksand like mud which woke me up. (A good friend of mine says she never tells her friends her dreams because they understand them better than she does.)

Both my parents grew up on farms; both of my grandmothers attended college. My maternal grandmother had been a principal, forced to resign when she married in her thirties. Although they struggled during the Depression, my mother's parents sent all four of their children to college. My Dad, on the other hand, was the only one of six children in his family to go to college. My parents felt disadvantaged having gone to rural schools. My Dad had wanted to be a veterinarian, but his grades were not good enough. Both of my parents revered education. Their message to us: Do not even think of bringing home anything but straight As. And do not expect rewards, either, even praise. It was simply expected. The highest praise might be, "pretty good for a scrub."

My Dad had a temper, but was not physically violent, and was incredibly patient with small children. I loved him and was his constant companion as my older brother and sister drifted toward communities of friends as they got older. I remember only two incidents. I was lying on the couch with my Dad watching TV in the dark as he put a hand in my underwear. He did not put his fingers inside me, nor stimulate me—I was seven and knew nothing of my own body. I froze and squirmed, knowing something was not right. Once when my Mom was away, I crawled into bed with him. (For years, I shared a bed with my older sister who could be mean. Like many young children, I would wheedle to sleep with my parents, doing so often during the six months my father was away getting training for his new job when I was about four.) He did it again in our half-awake, half-asleep state. I never got in bed with him again, blaming myself, but not really understanding. Nor did I ever again spoon with him on the couch. I have a memory of discussing it briefly with my sister, who was two years older, and she said he did it to her, too, although we never discussed it again. For more than fifty years, I kept this secret to myself until I recently told my husband and my therapist.

I now believe that I responded so strongly to the experience as a tour guide because it transported me back to this earlier incident, one with which I had never come to grips. Even if such events are processed, whatever that means, new ones can cause the eruption of the past trauma, engendering a cascade of feelings of shame and self-blame. When I was mauled by the husband of a Newcomb alumna at a fifty-year reunion luncheon my first thought was, "I cannot believe this is happening to me again!" as if somehow I might age out of sexism or sexual harassment or achieve enough to make me unassailable. I am transported back to being that little girl, freezing un-comfortably by being touched in a way she cannot understand by someone she loves. The shame is compounded, however, by what Rebecca Stringer calls (drawing on Lyotard) a "form of suffering that cannot be phrased in a shared idiom" (2013), the second-order wounding of having the wounding effaced (what philosophers are now calling epistemic injustice [Fricker 2007]). When the first person I told, an alumna and friend, says to me, "It's part of the job" I am transported back to my mother's failure to respond when I told her about *Dirty John*'s proposition or my sister's victim blaming over my experience as a tour guide. I lie awake all night until I conclude, no, it is NOT my job, nor any of my staff's: Tulane is not our pimp.[13] The literature talks about the second-order rape of police, prosecutors, and cross-examining defense attorneys (Krakauer 2015; Sanday 1997; Warner 2013), but less about the spirit-crushing failure of loved ones we tell to acknowledge our wounds and suffering. In one of the few exceptions, *Lucky*, Alice Sebold describes the pain of her family members questioning her behavior after she was raped at knifepoint.

Psychologist Jennifer Freyd is the expert at this betrayal and, in *Blind to Betrayal*, analyzes the doublethink such experiences generate. On the one hand, I loved my father dearly, still miss him, and think of him as a good person. On the other hand, he touched me inappropriately. How do I recon-cile these two things? One thing I know for sure is that I will never know if I keep it a secret.

While I was living in London, trying to scratch out the first few lines of a dissertation, a British friend, also a political scientist and feminist theorist who researched women and politics, told me her father had done the same to her after her mother died. She was older than I had been when it happened to me but had not yet left home for university. She told him never to do that again. I wish I had had the wherewithal to do that at age seven. What led her to confide in me? Had I told her what happened to me as a tour guide? I find it unlikely that I would have told her about my father. I was not even sure I remembered it then, or if I did, I was clearly submerged in the vault of memory, guarded by many defenses.

In her novel *A Thousand Acres*, Jane Smiley captures the social norms of rural Iowa life. She set herself the exercise of trying to write *King Lear* from the daughters' points of view. What could make them so hateful to their father? The answer turns out to be childhood sexual abuse. One of the most dramatic parts of the novel is when the adult daughter remembers her repressed childhood memory of knowing what her father was doing to her older sister and then remembering what he did to her. She finally talks about it for the first time with her older sister (the sexual abuse began after the death of their mother). They both had suffered and maneuvered so as to protect their younger sister, who ultimately refuses to believe them and sides with their father as he prepares to bequeath the farm to the next generation, an issue always fraught in farm country. My mother, an avid reader, hated the novel, objecting that sexual abuse did not mar all Iowa farm families. I found it riveting and powerful.

Feminist scholars are starting to theorize what they call a spectrum of violence. Sexual harassment does not just occur in the workplace, but occurs on the street, in bars and coffee shops, and on public transport. Experts on intimate partner violence encourage us to think of the cycle of violence—where the romance and contrition phase gets shorter and shorter until it disappears—as a slow homicide. Feminist scholars from Vicki Schultz (1997) onward, and African American women from slavery to Ida B. Wells and Rosa Parks, recognized the mistake of disaggregating each incident and then assessing harm one by one. Such analysis fails to see how such incidents accumulate. Now that we know more about the neuroscience of trauma, we can see how women live what sociologist Cecilia Menjívar labels women's private terror (2011). One does not need a diagnosis of PTSD to understand that a gauntlet of racism, sexism, and violence could lead women to experience the negative health effects of raised levels of cortisol and subsisting in a state of hypervigilance and anxiety.

Perhaps it is this hard-fought knowledge of women's experience more generally, more than being a survivor, a fellow traveler so to speak, that generates in me the desire, courage, and equanimity to bear witness to survivors in my class, through memoir, film, and the social science literature on rape. Molly Pulda argues that confronting open secrets that smooth over power imbalances in families, communities, and nations is the reason to write and read memoir today (Pulda 2012). I hope to heal myself through understanding and to refuse to be part of the wider societal erasure and denial while we collectively work toward prevention. I used to believe that these facts of my life determined who I was and was angry that I was so defined by events not of my own making. Beginning with the death of a parent, and counting episodes I have not recounted, as well as the ones described here, I score high on the Adverse Childhood Experiences (ACEs) test, disposing me toward depression and other adverse health consequences. Thanks to my leadership coach, therapist, and other teachers, I am now learning that re-framing, writing my own life story (Denborough 2014), is not some shallow form of wishful thinking; nor is it a way of denying my trauma nor sweeping my pain under the carpet and absolving others of judgment. Instead, rewriting my story to not feature victimhood so prominently is a way of showing myself compassion (Ngwenya 2016).

JUSTICE, COMPASSION, AND FORGIVENESS

In the 1970s, I heard Sara Weddington speak about how activists needed to learn to "put on their own masks first," as the airlines instruct, before attending to others. I rejected such advice as shameful self-indulgence. It has taken me a lifetime to accept what those who teach compassion know: that I must first show compassion for myself, for my own suffering. I must forgive myself for the choices I made that led to my victimization and forgive myself for freezing and not fighting back. I must forgive myself for keeping quiet. I must forgive myself for not doing enough to stop it. I think we can only begin to achieve justice and forgiveness and work toward prevention when we come out of the shadows and into the light. I need to understand why Roxane Gay, Jennifer Baumgardner's sister (2013), Thordis Elva (Elva and Stranger 2017), and others would choose to continue relationships with their rapists. Others have worked to understand that beloved teachers have raped someone else (Kamil and Elder 2015). As we start to put faces on the numbers, they are not all repulsive Harvey Weinsteins. Some are Bill Cosbys I grew up loving, or Al Frankens I worked to elect. (Zoe Whittall's gripping novel, *The Best Kind of People*, addresses how a family responds to having a beloved abuser in their midst.) Only after we share stories unflinchingly, as Mac McClelland has done, rejecting a hierarchy of trauma, will we start to figure it out.

Bravo for all the #MeToos. It's time for revolution.

NOTES

1. Just as Dr. Blasey Ford remembered most strongly Brett Kavanaugh and his accomplice's laughter, I still cringe as I remember my colleagues making jokes about what I had tried

to write anonymously about my tenure experiences in Political Science (Kenney and Sterett 1999).

2. When I have spoken about my work, several times my mother has shared that she is so glad that nothing like I have learned about has happened in our family. When I recently asked how she could say that, given the fact that I had been sexually assaulted multiple times, she replied, "Yes, but have you been raped?" Like the authors in Roxane Gay's anthology, I continually second-guess my own narrative, wondering if I am overclaiming, a common occurrence Manne documents (2018). Historian Ray Douglas shared with me this quotation from Micheline Maurel's account of her experience in a German labor camp, *A Camp Tres Ordinaire* (1957): "The question that I was always asked was the same: 'So, were you raped?' (That's the question I was asked most of the time.) Finally I was sorry I avoided that, I missed part of the adventure because of my fault, and it disappointed the audience. At least tell the rape of others."

3. Ironically, Estrich's gratitude for Ailes's support of her as a rape survivor led her to defend him against charges of sexual harassment (Farhi 2016), an additional case of how feminists end up undermining the cause by defending bad behavior (Hirschman 2019).

4. The literature on women leaders demonstrates how women, but not men, can be either competent or likeable but not both (Eagly and Carli 2007; Chatman and Ely 2015; Tinsley and Ely 2018). I choose to frame the assessment that I had no feelings as a recognition of competence.

5. I had very little contact with my mother during this period. She did take me home briefly, after I had my first migraine, although we did not know that is what it was at the time. I had a visual aura, was cognitively impaired, and could not open my locker. I think everyone assumed I was having a nervous breakdown. I had three days of a blinding headache and constant nausea. When I moved in with my foster family, they described my "spells" to a doctor in the family who diagnosed me and gave a narcotic. Slowly over a ten-year period, my mother and I reconciled. A good therapist helped me work through my feelings and share them with my mother.

6. The Swedish film *Lilja 4-Ever* (2002) is one of many that breaks my heart. Minnesota girls, I have learned, prized for their Scandinavian blonde and blue-eyed looks, are targeted at the Mall of America—the "safest" place for truant runaways to hide. They formed the largest category of those arrested for juvenile prostitution in Las Vegas on any given night. Native American girls have incidence levels off the charts, reflecting the intergenerational violence of trafficking native women in port cities like Duluth (Minnesota Women's Foundation 2008).

7. I loved the way *The Milkman* referred to no one by name throughout the entire novel, Constance Adler's beautiful memoir naming her ex-husband as simply "the yoga king," and Lara Naughton calling her rapist "the Jaguar Man."

8. Many rape victims wrestle with their own actions to "help" their rapist ejaculate to bring the assault to a climax, so to speak. See Ray Douglas's discussion of the shame and horror of dealing with a rapist who cannot sustain an erection, but also the accounts in *I Will Find You Anywhere* and *Lucky*. Thordis Elva also talks about how her rape seemed to go on forever, not the usual encounter of teenagers.

9. Examples include reading Kate Manne's *Down Girl* as well as the backlash against memoirs such as *I, Rigoberta Menchu* that Leigh Gilmore analyzes (2013), watching Jessica Valenti being hounded off of the internet, Professor Dauber being issued death threats for campaigning to hold Brock Turner accountable and Judge Persky who sentenced him to six months for raping an unconscious student (Ioffe 2018), Gamergate (Quinn 2017), and so on.

10. I had done a number of things Profeta (2019) recommends in his essay on preparing children for college—waited tables on the night shift, cleaned houses, lived on my own. But however mature I was, I was still vulnerable. While we are plotting to overthrow patriarchy, we need to do a better job of not treating young women in the workplace, in the freshman year of college (the red zone), in graduate school or academia as lambs to the slaughter, only able to learn from their own traumatic mistakes.

11. Once *Dirty John* sued my mother for palimony, a journalist wrote a story that included her picture on the front page of the *Des Moines Register* (Voss 1983). My mother said in that piece that the tipping point was finding him in bed with another woman.

12. Marta Hillers (1911–2001), a former KPD member who made her living writing for Nazi publications, is the author.

13. My boss was wonderfully supportive, urging me to not be too hard on myself for failing to find the perfect reaction in the moment. He recounted similar experiences of anti-Semitism that he regretted letting pass because of an inability to find the right retort on the spur of the moment.

REFERENCES

Adverse Childhood Experiences. https://www.npr.org/sections/health-shots/2015/03/02/387007941/take-the-ace-quiz-and-learn-what-it-does-and-doesnt-mean.
Anonymous. 2000. *A Woman in Berlin.* New York: Holt.
Babcock, Linda, and Sara Laschever. 2003. *Women Don't Ask: Negotiation and the Gender Divide.* Princeton: Princeton University Press.
Baumgardner, Jennifer. 2013. *It Was Rape.* New York: Soapbox Productions. http://www.jenniferbaumgardner.net/it-was-rape/.
Bechdel, Alison. 2007. *Fun Home: A Family Tragicomic.* Boston: Houghton Mifflin.
———. 2008. *The Essential Dykes to Watch Out For.* Boston: Houghton Mifflin.
———. 2013. *Are You My Mother?: A Comic Drama.* New York: Random House.
Brison, Susan J. 2002. *Aftermath: Violence and the Remaking of a Self.* Princeton: Princeton University Press.
———. 2014. "Why I Spoke Out About One Rape but Stayed Silent About Another." *Time.* December 1, 2014. https://time.com/3612283/why-i-spoke-out-about-one-rape-but-stayed-silent-about-another/.
Burns, Anna. 2018. *The Milkman.* London: Faber & Faber.
Campbell, Rebecca. 2002. *Emotionally Involved: The Impact of Researching Rape.* New York: Routledge.
Chamallas, Martha. 1993. "Jean Jew's Case: Resisting Sexual Harassment in the Academy." *Yale Journal of Law and Feminism* 6 (1): 71–90.
Chatman, Jennifer A., Laura Kray, and Robin Ely. 2015. "Modern Sexism at the Top: Gender Discrimination in High Echelon Roles." *Academy of Management Proceedings*, 2015 (1): 12584.
Cole, Alyson Manda. 2007. *The Cult of True Victimhood: From the War on Welfare to the War on Terror.* Stanford: Stanford University Press.
Connors, Joanna. 2017. *I Will Find You: A Reporter Investigates the Life of the Man Who Raped Her.* Reprint. New York: Grove Press.
Cooper, Helene. 2019. "Two Prominent Women Defend General Against Sexual Assault Claim." *New York Times.* July 30, 2019. https://www.nytimes.com/2019/07/30/us/politics/john-hyten-kathryn-spletstoser.html.
Covert, Colin. 1997. "The Anguished Life of Michael Dorris." *Star Tribune*, August 3, 1997. *StarTribune.com*.
Denborough, David. 2014. *Retelling the Stories of Our Lives: Everyday Narrative Therapy to Draw Inspiration and Transform Experience.* New York: W.W. Norton.
Dirty John. Podcast. https://wondery.com/shows/dirty-john/.
Douglas, Raymond M. 2016. *On Being Raped.* Boston: Beacon Press.
Eagly, Alice Hendrickson, and Linda Lorene Carli. 2007. *Through the Labyrinth: The Truth About How Women Become Leaders.* Boston: Harvard Business Press.
Elva, Thordis, and Tom Stranger. 2016. "Our Story of Rape and Reconciliation." Filmed October 2016 at TEDWomen 2016, San Francisco, CA. Video, 18:59. https://www.ted.com/talks/thordis_elva_tom_stranger_our_story_of_rape_and_reconciliation?language=en.
———. 2017. *South of Forgiveness: A Story of Rape and Responsibility.* New York: Skyhorse.
Erdrich, Louise. 2010. *Shadow Tag.* New York: Harper.
Estrich, Susan. 1988. *Real Rape.* Cambridge: Harvard University Press.
Farhi, Paul. 2016. "What Is Feminist Hero Susan Estrich Doing Representing Roger Ailes?" *The Washington Post*, August 4, 2016. https://www.washingtonpost.com/lifestyle/style/

feminist-hero-susan-estrich-fought-sexual-harassment-but-now-represents-roger-ailes-is-she-selling-out-or-standing-up/2016/08/04/904c22ce-5810-11e6-9aee-8075993d73a2_story.html.

Fierberg, Ruthie. 2019. "Why Heidi Schreck Stopped Her Very First Performance of *What the Constitution Means to Me*." *Playbill*. March 18, 2019. http://www.playbill.com/article/why-heidi-schreck-stopped-her-very-first-performance-of-what-the-constitution-means-to-me.

Fisher, Janina. 2017. *Healing the Fragmented Selves of Trauma Survivors: Overcoming Internal Self-Alienation*. New York: Routledge.

Francisco, Patricia Weaver. 2000. *Telling: A Memoir of Rape and Recovery*. New York: Harper Perennial.

Friedan, Betty. 1974. *The Feminine Mystique*. New York: Dell.

Freyd, Jennifer J., and Pamela Birrell. 2013. *Blind to Betrayal: Why We Fool Ourselves We Aren't Being Fooled*. Hoboken: Wiley.

"Friends of Ngong Road." 2019. *Friends of Ngong Road*. Accessed October 20, 2019. https://ngongroad.org/.

Fricker, Miranda. 2007. *Epistemic Injustice: Power and the Ethics of Knowing*. New York: Oxford University Press.

Gadsby, Hannah. *Nanette*. https://www.youtube.com/watch?v=5aE29fiatQ0.

Gay, Roxane. 2014. *Bad Feminist: Essays*. New York: Harper Perennial.

———. 2017. *Hunger: A Memoir of (My) Body*. New York: Harper Perennial.

———. 2018. *Not That Bad: Dispatches from Rape Culture*. New York: Harper Perennial.

Gidycz, Christine A. 2011. "Sexual Revictimization Revisited: A Commentary." *Psychology of Women Quarterly* 35 (2): 355–61.

Gilmore, Leigh. 2003. "Jurisdictions: *I, Rigoberta Menchú, The Kiss*, and Scandalous Self-Representation in the Age of Memoir and Trauma." *Signs* 28 (2): 695–718.

Gray-Rosendale, Laura. 2014. *College Girl: A Memoir*. New York: SUNY Press.

Hamilton, Laura T., and Elizabeth Armstrong. 2013. *Paying for the Party: How College Maintains Inequality*. Cambridge: Harvard University Press.

Harding, Kate. 2015. *Asking for It: The Alarming Rise of Rape Culture and What We Can Do About It*. Boston: DeCapo.

Hauslohner, Abigail. 2014. "It Should Never Be Too Late to Tell Your Story of Rape. 14 Years Later, This Is Mine." *The Washington Post*. December 18, 2014. https://www.washingtonpost.com/opinions/it-should-never-be-too-late-to-tell-your-story-of-rape-14-years-later-this-is-mine/2014/12/18/e596a6e2-771a-11e4-a755-e32227229e7b_story.html.

Herman, Judith L. 1997. *Trauma and Recovery: The Aftermath of Violence—From Domestic Abuse to Political Terror*. Reprint, Revised. New York: Basic Books.

Hirshman, Linda R. 2019. *Reckoning: The Epic Battle Against Sexual Abuse and Harassment*. New York: Houghton Mifflin Harcourt.

Ioffe, Julia. 2018. "When Punishment Feels Like a Crime." *The Huffington Post*. May 31, 2018. https://highline.huffingtonpost.com/articles/en/brock-turner-michele-dauber.

Kamil, Amos, and Sean Elder. 2015. *Great Is the Truth: Secrecy, Scandal, and the Quest for Justice at Horace Mann School*. New York: Farrar, Straus and Giroux.

Kenney, Sally. 1995. "Women, Feminism, Gender and Law in Political Science: Ruminations of a Feminist Academic." *Women & Politics* 15(3): 43–69.

———. 2008. "Gender on the Agenda: How the Paucity of Women Judges Became an Issue." *Journal of Politics* 70 (3): 717–35.

———, and Susan Sterett. 1999. "Tenure in a Chilly Climate." *PS: Political Science and Politics* 32 (1): 91–99.

Krakauer, Jon. 2015. *Missoula: Rape and the Justice System in a College Town*. New York: Knopf Doubleday.

Laymon, Kiese. 2018. *Heavy: An American Memoir*. New York: Scribner.

Ledbetter, Lilly, and Lanier Isom. 2012. *Grace and Grit: My Fight for Equal Pay and Fairness at Goodyear and Beyond*. New York: Crown.

Leys, Tony. 2018. "'He Was a Hero in Our Eyes': Southeast Asian Refugees Who Came to Iowa Mourn Former Gov. Robert Ray." *Des Moines Register*, July 10, 2018. https://

www.desmoinesregister.com/story/news/politics/2018/07/09/iowa-southeast-asian-refugees-governor-robert-ray/768356002/.

Lithwick, Dahlia. 2017. "How Judge Alex Kozinski Made Us All Victims and Accomplices." *Slate Magazine.* December 13, 2017. https://slate.com/news-and-politics/2017/12/judge-alex-kozinski-made-us-all-victims-and-accomplices.html.

MacKinnon, Catharine A. 1983. "Feminism, Marxism, Method, and the State: Toward Feminist Jurisprudence." *Signs* 8 (4): 635–58.

Manne, Kate. 2018. *Down Girl: The Logic of Misogyny*. New York: Oxford University Press.

Mardorossian, Carine M. 2014. *Framing the Rape Victim: Gender and Agency Reconsidered.* New Brunswick: Rutgers University Press.

Maurel, Micheline. 1957. *Un Camp Très Ordinaire*. Paris: Editions de Minuit.

McClelland, Mac. 2015. *Irritable Hearts: A PTSD Love Story*. New York: Flatiron Books.

McGlen, Nancy E., Meredith Reid Sarkees, and Foreign Policy Association. 1995. *The Status of Women in Foreign Policy*. Ithaca: Foreign Policy Association.

Menjívar, Cecilia. 2011. *Enduring Violence: Ladina Women's Lives in Guatemala*. Berkeley: University of California Press.

Miller, Chanel. 2019. *Know My Name: A Memoir*. New York: Penguin.

Minnesota Women's Foundation. 2008. *Status of Girls in Minnesota*. Minneapolis: Minnesota Women's Foundation and Institute for Women's Policy Research.

Möller, Anna, Hans Peter Söndergaard, and Lotti Helström. 2017. "Tonic Immobility during Sexual Assault—a Common Reaction Predicting Post-Traumatic Stress Disorder and Severe Depression." *Acta Obstetricia et Gynecologica Scandinavica* 96 (8): 932–38.

Morgan, Leslie. 2009. *Crazy Love: A Memoir*. New York: St. Martin's Press.

Murphy, Evelyn F., and E. J. Graff. 2006. *Getting Even: Why Women Don't Get Paid Like Men and What to Do about It.* New York: Simon & Schuster.

Newcomb Institute, Tulane University. n.d. "Sally J. Kenney, PhD, Bio." Accessed October 27, 2019. https://newcomb.tulane.edu/content/sally-j-kenney-phd.

Ngwenya, Dumisani. 2016. "'Our Branches Are Broken': Using the Tree of Life Healing Methodology with Victims of Gukurahundi in Matebeleland, Zimbabwe." *Peace and Conflict Studies* 23 (1). https://nsuworks.nova.edu/pcs/vol23/iss1/2.

Nussbaum, Martha C. 2017. "Why Some Men Are Above the Law." *Huffington Post*, January 15, 2017. https://www.huffpost.com/entry/why-some-men-are-above-the-law_b_8992754.

Pereda, Noemí, Georgina Guilera, Maria Forns Santacana, and Juana Gómez-Benito. 2009. "The Prevalence of Child Sexual Abuse in Community and Student Samples: A Meta-Analysis." *Clinical Psychology Review* 29 (4): 328–38.

Profeta, Louis. 2019. "A Very Dangerous Place for a Child Is College." June 29. https://www.linkedin.com/content-guest/article/very-dangerous-place-child-college-louis-m-profeta-md/?fbclid=IwAR3QvOJ7WnhMzX3OaoXHdXh9Dtj9hNVce7UKpQWp7nubsri5-ce6Wi_NI-c.

Pulda, Molly. 2012. "Unknown Knowns: State Secrets and Family Secrets." *Biography* 35 (3): 472–91.

Quinn, Zoë. 2017. *Crash Override: How Gamergate Nearly Destroyed My Life, and How We Can Win the Fight Against Online Hate*. New York: Public Affairs.

Rukeyser, Muriel. 2006. "Käthe Kollwitz." *The Collected Poems of Muriel Rukeyser*. Pittsburgh: University of Pittsburgh Press

Sanday, Peggy Reeves. 1997. *A Woman Scorned: Acquaintance Rape on Trial*. Berkeley; London: University of California Press.

———. 2007. *Fraternity Gang Rape: Sex, Brotherhood, and Privilege on Campus*. 2nd Edition. New York: New York University.

Schauben, Laura J., and Patricia A. Frazier. 1995. "Vicarious Trauma: The Effects on Female Counselors of Working with Sexual Violence Survivors." *Psychology of Women Quarterly* 19 (1): 49–64.

Schultz, Vicki. 1997. "Reconceptualizing Sexual Harassment." *Yale Law Journal* (6): 1683–1806.

Sebold, Alice. 2002. *Lucky*. Boston: Back Bay Books.

Seccuro, Liz. 2011. *Crash Into Me: A Survivor's Search for Justice*. New York: Bloomsbury.

Senn, Charlene Y. et al. 2015. "Efficacy of a Sexual Assault Resistance Program for University Women." *New England Journal of Medicine* 372 (24): 2326–37.

Smiley, Jane. 1992. *A Thousand Acres*. New York: Ballantine.

Stern, Dr. Robin. 2007. *The Gaslight Effect: How to Spot and Survive the Hidden Manipulation Others Use to Control Your Life*. New York: Morgan Road Books.

Stern, Jessica. 2011. *Denial: A Memoir of Terror*. New York: Ecco.

Stringer, Rebecca. 2013. "Vulnerability after Wounding: Feminism, Rape Law, and the Differend." *SubStance* 42 (3): 148–68.

Taylor, Shelley E. et al. 2000. "Biobehavioral Responses to Stress in Females: Tend-and-Befriend, Not Fight-or-Flight." *Psychological Review* (107) 3: 411–29.

Tinsley, Catherine H., and Robin J. Ely. 2018. "What Most People Get Wrong About Men and Women." *Harvard Business Review* 96 (3): 114–21.

Toews, Miriam. 2018. *Women Talking*. Toronto: Knopf Canada.

Valenti, Jessica. 2016. *Sex Object: A Memoir*. New York: HarperCollins.

Voss, Melinda. 1983. "I Was Charmed, Deceived, Says Widow in Palimony Suit." *The Des Moines Register*, November 27, 1983. Page 1.

Wade, Lisa. 2017. *American Hookup: The New Culture of Sex on Campus*. New York: W.W. Norton.

Warner, Ashley. 2013. *The Year After: A Memoir*. New York: CreateSpace.

Whittall, Zoe. 2016. *The Best Kind of People*. Canada: House of Anansi.

Chapter Seven

Survival Stories

Transforming Terror to Power

Lynn Z. Bloom

ESCAPING THE RAPIST

In the 1970s and 1980s I taught undergraduate courses in Women Writers, when the authors and points of view were new to the students reared, at the time, on tales by great, white, mostly dead, men. These courses were not only writing-intensive but discussion-intensive, full of surprises for the students and often for myself, as well. One day the students—mostly women—began arguing about Joyce Carol Oates's "Where Are You Going, Where Have You Been?" Some claimed that Arnold Friend, "thirty, maybe," who invades Connie's driveway in "an open jalopy, painted a bright gold," his eyes hidden behind mirrored, metallic sunglasses, is in love with the pubescent teenager about whom "everything has two sides to it, one for home and one for anywhere that was not home." Others asserted that from the moment they met, Arnold's "Gonna get you, baby" signaled the abduction with which the story concludes. Though he does not lay a finger on his victim, Friend does, they pointed out, threaten to burn down her house and kill her parents—scarcely acts of love. After screaming for help into a disconnected phone until she loses her breath, Connie has no more voice and walks sacrificially out into the sunlight and Friend's mockingly waiting arms: "What else is there for a girl like you but to be sweet and pretty and give in? . . . You don't want [your family] to get hurt. . . . You're better than them because not a one of them would have done this for you."

Such compelling evidence clinched the debate, and I decided to reaffirm the students' interpretation with a life-saving story of my own. "A decade earlier," I began, taking a deep breath. I had never thought I would tell this story to my students. I rarely told it to anybody. "My husband, adolescent sons, and I were camping in Scandinavia. But it was a dark and stormy night in Stockholm, so we decided to spend the night in a university dorm converted to a youth hostel for the summer. At 10 p.m., the boys tucked in, Martin and I headed for the showers down the hall. He dropped me off in front of the door decorated with a large, hand-lettered sign—*Damar. Women. Frauen. Dames.*—and went to the men's shower at the other end of the long corridor. As I groped for a light switch in the pitch black room, it struck me as odd that the lights were off at night in a public building. The room was dead silent, not even a faucet dripping. I walked past a row of sinks to the curtained shower stall closest to the window, where I could leave my clothes and towel on the sill."

"As I turned, naked, to step into the shower, a man wearing a bright blue tracksuit and blue running shoes shoved aside the curtain of a shower stall across the aisle and headed toward me. I began to scream in impeccable English, 'Get out! You're in the women's shower.' He kept on coming. My voice had the wrong words, the wrong language. I screamed again, now into his face, looming over mine as he hit me on the mouth. I screamed again, 'Get out!' as he hit me on the cheek. My mouth was cut. I could taste the salty blood as he hit me again in the head. I began to lose my balance. 'If he knocks me down on the tile,' I thought, 'he'll kill me.' Then I thought, still screaming, 'I don't want my children to hear this.'"

"Then time slowed down, inside my head, the way it does just before you think your car is going to crash when it goes into a skid, and the voices, all mine, took over. One voice could say nothing at all for terror. I had never been hit before in my life. How could I know what to do? The man in blue, silent, continued to pummel my head, his face suffused with hatred, his eyes vacant. Another voice reasoned, 'I need to get my clothes and get out.' 'But to get my clothes I'll have to go past him twice. I should just get out.' Still I couldn't move, the whirling blue arms continued to pound me, I was off balance now and afraid of falling. Then the angry message came, etched in adrenaline, 'I didn't ask for this, I don't deserve it, and I'm not going to take it.' I ran naked into the corridor."

The bell rang. "You're right," I said. "Oates's story is about violence, not love." The students, whose effervescent conversation usually bubbled out into the corridor as they dispersed, filed out in silence.

That was on a Thursday. The following Tuesday, an hour before our next class meeting, a student, svelte and usually poised, came into my office, crying. "What's the matter?" I asked. "Saturday night," she said, "I was walking home alone—I live alone—and heard the phone ringing in my apartment. When I rushed in to answer it I must have left the door open. Because after I'd hung up, when I went into the kitchen a man stepped out from behind the curtain, grabbed me from behind, and shoved a gasoline-soaked rag over my face. As he began to wrestle with me, he ripped my shirt trying to throw me down. Suddenly I heard your voice in my head, repeating the words you'd said in class, 'I didn't ask for this, I don't deserve it, and I'm not going to take it.' I ran, screaming, into the street and flagged a passing policeman. You saved my life."

"No," I said, "you saved your own life" (Bloom 824–25).[1]

TEACHING SURVIVAL STORIES

My Teaching History

My teaching career began in the buttoned-up, buttoned-down era of New Criticism. As readers we were instructed to separate the dancer from the dance, and thus to regard a work of literature as independent of its author. We were not to let any biographical information contaminate our reading. As TAs, we were to keep our distance, concentrating on the work as a self-contained aesthetic entity, sealed off from the external world. Our reactions to it, and those of our students, didn't matter; they only cluttered up the possibility of concentrating on the pure work itself. Fortunately, I soon got over this injunction. My first tenure-track job gave me the confidence to admit that I was a human being who cared about what we were reading. I encouraged my students to express their opinions, as long as they could back them up with evidence from the text. Students could also entertain evidence from alternative critical readings, but not—in those good old bad old days—what they knew from real life. My classes became lively and fun, although I was careful to keep my biography out of the picture, no matter what was going on in my life at the moment. That level of engagement remained constant for fifteen years.

Flash forward to the Women Writers class discussion of "Where Are You Going, Where Have You Been?" When some of my students simply could not see that Arnold Friend had arrived in a weird convertible jalopy "painted a bright gold that caught the sunlight obliquely" to abduct naïve Connie, "bathed in a glow of slow-pulsed joy that seemed to rise mysteriously out of the music" always beating in her "airless little room" (Oates 254), I surprised myself by telling my own powerful escape story in hopes of showing them that she could have been active in her own defense. In coming out as a human being, and having escaped a near rape, I was—I thought—demonstrating that Connie could have fought back and tried to run away from this menacing man concealed, as is his silent sidekick Ellie Oscar, behind metallic sunglasses that "mirrored everything in miniature" (254). Friend cannot stand erect without losing his balance because "his feet did not go all the way down into . . . boots [that] must have been stuffed with something so that he would seem taller" (263); he, too, is vulnerable. Whatever the outcome, she is isolated and outnumbered by this sinister pair; it did not occur to me that in emphasizing my own lifesaving message I was also giving them language for saving their own lives—"I didn't ask for this, I don't deserve it, and I'm not going to take it." I am aware that not every female has the option of successfully fighting back. If she is isolated, underage, subject to child abuse or gang rape, or otherwise unprotected during war, migration, or other contexts of social upheaval. She may have no recourse. But this message, like the characteristics of rape stories I discuss later, can provide the exemplary model for gaining knowledge and power, and the potential for resistance.

To this day, forty years after the rape attempt, if the lights are out when I open a public restroom door, I turn them on with trepidation. If the lights are on and I'm alone in a restroom, I automatically survey the stall doors to see whether there are any feet below—although these days the shoes are often unisex and thus ambiguous. It's clear as I write this essay that although this story is seldom in the front of my mind, the rapist's blue running suit is lurking there in the back.

Full Disclosure

In our current era of oversharing, when selfies and a constant Twitter feed make every private moment public, it may be surprising that even as late as the 1980s many faculty members—myself included—believed it was unprofessional to share personal information with our students, especially undergraduates. After all, the course wasn't about me; I had a life outside the classroom, as did the students. Although we were friendly, we were neither peers nor pals. Moreover, we had a university-sanctioned obligation to concentrate on the course content—and, to this day, we still do. Yet because art is a witness to life, as well as an interpreter of it, it is arbitrary and unrealistic to wall off the students' prior experience and understanding of life for fear of complicating, even contaminating, their reading. Over the years undergraduate teaching in the humanities has become progressively more student-centered, so the classroom serves as a context where art—whatever the subject—meets life.

TELLING THE TEACHER'S PERSONAL STORY: BEST PRACTICES

What Is the Appropriate Context?

Under what circumstances is it appropriate for teachers to bear personal witness to an intimate, shocking, deeply personal story and thereby to set an example for their students to respond in kind? Obviously, these personal stories don't all have to be related to rape; survival, like illumination, can include a host of topics. But because the focus of this book is on rape and rape culture, and I am perforce concentrating on this topic, I must approach this discussion of teaching with some important considerations of best practices that provide the lens through which to view the ensuing analysis of the conventions of rape stories. There is, of course, no single right answer to this question, because the context is so important, and that is determined by a— one hopes—symbiotic relationship between teacher, students, and material.

What Story to Tell?

To tell the bare, good bones of the story and count on the students to fill in the gaps will help to keep the course focused on the work at hand—where it belongs. There is, of course, an ending beyond the ending in the attempted rape story I told the class. When, naked, I tried to escape the potential rapist by fleeing into the corridor beyond the shower room, I was startled to see the hall crowded with other hostel guests, all men, silent and still. They had heard me scream; indeed, I was still screaming, but no one had crossed the threshold of the door emblazoned "Women." My husband, who had never heard me scream in twenty years of marriage, came running to aid the person in distress, and, as Martin was enveloping me in his raincoat (which doubled as his bathrobe—we travel light), the assailant emerged, gazed without expression at the flash mob, and retreated to the shower room. There is, of course, much more to this story. Two trips to the Stockholm police station to address this "very unSwedish" event. A call to the American embassy lawyer—"Swedish law favors the criminal. He'd have had to kill you before they'd arrest him." A social invitation from the Head of the Swedish Interpol to his home the next evening; he also found us another hotel. Our immediate decision to "take back the night" and continue on our Scandinavian vacation rather than to return to the US and let the assailant control our lives. Our automatic decision to shield our young sons from the knowledge of what they had slept through. An American lawyer's reaction when I told him about the rape attempt on our return. "Surely," I said, "this failure to follow up wouldn't happen in the States." He laughed. "A lady professor's case would be treated seriously. But if you were a poor black girl, forget it." There is, of course, more to the story, and again more because a rape story never ends.

But I have already told you here 279 words beyond the original ending, and the more I say the farther the narrative escapes from the real point I want to make in telling the tale: "I didn't ask for it, I don't deserve it, and I'm not going to take it." That life-saving message of empowerment and the strength passed on to the student who used it to save her own life is where that tale should stop for most audiences, except for purveyors of criminal justice.

The reason I'm elaborating on these details here is to illustrate how students (or anyone) writing their own rape story might initially include everything they can remember as a way of gaining understanding and consequently power and control over the narrative. No topic should be censored (see Appendix 1, on the problems with trigger warnings). It could be very important to do this at the outset, yet even with that liberty they won't remember everything (my clothes were retrieved from the shower room—but when? by whom?). Moreover, as Brownmiller points out in *Against Our Will*, her revolutionary anatomization of the subject, there are many kinds of rape, ranging from bride capture, child molestation, and date rape to incest, mob rape, and statutory rape. Brownmiller's index identifies twenty-two functions of rape, including seventeen that pertain to Arnold Friend's abduction of Connie in "Where Are You Going?": as "act of manhood, adventure, conquest over women, discipline, entertainment, heroic, humiliation, intimidation and threat, power, 'recreation,' reward, seduction, sexual initiation, social control mechanism, terror, 'theft' of virginity, and 'trespass'" (Brownmiller, 465). Ultimately, by hearing her own story, which may fit multiple categories, the student writer will find its center of gravity, focus on that, and cut out the extra material. Sharing the story with a peer writing partner who can comment as a sympathetic outsider can be very helpful in pointing out both gaps and overelaboration.

Why Tell the Story?

A teacher should tell a personal story only when the story will enhance and illuminate the material at hand, never simply for its own sake. That it can provide a model for student survival as well as an analogue to understand the readings is a real-life bonus. The more intimate the story, the more personal the students will understand it to be. To avoid autobiographical distractions, the teacher can control the discussion by identifying in advance some specific points of relevance for the students to address. If the story doesn't fit the course or the subject at hand, even if it's a really, really good story, to tell it would be an invitation to focus inappropriately on the instructor—a gratuitous intrusion of ego in a context where she already has the upper hand. Don't go there!

When to Tell This Story?

Even when an intimate, personal story is appropriate for the subject du jour, the teacher shouldn't tell it too early in the semester, until the class has learned to trust and talk to one another. Although telling a personal story might seem best suited for a small class, it can be told even in a large lecture format. In any venue, the storyteller needs to be in control of both the delivery and discussion of the material. Unless it's an obvious fable or allegory, the story should be true, well told, meaningful to the teller and to the audience. Storytelling, like lecturing, is an art that requires advance practice in tone, breath control, diction, and timing, as with stories told on *This American Life*, *The Moth*, or the *New Yorker* podcasts. Rehearsal, with feedback from a trusted listener or two, can enable the teller to judge the pacing, enhance the drama, and avoid narrative distractions during the actual performance, such as crying, or laughing at one's own jokes. Yes, teaching is a performing art, but if the story is too tough for the teacher to tell without breaking down, then it's too tough to be inflicted on the students.

Who Is the Audience?

In considering audience, ethical and pedagogical concerns become inseparable. The first line audience for teachers' stories is, of course, their students, with whom they have presumably developed rapport by the time of the telling. To hear a story often makes listeners want to tell their own, right back. But when the stories are profoundly personal, possibly confessional, students should not be expected to reciprocate with a confessional story of their own. That can be an option, but never a requirement.

The following ethical principles are fundamental and cannot be compromised. The class, whether an English class or any other academic subject, is NOT a therapy session, and the instructor is not practicing therapy without a license, despite the wide application of James Pennebaker's Expressive Writing Therapy in a variety of other contexts.[2] HIPAA principles should prevail in the classroom as well as in the doctor's office: no one—student or teacher—should be required to disclose private information against their will. Students who choose to engage with this (or any other) sensitive topic can decide whether they want the entire class, a smaller subset, or only the teacher to see it.

What Happens When the Story Escapes the Class?

Where does the teacher's responsibility for student stories engendered by her class begin and end? If a student has prepared a story for class, within an established safe space for candid commentary and dialogue, who assumes responsibility for the consequences if the writer tells that story to additional audiences—such as a therapist, victims of a comparable assault, police, lawyers, social media, publication?[3] One could simply say the student is an adult who, as a writer, owns her own story and can do whatever she wants with it. This is certainly true. Yet if the student has made herself vulnerable in telling a rape story, deeply intimate and profoundly personal, this is quite different from the usual academic paper, and the new author may need ongoing professional protection and advice.[4] Today's assaultive climate of rancorous discourse exposes women, nominally private citizens, to public flogging—

hard for a person of any level of maturity to withstand, let alone a relatively immature student. At the very least, the storyteller—and the teacher—will need to consider how specific the author can be in identifying and writing about her assailant, for the accused has rights, as well as the victim. If her tale began as a story in school, will that school protect her in an off-campus venue, such as a court of law?

In this discussion I have taken for granted that the audience will be on the victim's side, and sympathetic to her testimony. But what if they're not? A story that could be life-saving in one context could be life-threatening in another. Should the writer fear retaliation or other forms of personal attack? Anita Hill's testimony during the confirmation hearings of Clarence Thomas for Supreme Court Justice was utterly credible, utterly denied, and Hill was subjected to vehement character assassination by Thomas and others. Twenty-seven years later, after testifying about a teenage sexual assault by Supreme Court nominee Brett Kavanaugh, Christine Blasey Ford suffered death threats to herself and her family, and had to move four times. Rape stories have to be told, but at what cost? With what protection?

Grading

If this component is graded, the criteria should pertain to ordinary class expectations—for instance, clarity, organization, and supporting information of an argument or claim. The grade is not contingent on the student's emotional investment in the topic, amount of pain and suffering, extent of personal disclosure, or other factors not generally applicable to other work in the class.

PEDAGOGICAL ISSUES

In this time of the #MeToo movement, what do we expect students to know and be able to do as a consequence of hearing the story or comparable stories?

Conventions of Rape Stories

Talking the talk helps anyone—students and teachers, storytellers all—to walk the walk; familiar terms can help us talk about even the most challenging stories. A quick review of the definitions of common terminology helps: *theme, setting, plot, character, motive, action, denouement* (this fancy word says more than its plain alternative, *end*), *symbolism*, and what Tom Wolfe calls "details of the status life," information about a person's house, neighborhood, recreation; what they eat, wear, drive; how they talk and behave and handle money. In addition to the basics of the genre, it can be especially useful to draw on the concepts below when analyzing a rape story. Although my students understood the conventions of the genre of the short story, had they been aware of the conventional characteristics of rape stories, the argument over whether Arnold Friend was a sincere suitor or a skulking rapist might not have occurred.

In that case, I wouldn't have needed to tell my attempted rape story to settle an argument. However, the time had come to tell that story in class as a way to encourage the students to understand the real-life implications in general of such a story, and to consider in particular its relevance to their own lives. So I'd probably have weighed in anyway, to begin a conversation that the students could pursue if they wished.

Literary, Narrative Conventions, Whether the Story Is Fiction or Non-Fiction

Here's what the students can understand about the genre, even though there are exceptions to these general conventions, and variations on the theme. I am assuming that Joyce Carol Oates's widely taught "Where Are You Going, Where Have You Been?" is so familiar that it can serve as a case in point, and that readers of this essay can supply supporting evidence as necessary. Teachers as well as students are free to illustrate the ensuing analysis with other stories ad lib, beginning with familiar fairy tales, such as "Little Red Riding Hood," or real-life stories of their own.

Character

- The *principal character*, often the narrator, is a female pretty enough to know that others—especially boys and men—also think she's pretty. She is the intended victim of an attack, actual or potential.
- The *attacker* is male, who may be casually or well known to her, or he may be a stranger. He is older and stronger than she, and more powerful in various ways—physically, socially, institutionally, economically, politically. He is likely to be the mysterious stranger who comes to town, the bearer of alien ways. He is up to no good, and will leave as quickly as he came. There may be something "off," or weird about this character that signals trouble to more sophisticated people, but which his intended victim doesn't know how to process, even if she recognizes its oddity.
- The main character is virginal and vulnerable. She is innocent and/or trusting, not suspecting that violence will occur. She is physically weaker than the assailant, and she is often defenseless because she is naïve and cannot imagine, let alone anticipate, what evil awaits. Although she may consider herself sophisticated, readers know better.

- If she has heard cautionary tales from others, particularly women, she has discounted or denied them. Do young girls ever listen to old wives' tales? Or to the town gossip?
- Even if she is worldly in some respects, even if she or someone she knows has even been exposed to rape or other violence, she isn't prepared for the attack du jour.

Inciting action, an attack:

The various ways the assailant and victim meet, the ways he makes connections with her, and escalates his demands and/or deceptions constitute the narrative crescendo. The tension builds as the danger mounts to the climax, signaled by real or implied threats, which lead to the moment of attack. The denouement is triggered by the victim's capitulation—either acceding to demands or threats, or innocently walking into a trap. The Damoclean sword of rape is likely to remain in suspension, ready to be plunged into the victim by the time the story ends, rather than to actually have done the dastardly deed. Note: The rape plot is not to be confused with the seduction plot, in which the woman, single or married, young or older—is infatuated with the seducer and willingly abets his demolition of her previously untroubled existence. Rape plots are more likely to be the spine of short stories; seduction plots can be of much longer narrative duration, with many perorations and variations, as in the plots of *Madame Bovary* and *Anna Karenina*.

- At the time of the attack, the main character is either physically or psychologically alone or without support, just as she may later be without resources to either abet her escape or aid in her recovery/rehabilitation.
- If a social context provides the venue for the rape, the culture of that context often protects the rapist—such as membership in a family, a church, or a fraternity, or another educational or work setting.
- The victim may be ashamed, angry, fearful, hurt, reluctant to tell the story or even to acknowledge it to herself, particularly if there is a culture of silence or denial.
- So there may be a long time lapse between the event and the telling, if in fact the story is ever told.
- The victim may not remember all the details precisely. Although this is very likely true of every memory, not just rape, the imprecision of memory can present problems for the victim's testimony.
- Why and when and under what circumstances does she finally decide to tell her story? Her language is often tentative and/or overdetermined by the conventional discourse on the subject. In fiction, the omniscient narrator may tell the story unbeknownst to the victim.

- If she is telling her own story, the victim may have to overcome her own and familial or cultural resistance before she can speak.
- Who hears the victim's story, how soon after the rape or rape attempt, and for how long afterward is the story valid? There is no single or comprehensive answer for this, in fact or in fiction.
- If there are no witnesses, who is to be believed? The narrator is generally reliable, and in most stories for a general readership she provides the grounding in both accurate information and point of view to make the story credible and the reader sympathetic to the central character/rape victim.
- What's the point? The telling may be cautionary, therapeutic, confessional, didactic, or more. What does the author want the outcome of the telling to be? Awareness? Anger—individual or collective? Action—relief, revenge, healing, help?

Conclusion

"And ye shall know the truth, and the truth shall make you free." John 8:32.

It is tempting to assume that telling a rape story will bring agency and empowerment to the teller, and with it liberation from shame, embarrassment, fear, or other debilitating emotions. However, given the variability of tellers, stories, listeners, timing, and contexts of both the rape and the narrative, there is no guarantee that either empowerment or liberation will occur, either immediately or in the future. Nevertheless, simply telling the story can provide considerable relief to the teller, as numerous analyses of Pennebaker's Expressive Writing Therapy method reveal.[5]

In addition to possible therapeutic benefits to the individual, the power of telling one's rape story has potential resonance in discussion with men as well as with women, not only with victims and possible assailants, but with potential defenders as well, irrespective of gender. As with other social movements, a critical mass can emerge that has the potential to lead to position statements, policies, action, social change, as we are currently experiencing with the #MeToo movement. "Well-behaved women seldom make history," as historian Laurel Thatcher Ulrich observes in the introduction to her book *Well-Behaved Women*: "Some history-making is intentional; much of it is accidental. People make history when they scale a mountain, ignite a bomb, or refuse to move to the back of the bus. But they also make history by keeping diaries, writing letters, or embroidering initials on linen sheets. History is a conversation and sometimes a shouting match between present and past, though often the voices we most want to hear are barely audible. . . . Some people leave only their bones, though bones too make a history when someone notices" (Ulrich, xxxiii). Rape victims make history, become history when they tell the truth. Teachers can help these soft and muted voices to become loud and clear as they express the powerful truths that shall make them free.

APPENDIX: TRIGGERS AND TRIGGER WARNINGS

Broadly defined, a trigger warning is intended to alert students that what they are about to "read or see in a classroom might upset them or, as some students assert, cause symptoms of post-traumatic stress disorder in victims of rape or in war veterans" (Medina). Rape has become a particular focus of trigger warnings in recent years, just as the #MeToo movement has—paradoxically—encouraged disclosure and discussion of the topic. When both options are possible and politically sanctioned in contemporary classrooms, how can teachers decide what to do?

Life itself is full of triggers, and literature unpacks and exploits these. My surmise is that any literature course in any language, any culture, any period of time, for any level of reader could be prefaced with a warning about multiple triggers. Happy families may be all alike, but conflict, violence, power struggles, pain, agony, distress, and sex—singly or in combination— are literary motifs worldwide, translated as well into film, video, music, art, from Beowulf to Virginia Woolf, *Macbeth* to *Maus*. These topics permeate the media and the culture so generally that it would be hard to avoid them in or out of the classroom, which is not an island but a part of the main.

Triggers embedded in *Romeo and Juliet*, for instance, might include *gang fighting, child marriage* (Juliet is 13), *poison, suicide*—each with portentous consequences to the characters in the play, and potentially for many readers, as well, including teenagers (*West Side Story* scenario or not) in whose lives these topics are of pressing contemporary relevance. Yet to read or view the play with these key words as the operative concepts would eliminate its essence—the romance, the passion, the beauty, the poetry—as well as the irony and the tragedy. It almost goes without saying that such a reductive trigger-warning reading would be a serious injustice to both the play and its many audiences by substituting key words with nominally simplistic meanings for the nuanced complexities of the original language.

Yet colleges may feel pressured by both students and parents to provide trigger warnings. If so, those who establish the policy (administrators? counselors? faculty? students?) would need to decide how nuanced a trigger warning can, should, or must be. Would a single, generic notice placed in the course catalog suffice—analogous to the Motion Picture Association of America R (Restricted. Under 17 requires an accompanying parent or adult guardian) or NC-17 (Adults Only; No One 17 and Under Admitted) rating? Note that the cutoff age is 17; older than that is considered adult, as are most college students. Colleges traditionally provide an environment for a truly liberal education, for intellectual and personal growth, where students and teachers can—and should—engage in a free play of ideas, including many that are disturbing or that contradict their own beliefs. Even if the students graduate with the beliefs and values they held when they entered firmly intact, these principles will be stronger for having survived challenges. Trigger warnings threaten to curtail the essence of a liberal education.

Yet if it's a college policy to alert students to potentially upsetting course content, in addition to minimalist trigger warnings posted in the course catalog, warnings would have to be elaborated on in the course syllabus, either categorically or specific to each work studied.

Although for space reasons a published trigger warning itself has to stick to the core terms, such as "rape" or "violence," these may have a wide range of connotations for student readers—or any others. Like Justice Oliver Wendell Holmes's famous example of "falsely shouting *fire* in a theater and causing panic," there is scarcely any key word whose meanings are not variable, dependent on context, genre and the conventions of that genre (such as satire, or tone of voice which can reinforce, undercut, or negate the apparent meaning), cultural norms and understanding. The definition of *rape* elicited 138 million hits on Google (July 13, 2019). Even allowing for redundancy, the definition of rape varies historically and culturally, depending on context—medical and legal (which have innumerable variations), as well as from individual to individual, situation to situation, tribe to tribe, nation to nation.

There is more danger, I believe, in using trigger warnings than in eliminating them. If an entire curriculum is bristling with trigger warnings, as it would be in many liberal arts courses, the focus on triggers—reductive, restrictive, and simplistic—could deter a student from taking a course that might, in fact, be illuminating. If, despite such a warning, the student enrolled in the course anyway, a syllabus punctuated with trigger warnings could obscure the works themselves. The very presence of the trigger words, general or specific, might function as a lens through which students would read the work, rather than coming to it without restrictive preconceptions. A college education should open up minds, not shut them down; it should encourage students to think for themselves, to make their own judgments, to think and read and write with agency and authority. A trigger warning does too much of that thinking for them, and too narrowly.

Trigger warnings would be hard to apply without wrecking the course integrity, structure, and fairness. If students could opt out of reading on a work-by-work basis, this local option would have the potential for destroying the course's communal conversation and ruining the intellectual structure of a carefully constructed syllabus or curriculum. If the teacher needed to allow substitutions on a work-by-individual-work basis, the class could devolve into a clutch of individual tutorials in works that wouldn't necessarily be equivalent to the original, in substance or in intellectual demands. An administrative night-mare would occur if each substitution had to be negotiated—and with whom?—the student? the department or college curriculum committee?

Having raised all these complications, I conclude with a Thoreauvian solution, "Simplify, simplify, simplify." If a student is potentially trauma-tized by the subject or is likely to be, then she shouldn't take such a potential-ly threatening class in the first place. However, as her education unfolds, with greater maturity and exposure to many new subjects and points of view may come a new willingness to step into an ever-widening pool of fresh ideas and expose previously traumatizing experiences to the healing sunshine of insight.

NOTES

1. This excerpt is reprinted with permission from Lynn Bloom, "Teaching College English as a Woman," *College English*, November 1992, 824–25.

2. There is an enormous amount of literature focusing on the research (from the 1980s onward—over 200 studies) of social psychologist James Pennebaker, who developed Expres-sive Writing Therapy, a highly successful therapeutic program. Participants were instructed to write—with no feedback and no expectation of any—in twenty-minute sessions for four con-secutive days, in response to the prompt: "Write about your deepest emotions and thoughts about the emotional upheaval that has been influencing your life the most. In your writing, really let go and explore the event and how it has affected you. . . .You might begin to tie it to other parts of your life. For example, how is it related to your childhood and your relationships with your parents and close family . . . . your work, and your place in life? And above all, how is this . . . related to who you have been in the past, who you would like to be in the future, and who you are now?" (Pennebaker, 33). His guidelines include: 1) Create your own space, both figuratively and literally, where you are comfortable writing. 2) Write about something that is extremely personal and important for you. 3) Write continuously. Don't worry about spelling or grammar. 4) Write only for yourself. 5) Deal only with events or situations that you can handle now (31–32). "People who are able to construct a story, to build some kind of narrative over the course of their writing seem to benefit more than those who don't," Pennebaker says. "In other words, if on the first day of writing, people's stories are not very structured or coherent, but over the three or four days they are able to come up with a more structured story, they seem to benefit the most" (Griffith). Making a story out of a messy, complicated experience may make the experience more manageable; "writers discover significance and meaning *as they write*" (Pennebaker, 121). Even this small amount of writing has been helpful in dealing with stressful events and life circumstances, including breakup with a life partner, death of a loved one, and natural disasters. Research studies have shown that Expressive Writing Therapy has also con-tributed to improvements in the writer's mental and psychological state, including "Feeling more positive emotions, Feeling healthier, Drinking less alcohol, Taking fewer drugs, Eating more healthily . . . Experiencing more honest and open relationships with others; Finding it easier to focus on work and get things done; [and] Noticing a greater sense of meaning in [the writer's] life" (Pennebaker, 42–43). Expressive Writing Therapy is also credited with amelio-rating a wide range of medical problems, including lung functioning in asthma, pain and physical health in cancer, and immune response in HIV infection (Whole Health).

3. In order to publish "Teaching College English as a Woman," the essay with which "Escaping the Rapist" concludes, in *College English*, the journal's sponsoring organization, the National Council of Teachers of English, took out libel insurance—for the first time in its then (1992) seventy-five-year history. I named no names. I never even knew the assailant's name. I

received only congratulations on the essay—many from men who found it eye-opening—and as far as I knew, no one ever sued the NCTE.

4. Some institutions may require instructors to be mandatory reporters of sexual assault, and instructors inform their students (usually on syllabi) that they may have mandatory reporting obligations. Thus, students realize that what they share in class or written assignments might trigger a professor's mandatory reporting requirements. See Brown 2018.

5. In fact, Brown and Heimberg tested the "Effects of Writing About Rape: Evaluating Pennebaker's Paradigm with a Severe Trauma" with eighty-five undergraduate women who had experienced attempted or completed rape, and found that writing about the traumatic event in some detail decreased "symptoms of dysphoria and social anxiety."

REFERENCES

Bloom, Lynn Z. 1992. "Teaching College English as a Woman." *College English* 54, no. 7 (November): 818–825.

Brown, Elissa J., and Richard G. Heimberg. 2001. "Effects of Writing About Rape: Evaluating Pennebaker's Paradigm with a Severe Trauma." *Journal of Traumatic Stress* 14, no. 4 (October): 781–790. https://link.springer.com/article/10.1023/A:1013098307063.

Brown, Sarah. 2018. "Many Professors Have to Report Sexual Misconduct, How Should They Tell Their Students That?" *The Chronicle of Higher Education.* August 16, 2018. https://www.chronicle.com/article/Many-Professors-Have-to-Report/244294.

Brownmiller, Susan. 1975. *Against Our Will: Men, Women and Rape.* New York: Fawcett.

Griffith, Vivé. "Writing to Heal." https://www.emotionalaffair.org/wp-content/uploads/2013/05/Writing-to-Heal.pdf.

Medina, Jennifer. 2014. "Warning: The Literary Canon Could Make Students Squirm." *New York Times*, May 17, 2014. https://www.nytimes.com/2014/05/18/us/warning-the-literary-canon-could-make-students-squirm.html.

Oates, Joyce Carol. 2006. "Where Are You Going, Where Have You Been?" *Epoch*, Fall 1966. Rpt. in *High Lonesome: New and Selected Stories 1966–2006.* New York: HarperCollins, 249–66.

Pennebaker, James W., and John F. Evans. 2014. *Expressive Writing: Words that Heal.* Enumclaw, WA: Idyll Arbor.

Ulrich, Laurel Thatcher. 2007. "The Slogan." *Well-Behaved Women Seldom Make History.* New York: Knopf, xiii–xxxiv.

"Whole Health: Change the Conversation." Therapeutic Journaling Clinical Tool Integrative Medicine Program. Accessed August 18, 2019. http://projects.hsl.wisc.edu/SERVICE/modules/12/M12_CT_Therapeutic_Journaling.pdf.

Chapter Eight

Layers

Academia, Autobiography, and
Narrative as Refuge and Struggle

Katrina M. Powell

My therapist says I have post-traumatic stress disorder (PTSD). I don't want to tell anyone I have PTSD, especially not my colleagues or students. I don't want this to be my story. I have carefully constructed a persona that has buried this story. But it is my story, and I'm learning that being able to tell it without falling apart can lead to healing.

When I returned to therapy recently after many years, my therapist asked me to write down all the times over the years I had been harassed or assaulted. My list contained twenty-five items. But, while compiling it, I remembered a time recently when a colleague angrily accused me of not respecting him because I pointed out that his comment could be considered sexist. I'm including that time on the list too (see "End Matter: Layers"). To tell my therapist about one instance leads to remembering another, then another. I've relegated this layered list to the "End Matter"—on purpose. I've chosen this container where the "End Matter" is pushed to the background and stories of surviving are the focus.

While negotiating these layers of experience over the years, academia has been both a place of refuge and struggle. As a professor of rhetoric and writing and former director of Women's and Gender Studies, I work with many students and faculty who have their own stories to tell. Nearly every day in my work, I hear or read a story that reminds me of my own, like Laurie Halse Anderson's recent work, *Shout*, where she says, "When I wasn't stoned the only thing that helped me breathe was opening a book" (76). Studying rhetorics of autobiography has sustained and carried me through very difficult times. Feminist theory and autobiography studies provided a language for what I had experienced. Readings in these disciplines have also made me very anxious about writing my own experience, as I wish I could write like the authors I admire. In graduate school the autobiographical texts I read by Dorothy Allison, Audre Lorde, Mary Karr, Cherríe Moraga, and others created spaces for me to survive, to know I wasn't alone. Over the years, additional writers like Roxane Gay, Suzanne Scanlon, Maggie Nelson, and many others have demonstrated how the crafting of the story holds just as much significance as the content does. Scholars have discussed the ways that narrativizing trauma is rooted both in storytelling and Westernized notions of the truth, making for fascinating study as writers recount their memories and audiences inspect them for "facts." Cathy Caruth's *Unclaimed Experience: Trauma, Narrative, and History* (1996) and Dominick LaCapra's *Writing History, Writing Trauma* (2001) are examples of trauma studies examining the nature of writing and narrative when it comes to documenting traumatic events. The tension between truth-telling/testimony/reparations and remembering/narrating/repairing individual and collective memories is addressed by many writers and scholars both in content and form (e.g., Gilmore's *Tainted Witness* 2017; Kaplan's *Trauma Culture* 2005; Miller and Tougaw's *Extremities: Trauma, Testimony, and Community* 2002; Rothe's *Popular Trauma Culture* 2011).

Furthermore, scholars in autobiography are (re)engaging with narratives of rape trauma within the context of the #MeToo movement (Borg 2018; Michael 2019; Pellegrini 2018). A collection from McSweeney's, *Indelible in the Hippocampus: Writings from the Me Too Movement* (Oria 2019), publishes poetry, essays, and fiction from a variety of writers, highlighting the far reach of violence against women and underrepresented groups. With these recent texts and literary study, it's no accident that autobiographies and memoirs have become more popular than ever. We may, as some critics say, be hungry for voyeurism, consuming others' tragedies for a thrill. But such autobiographical texts may also be increasingly gaining readership because many of us are relieved to know that we're not alone as well. And, we may look to these texts to teach us how to survive and thrive despite our pasts.

When I listened to Christine Blasey Ford testify last year, I wondered, "How could she do that? How could she share what was likely an unprovable story? How could she be telling my story? How could it be that she was telling so many women's stories and it still didn't seem to matter to decision-makers?" Her testimony was a shock wave that sent me back to 1987, to a time and to a place I did not want to return. After hearing her testimony I went to bed for days and watched *Law and Order: Special Victims Unit* reruns. I was confused and scared at how her story could so accurately describe mine, even if the details were different. What was clear was that she had done the work to heal and, because she had, she could document her past experience for the country to see. Unlike Blasey Ford, I have carefully avoided the past. But here I describe how teaching has anchored me despite my chaotic past and why now I face the work that needs to be done to heal.

* * *

I had my own dirt bike when I was seven years old. My uncle Stacy handed it down to me. It was a Honda 70 minibike that I rode all over our farm, creating pretend adventures for myself, jumping groundhog holes. I also have a photograph of myself bounding from rock to rock along the creek bed of the Robinson River in Shenandoah National Park. That girl was adventurous. That girl got in trouble for not wearing her helmet because she loved to feel the wind in her hair. That girl loved school and loved reading and couldn't wait to get out of the southern town that felt too small for a geeky, mouthy girl with big dreams.

When I was about thirteen, my father took my sister and me to an air show. We saw the Thunderbirds. There were lots of military personnel giving tours. I was most intrigued by the woman pilot climbing out of the cockpit, wearing her olive-green flight suit. I wanted to wear a flight suit like that. I wanted to fly a plane like that. So, at forteen I told my dad I wanted to go to the United States Air Force Academy (USAFA, pronounced you-sah-fah), his alma mater. For the next few years he and my mom helped their daughter achieve this dream. They woke up early every morning to run with me while I broke in my combat boots. Dad built a pull-up bar so that I could pass the physical fitness test. Mom helped me fill out the mountains of paperwork. They helped me secure a Congressional nomination. Dad gave me flying lessons and I soloed at sixteen in a Cessna 150. Then, for a brief time, I went to USAFA. I made it through basic training, then the Doolie year, then survival training, and then wore my flight suit to fly a sailplane in the Colorado mountains.

But during my Third Degree year (sophomore), layer number 17 (see "End Matter: Layers") happened. The bar of hallway light came through the slowly opening door as he crept in. He climbed up. He whispered. He pressed his fingers into my face as his palm covered my mouth and nose. He made fun of my "grandma" nightgown. I wasn't a virgin. I wasn't not already a rape survivor. I shook my head, tried to breathe. He whispered, "Shhhh." He held me down. I sort of froze but mostly I just couldn't believe it. I couldn't believe that I couldn't force my way out of it. I was stunned. I just wanted it to be over.

By the time I was raped at USAFA, I had already been groped, pawed at, ogled at, and pressured to have sex many times. So had most of my girlfriends. But I naively thought USAFA would be different. I assumed that I could fight anyone off if I needed to. My dad taught me defensive moves. I was strong and athletic. I went to an elite college. There wouldn't be any of "those" kind of guys at USAFA, I assumed. In basic and survival training we had been instructed in unarmed combat and taught how to kill the "enemy." I genuinely believed that I could take care of myself. So I didn't expect what happened.

I don't remember exactly how I reacted in the days that followed. I was in shock. I just wanted to sleep. I remember the next morning standing in formation before classes, the sun reflecting off the Cadet Chapel and the Colorado Rockies, not sure what to do. I willed myself not to think about it and, in fact, I didn't have time to think about it. Final exams were coming up.

Then I got sick. For weeks I couldn't get out of bed. I finally went to sick call and I remember the nurse suggesting that I might not have the flu. "Then what is it?" I asked. She just cocked her head, pursed her lips, and looked at me, waiting for me to get it. It finally occurred to me that I might be pregnant. But it was clear the military nurse did not want to discuss it with me—she knew I'd be kicked out of USAFA. So I looked in the yellow pages for a clinic in downtown Colorado Springs. I didn't have a car but got a ride from an upperclassman who dropped me off a few blocks away. "Here?" he asked, confused. "Yeah," I said. No one knew, no one went with me.

Afterward, I lied to the nurse that I had a ride home and I stumbled to the Sears department store across the street. I found the bathroom and laid down on the red pleather couch. I don't know how much time passed before I opened my eyes, looking up to see two older women looking down at me. "Are you alright, dear?" I went back to campus and failed my economics and mechanical engineering exams. I got a B on my English paper.

Major Thompson, my English professor, asked me to be an English major. "Your writing shows promise," he said. Those introductory classes in English studies brought me back to my desire to read everything I could and to find the stories that helped me. I left USAFA after my sophomore year and finished my English degree at Mary Washington College, where I learned to focus not on my pain but on journalism and women's literature. Whenever anyone has asked me why I left USAFA, I said that while I did fine with the military training and loved flying, I struggled with academics. "My rural high school didn't prepare me," I said.

Years later I read an opinion piece by Ellen Goodman (2003) in the *Boston Globe* about the sexual abuse scandal at USAFA that made national news. She says,

> In a pattern that defines the abuse of power, sexual assault became a form of hazing that strong young women were supposed to "take." Christine Hansen, director of the Miles Foundation, a military victim support group, says assault becomes a "rite of passage." One upperclass female cadet is said to have told a new cadet, "If you want a chance to stay here, if you want to graduate, you

don't tell. You just deal with it." . . . Many of the strong young women who came to Colorado Springs to be empowered ended up feeling powerless. Some "took" it. Some complained to an administration that, as often as not, turned on them. (Goodman 2003, 17)

I remember the shock of reading the truth of my experience in Goodman's reporting. Though I had left the academy in 1988, the culture had not changed much. I felt less alone but also more ill-equipped to do anything about it. It stung, too, to learn that it's typical for trauma victims to have difficulty concentrating and that slipping grades were not unusual. I wondered, "What if I'd known that in 1987? Would I have stayed?"

At Mary Washington I focused on my schoolwork, becoming practiced at ignoring pain. After graduation I worked as a journalist and then as a technical editor. I figured out I wanted to go to graduate school, but I was vacillating between a PhD and an MFA. I got accepted to a PhD program. But I had also applied to the Bennington Writers Workshop the summer before, and I went to see if becoming a short story writer was feasible for me. For the application to Bennington, I submitted a short story that was about an abortion. The late Lucy Grealy, author of *Autobiography of a Face* (2003), was my professor during the two-week residency. I had read her memoir and was struck by her defiance to be controlled by the circumstances of her life. In her memoir she says, "Life in general was cruel and offered only different types of voids and chaos. The only way to tolerate it, to have any hope of escaping it, I reasoned, was to know my own strength, to defy life by surviving it" (Grealy 2003, 45). In her work I saw that other people who suffered, for whatever reason, were trying to gain control of that suffering through writing.

After writing new stories at Bennington, Lucy met with me about the abortion story and the several stories I'd written during her workshop, including one about survival training in which the characters rubbed camouflage face paint on each other's faces. She encouraged me to focus on this story to revise—not the abortion story. "Everyone's had an abortion," she said. "Not everyone has smeared camouflage on someone else's face and found it sensual. Craft *that* story," she said. I found her advice liberating. I didn't feel a need to write about the abortion anymore and that freed me to focus on something other than a painful past. More importantly, I figured out that I really wanted to teach writing, to hold workshops like she did, to study how writers craft a narrative out of life events.

After Bennington, I happily went to the University of Louisville to earn a PhD in rhetoric and writing. I got married and divorced within a year—married because I was good at pushing through and ignoring giant red flags and divorced because I couldn't take the violence (see number 22 in "End Matter: Layers"). Again I willed myself not to think about it. But this time my studies made me happy. And I had a laser-like focus while writing my dissertation. I was getting very practiced, through study and drink, at suppressing memories and pain. Thank god for literature. It saved my life. I read Dorothy Allison for the first time when a friend gave me *Two or Three Things I Know for Sure* (1994). She says in this brief memoir/performance piece: "For years and years, I convinced myself that I was unbreakable, an animal with an animal strength or something not human at all. Me, I told people, I take damage like a wall, a brick wall that never falls down, never feels anything, never flinches or remembers. I am one woman but I carry in my body all the stories I have ever been told, women I have known, women who have taken damage until they tell themselves they can feel no pain at all" (Allison 1994, 38). When I read Allison's words, I wept. Though her particular experience was different than mine, she crafted her story in a way that felt like she was telling my story.

I was taking courses in feminist theory, feminist autobiography, and rhetorical theory. While my dissertation did not focus on autobiographical texts, I was examining students' disciplinary self-representations. So I created a theoretical framework that used autobiography theory. In my first book about displacement narratives by families forcibly removed from their homes in Shenandoah National Park, I used a similar theoretical framework to understand how the displaced represented themselves to institutions of power. My desire to understand how writers, whether published authors or not, represented their experience for a desired outcome was fueled by my desire to understand how people can write from trauma to achieve social change. The courses that I created and teach, such as "Rhetorics of Social Justice" or "Literacy, Culture, and Power" all work to understand the ways that power dynamics operate within a writer's story, whether it's in the form of an essay, letter, film, or any other genre.

When I research displacement narratives, I often use oral history methodologies to understand how people tell stories about their displacement. Interviewing people about their experiences was (and is) an extension of my early days as a reporter. After becoming an academic, I decided to use oral history as a research methodology when I was researching families who had been displaced from Shenandoah National Park. I contacted descendants in order to find out more information and, in doing so, heard amazing stories about their ancestors. It quickly became clear that recording these stories would be a great resource in understanding the history of the park. I enrolled in Columbia University's Oral History Institute and started using oral history methodology to interview displaced populations. Looking back, I can see that I avoided my own past by filling my time with the narratives of other people. For my current oral history book project with Voice of Witness, *Resettled: Beginning (Again) in Appalachia*, I taught training workshops about how to conduct interviews with people who had experienced trauma. Always in the back of my mind is an understanding that my own traumas influence how I interact with narrators. No matter the subject matter, I'm often triggered during these interviews. I think I feel compelled to do this kind of research as a way to connect, even though I don't share my own experience with interviewees.

I was confronted with my tendency to avoid my own story while living in Louisiana. While an assistant professor at Louisiana State University (LSU) I raised enough funds to invite Dorothy Allison to speak and conduct a writing workshop on campus. After reading and teaching her work, it was incredible to talk to her about writing. After her lecture, she sat on my couch having iced tea while I prepared snacks for her reception. "What are you writing?" she asked. I listed the variety of academic articles I was writing for tenure. "Yeah," she said. "What stories are you writing?" Like Lucy Grealy, she sensed I had other things to say but couldn't yet. She insisted that "work" was writing stories and while I agreed with her, I couldn't write my own. In any case, I learned from her how to hold a great workshop and I incorporated her techniques into my classes.

The first time I taught autobiography at LSU was when autobiography scholar James Olney, who was close to retiring, asked me to teach the course for him. I focused the course, "Autobiography: Constructs of the Self," so that it examined "how self-construction across genres—novels, memoirs, or ethnographies—is a performance: a self-conscious act calling conventions of writing and representation into question" (Powell 2008, 135). In the variety of autobiography courses I've taught since then ("Autobiography as Activism," "Rhetorics of Autobiography," "Feminist Autobiography," and "Gender, Performance, and Autobiography"), I ask students to consider issues of power and subjectivity and how these contested concepts have influenced theories of identity and the body (Smith and Watson 2008; Gilmore 1994). A combination of rhetoric and creative writing pedagogy, my autobiography classes address rhetorics of autobiography by examining autobiography theory, memory and trauma studies, displacement studies, and narrative theory.

As I've taught courses in autobiography over the years, I don't focus on St. Augustine as the first autobiographer, but rather Sappho. While St. Augustine is often lauded as the first to narrate a life, feminist scholars argue for Sappho's autobiographical lyric poetry as the first. She was often ignored, however, because her writing exists in fragments—bits of her poetry on pieces of disintegrating parchment. Because there has been a particular linear and "masculine" quality defined for autobiography, many writers like Sappho, Julian of Norwich, and Anne Sexton have been criticized as not conforming to the autobiographical pact. Drawn to feminist autobiography scholars such as Gilmore (1994a, 1994b) and Smith (1994), however, I became interested not only in the recovery of many women's texts but also in the ways that form and resistance to form were indicative of resistance to

Chapter 8

social norms more generally. As far as Sappho's fragments, classicist Anne Carson (2003) argues that what we have left of Sappho's poetry is "magical." As I discuss elsewhere, Carson

> provides for us a methodology for archiving that finds fragments and gaps as not only tolerable but actually the state of reality. In her translation of Sappho's poetry, Carson's method includes editing Sappho's fragments as they exist, making the fragments and gaps visible and explicit . . . to reveal the "layers of time" and to uncover the various uses and interpretations of the artifact. (Powell 2018, 29–30)

Carson's argument that "the space where a thought would be, but which you can't get hold of" (qtd. in Aitken 2004) emphasizes how memory is experienced versus how memory is narrated. In autobiography courses, then, when we read the works of writers such as Kazim Ali (2009), Renaldo Arenas (1994), Suzanne Scanlon (2015), Maggie Nelson (2009), and others, we can talk about how the form evokes the message(s) of the content. When I discuss these aspects of autobiography with students, I feel very happy. Studying writing and oral history as performance and performativity (Pollock 1998; Pollock 2005) is the exact kind of work that sustained me during graduate school and has since sustained me as a scholar. The pleasure of working with students to understand the nuance of an author's form has been a key to my survival.

Understanding this aspect of autobiography from a scholarly perspective has also had an enormous impact on my personal health. My own flashes of memory felt disconnected, unstructured, wrong. But Anne Carson and others show us that these alternative ways of representing memory and life are more true to the embodied experiences themselves. While my memories were fragments, understanding the narrative of those fragments helped instill in me a confidence that they weren't wrong, even if they were disjointed.

Though my classes are focused on the rhetorical dimensions of autobiography, I assign students to write a creative piece in addition to their research essays. As I explain,

> This creative piece can take any form: poetry, essay, short story, novel chapter, song lyrics, painting, digital storytelling. In fact, I ask students to experiment with form and content. Depending on their approach, I also ask them to merge scholarly with personal life by making generic features visible, inviting interpretation from the audience, or reiterating notions of performativity discussed throughout the course. This assignment is based on my own workshop experience with Dorothy Allison, who suggested that it is not the fact of a life that makes a story but the way it is crafted and performed. In this way, the control over the event—in some cases trauma—lies with the writer. (Powell 2008, 140)

While I require this creative project, I emphasize that no one is obligated to tell a "true" story, no one is obligated to share a secret—the focus is on craft. I've received amazing projects including a short story about education in Puerto Rico, a Korean folk song, a digital story with film shorts taken in Alaska, self-portraits in watercolors, and handmade books, among many other extraordinary projects. I get emails periodically from alumni when they've published something they worked on in class.

Usually students perform their projects at a coffee house or pizza shop, so that the public-ness becomes a part of understanding the way that life writing can be constructed and performed. But in spring 2018, after the election (and just after Blasey Ford's testimony), I moved the performance to my house. This particular group of students was very close and they were sharing very painful experiences. I knew from their drafts that the topics included sexual assault, coming-out stories in which families rejected them, suicide, self-harm, and other traumatic content. I had the sense that we shouldn't perform in public (at least not yet), that we should have a safer space. So I served them a lasagna dinner. We moved the furniture to accommodate several guitars, a video projector, screens, and installations.

Before that night, I'd been having a hard time getting out of bed because of Blasey Ford's testimony. I'd been feeling alone and unable to share with anyone what I had been through. Then, there I was in my living room listening to people in their twenties and thirties bravely sharing their survivor stories. It dawned on me that I had never shared my story with students. I've always felt strongly about *not* doing that myself. Unlike Lynn Bloom, who articulates in her chapter in our book, I had never used my story to make a point or to show empathy. Instead, I had told myself that I withheld my story because I wanted the class to focus on the students and their development as scholars and writers. Furthermore, I was determined not to make this course about therapy. I was committed to mirroring Dorothy Allison's approach of focusing on crafting the story as a way to control it, not on the trauma itself.

But in my living room that night, I wondered: "I'd asked them to be vulnerable. Shouldn't I be as well?" It wasn't the first time I'd wondered this over the years. Indeed, I'd read Lynn Bloom's "Teaching College English as a Woman" in graduate school—I knew the power of autobiography. In the past, though, it'd been easy to say no because I was not anywhere near ready to reveal my own past. But the students' courage astounded me. I had been afraid. I had hidden in bed watching "SVU." They, on the other hand, stood up and resisted the stories inscribed on their bodies (Spallacci 2019). They listened intently to each other tell difficult stories in creative, funny, heartbreaking, masterful ways, and they supported each other, *as writers*. What I realized in that room of caring, beautiful people is that I *could* share, that it would be safe to do so. I didn't, though. And I probably won't in a classroom setting, at least not until I figure out a way to do so without turning too much attention away from the students' work. But the important point here is that as a teacher I feel like I should be willing to engage in the projects I ask my students to do. The writers who we discuss in class were there in my living room, challenging me as I had challenged the students. I could hear Audre Lorde saying in *The Cancer Journals*, "I'm doing my work, come to ask you, are you doing yours?" (1980, 21) and Cherríe Moraga saying in *Loving in the War Years*, "Without an emotional, heartfelt grappling with the source of our own oppression, without naming the enemy within ourselves and outside of us, no authentic, non-hierarchical connection among oppressed groups can take place" (2000, 53).

Years of teaching have helped quell my own demons. I spent years muddling through bad relationships and destructive behavior, which I've learned through therapy, were ways to cope. After the 2016 election and the #MeToo movement, however, the issues have been brought to the forefront of our cultural discussions. I didn't participate in #MeToo on Twitter. I'm still very uncomfortable sharing this story and I deeply believe in the right *not* to tell one's story. But as I've read the increasing number of essays, including those in the last few months by Michelle Alexander (2019), Patti Davis (2018), and Pramila Jayapal (2019), and articles about Hannah Gadsby (Shapiro 2019) and E. Jean Carroll (Davis 2018), among others, the connection between the critical moment for *Roe v. Wade* and the #MeToo movement has taken on a renewed sense of urgency.

When Blasey Ford shared her testimony last October, I was in the car for 4 hours and able to listen to the entire hearing. All the years that I'd been able to maintain solid ground by reading and teaching suddenly rushed out from under me. The memories came flooding back. When I got home later that weekend, I got in bed and couldn't get out for three days. When I went back to campus the students looked to me in the way they had after the 2016 election. They needed a way to process what was happening. I realized I could hardly help them. I could hardly take care of myself. And I couldn't quite understand. The country has seen ineffective presidents. But this was a full-out dismissal of women. I was stunned at the way the presidential candidate stood menacingly behind Hillary, at the way the Supreme Court candidate yelled in anger at the accusation, at the way that a substantial number of people didn't care and voted them in anyway. The message is that they care more about money than women. So it wasn't just one person. It was the whole country, it seemed. And it was an affirmation of what I knew to be true when I was nineteen in 1987—that if I'd reported the rape, no one would have cared and probably they would have been concerned for his career and not my well-being (see "End Matter: Layers," number 16).

When I watched "SVU" in bed, my husband and son noticed I didn't "feel well." When I had lived alone it was easier to retreat for days. In addition, my students were looking to me to help them through the difficulty of the confirmation and I had nothing for them. So I went back to therapy for help in putting myself back together. My therapist was curious why, given my experience, I had chosen "SVU" to binge-watch. I wondered too, as I had taught students Sarah Projansky's (2001) *Watching Rape* about our culture's obsession/fantasy with seeing women hurt. But in the formulaic "SVU," there is also the fantasy of fighting back, of testifying, of telling, and even if the court case at the end didn't end in favor for the survivor, at least the survivor was heard and advocated for. I had been in a controlled state for years, holding steady, and I was afraid if I started recounting the layers of my own experience that the floodgates would open and I wouldn't be able to close them. As Roxane Gay (2017) says, "All too often, what 'he said' matters more, so we just swallow the truth. We swallow it, and more often than not, that truth turns rancid. It spreads through the body like an infection" (*Hunger*, 35). This is how I felt, but with my husband and son looking on with worried faces, I knew I had to get up, again, and come back to the world for them. I had to come back for my students. I had to come back for any other person who feels alone.

Women's right to privacy and right to decide about their own bodies is in danger. When I watch *The Handmaid's Tale* on Netflix it's frightening how realistic it is. I'd sneaked Atwood's (1985) novel from my mom's bookshelf in high school, as I'd done for years reading Doris Lessing's *The Golden Notebook* (1962) and John Fowles's *The French Lieutenant's Woman* (1969). It had seemed so fantastical to my 15-year-old self that Atwood's story could come true. Her novel and other feminist texts had been on the margins of popular discourse. But now to see popular film, news, podcasts, and television shows filled with innovative, critical, and creative ways highlighting the issues and exposing criminals is a sea change. At the same time, the repealing of reproductive rights and closing of health access facilities to women makes Atwood's novel frighteningly real.

What I appreciate about the layering of the work by Scanlon (2015), Nelson (2009), Gloeckner (2000), or Gay (2017) in their texts is that they disrupt the idea that a trauma happens once and then it's dealt with and then we move on. Their texts repeat, circle back, and return to the ways that memory reoccurs around a trauma. Jerome Bruner's (2004) theories about life as narrative have influenced the ways we understand trauma and autobiography. But feminist theorists point out that narratives that disrupt temporality and attend to the ways that experience is held in the body more accurately reflect the experiences of women and underrepresented groups, particularly those who have suffered trauma. Autobiography as form(s) becomes a way to resist cultural codes, inscriptions forced upon the body. So while autobiography has been criticized as being self-indulgent, it is in fact an act of resistance (Smith and Watson 1998; Spallacci 2019). In *The Cancer Journals*, Audre Lorde (1980) discusses the ways that we are made invisible to each other, so that we can't support each other. By speaking out, many people are becoming known to each other, as a resource to others who might need them. While my instinct is to hide, I won't any longer because I want others to know that they have support. I honor the need to self-protect by remaining silent. But what I hope this chapter illustrates is that many life narratives are available to help us to know that we are not irrevocably damaged.

I'm exhausted from the work of healing. But I don't want to be tired. I have so much I want to do. And I don't want to let the tiredness I know comes from the mental exhaustion of reliving these layers every day of my life have so much impact on what I can get done. I don't want my son to have memories of me hiding from the world because I couldn't face my shit. At work I reexperience almost every day some aspect of the past and can't focus and I want to flee from the confines of the room I'm in. I can feel the floor rushing up whenever this happens and my instinct is to retreat. Frankly, some days I don't know how I survive. But I do know that the friendships of several loving beautiful women have helped me (thank you L, J, J, C, KH, A, K, J). Part of the reason I went back to therapy was because I was burdening them, repeating myself, not really getting better. Despite how hard it is, I'm doing this work because my students inspire me, I want to be there for them, and I want to be fully present for my family.

I've been trying to recover for over thirty years. Some family and close friends know, but I don't share it often. My students and co-workers don't know. I don't want them to know. When I told my parents about it (ten years after it had happened), I yelled at them that I felt forced to tell. I wanted the secret to remain mine because if I kept it secret, I could control it. But I learned from writers like Dorothy Allison how the secret controlled me. I won't be recovered after writing this chapter, I know. But I already feel like contributing to this volume has moved me forward and I have hope in this collection as a resource for people who need it.

I've wondered lately how my life would've been different if I'd given my parents a chance to help me when I was hurt. My mother is a problem solver. I wondered, "What if I had shared my story with her earlier? Maybe I wouldn't have been as vulnerable to further attacks. Maybe I would have healed so much earlier." I didn't give her a chance to help me. I didn't give my dad a chance to mourn the loss of a dream with me. I wish I had.

While it took me more than ten years to share the trauma with them, they knew something had happened. When I came back from USAFA so different, so changed, and so angry, all they could do was say, "Let's go hiking." They took me back to the hiking trails in Shenandoah National Park where I'd been a happy, strong, confident girl. Indeed, studying the displacement of families from that area, and reading their letters wishing they could stay in their mountain homes, helped me realize how healing the landscape was for me.

While I regret not asking for my parents' help, I do not regret my ability to stand up and show up, despite getting knocked down time after time. What I also have to learn now at fifty-two is that showing up for everything can also mean avoiding the pain and avoiding the self-care necessary to heal. I am grateful to the contributors to this volume such as Ari Buford who suggest that hearing other survivors' stories provides a critical reason to keep surviving. Likewise, Dawoud Bey's recent exhibit at the Art Institute of Chicago, "Night Coming Tenderly, Black," evokes the Langston Hughes poem and delves into the trauma of slavery to understand present-day individual healing within that history. He is committed to "seeing deeply" in his photographs and doing so, according to Bey, is a process of self-liberation. I can't hope to be something positive in this critical moment of reproductive rights and gender-based violence without doing the kind of work that Bey suggests. I've tried to do it privately. But this volume has given me the opportunity to think about the implications for me to do this publicly, and the ethical responsibility we have to each other to provide support. That's not to say, however, that silence isn't a form a resistance—it is. But I have felt challenged by Audre Lorde to break my silence, buoyed up by the courage of my students, to let others know they're not alone.

END MATTER: LAYERS

1. 4 years old, at daycare an older boy pulled down my pants.
2. 8 years old, on a school bus older boy gestured suggestively while singing KC and the Sunshine Band's "I'm Your Boogie Man."
3. 9 years old, swimming with friends of my cousin's parents, adult men skinny-dipped.
4. 10 years old, step-cousin rubbed my chest while bunch of kids were in the back of the truck.
5. 12 years old, playing with uncle's CB radio, truckers said to me, "Get in my truck little girl, I show you something big to suck on."
6. 12 years old, trip to the skating rink, older boy (seventeen) kissed me in the van.
7. 13 years old, uncle takes step-cousin and me skiing, he gets drunk in the lodge, says to me, "Boys will want to get into your 'pussy.'" Same night, he drives drunk, passes out, 14-year-old step-cousin (same one in number 3) tries to drive and wrecks. I leave accident scene and walk to a friend's house.
8. 13 years old, walking to parents' office after school, older girl and boy stop me and say, "Who do you think you are, acting too big for your

britches. You better watch it or you'll be sorry." Later in basketball and softball practices, pushed, shoved, threatened by same girl.

9. 13 years old, 15-year-old stepbrother of kids I babysat touched my chest without asking.

10. 13 years old, sleepover at friend's house where boys and girls spent the night, woke up in the night with a boy's hand down my pants.

11. 14 years old, first real boyfriend pressured me to have sex, asked why I always "shot him down."

12. 14 years old, changing classes in high school, boys leered at, touched, flirted, pushed many of us girls. One boy in particular flirted, very suggestively, and when other boys saw the attention from him, called me a slut for flirting with "black boys."

13. 16 years old, lifeguarding, pulled out a teenager my age who was drowning, who had jumped in because his friends dared him, on whom I performed mouth-to-mouth and afterward the parents and other kids called me a "[n-----] lover" and one parent asked "how could you let your lips touch that [n-----]?"

14. 16 years old, went to a friend's where we got very drunk, boys showed up uninvited, one pushed me in a room and had sex, I was incoherent and couldn't consent. This boy had been another friend's boyfriend and when she found out, she blamed me for betraying her.

15. 18 years old, went to USAFA, daily harassing comments about all women's bodies by the upperclassmen, one yelled at one of my male colleagues to carry my rifle because he thought I was struggling . . . when I refused to let him take my rifle, they got pissed at my colleague for not "taking care of the girls." When I won a sharpshooter contest, they all couldn't believe a girl had done it. The celebration I might have had was tainted by the sexism. This is one of many daily incidents among my women colleagues where we were constantly harassed about our physical attributes/capabilities/belonging. When I won the pugil stick competition (women only) an upperclassman whispered *you're a dyke* in my ear, as if that would threaten or belittle me.

16. 18 years old, woke up to an upperclassman in my bed, rubbing my body, saying, "Come on, Powell, come on." When my roommate turned on the light he fell out of the bunk and ran out and slammed the door, leaving my roommate and I looking at each other in shock. A few seconds later he threw open the door and said, "You better be ready for the morning run, Powell!" When I reported him to the commanding officer, he asked if I really wanted to formally report it because if I did, "You could ruin this young man's career."

17. 19 years old, partied with friends in the dorm, got drunk, went back to room for curfew, not allowed to lock our rooms at night, woke up to

one of my friends on top of me, forcing my nightgown up, assaulting me. When I started to protest, he put his hand on my mouth and whispered in my ear, "Shhh, you'll wake up Catherine"—my room-mate. With his other hand held my hands so I couldn't push or scratch him. His weight held me down. His hand was over my nose so I couldn't breathe.

18. 20 years old, after being raped decided to have an abortion. After-ward, stumbled across the street to the Sears and passed out on the couch in the women's room and woke to women leaning over me with worried looks, one with a Sears nametag that read "Alice" who said, "Must be another one from that clinic across the street."

19. 20 years old, went out with friend from high school who got mad when I wouldn't park with him and dropped me at home early.

20. 20 years old, decided to break up with boyfriend. He showed up unannounced at my house where I lived with 3 roommates, forced his way in, tried to take my dog, threw me across the room when I wouldn't let him take her, roommates called the police who arrested him. Roommate took me to police station. The officer said, "You could file a complaint but mostly what I see is women like you not following through so don't waste my time if you're not gonna follow through."

21. 22 years old, worked at Holiday Inn as waitress where the cook yelled at all of us, was glad when I got "promoted" to cocktail waitress in the hotel bar, but when I complained about customers touching my ass my boss said, "well you'll get better tips."

22. 28 years old, within a year of getting married, I woke up to him forcing himself on me while I was asleep. I said no and he wouldn't stop. I didn't struggle, I just kept saying no, no, no, no, no, no, no. I left the next day.

23. 31 years old, after divorce, boyfriend fractured my arm in a drunken argument.

24. 34 years old, drunken colleague overstays his welcome.

25. 48 years old, in a meeting and pointed out to male colleague that his comments regarding a course about gender could be interpreted as sexist. He pointed his finger at me and said in a booming voice, "You don't know me. You have no respect for who I am by saying that."

REFERENCES

Aitken, Will. 2004. "Interview with Anne Carson: The Art of Poetry No. 88," *Paris Review* 171. https://www.theparisreview.org/interviews/5420/a-href-authors-3109-anne-carsonanne-carson-a-the-art-of-poetry-no-88-a-href-authors-3109-anne-carsonanne-carson-a.

Alexander, Michelle. 2019. "My Rapist Apologized: I still needed an abortion." *New York Times*, May 23, 2019. https://www.nytimes.com/2019/05/23/opinion/abortion-legislation-rape.html.

Ali, Kazim. 2009. *Bright Felon*. Middletown: Wesleyan University Press.

Allison, Dorothy. 1995. *Two or Three Things I Know for Sure*. New York: Penguin.

Anderson, Laura Halse. 2019. *Shout*. New York: Viking.

Arenas, Renaldo. 1994. *Before Night Falls*. New York: Penguin Books, reprint edition.

Atwood, Margaret. 1985. *The Handmaid's Tale*. Toronto: McClelland and Stuart.

Blasey Ford, Christine. 2018. "Written Testimony of Dr. Christine Blasey Ford, United States Senate Judiciary Committee, September 26, 2018." https://www.judiciary.senate.gov/imo/media/doc/09-27-18_20Ford_20Testimony.pdf.

Bloom, Lynn. 1992. "Teaching College English as a Woman." *College English* 54 (7): 818–25.

Borg, Kurt. 2018. "Narrating Trauma: Judith Butler on Narrative Coherence and the Politics of Self-Narration." *Life Writing* 15 (3): 447–65.

Bruner, Jerome. (1987 original) 2004. "Life as Narrative." *Social Research* 71 (3): 691–710.

Carson, Anne, ed. 2003. *If Not, Winter: Fragments of Sappho*. New York: Vintage.

Caruth, Cathy. 1996. *Unclaimed Experience: Trauma, Narrative, and History*. Baltimore: Johns Hopkins University Press.

Davis, Patti. 2018. "I understand why E. Jean Carroll doesn't want to use the word 'rape.' I didn't, either." *Washington Post*, June 25, 2018. https://www.washingtonpost.com/opinions/i-understand-why-e-jean-carroll-doesnt-want-to-use-the-word-rape-i-didnt-either/2019/06/25/af9f7aa0-9777-11e9-830a-21b9b36b64ad_story.html.

Fowles, John. 1969. *The French Lieutenant's Woman*. New York: Little, Brown and Company.

Gay, Roxane. 2017. *Hunger: A Memoir of (My) Body*. New York: Harper Collins.

Gilmore, Leigh. 1994. "The Mark of Autobiography: Postmodernism, Autobiography, and Genre." In *Autobiography and Postmodernism*, edited by Kathleen Ashley, Leigh Gilmore, and Gerald Peters, 3–18. Amherst: University of Massachusetts Press.

———. 1994. "Technologies of Autobiography." *Autobiographics: A Feminist Theory of Women's Self-Representation*. Ithaca: Cornell University Press, 65–105.

———. 2017. *Tainted Witness: Why We Doubt What Women Say About Their Lives*. New York: Columbia University Press.

Gloeckner, Phoebe. 2000. *A Child's Life and Other Stories*. New York: Frog Books.

Goodman, Ellen. 2003. "Lessons in war, abuse of power." *Boston Globe*, April 10, 2003. https://www.newspapers.com/newspage/442880154.

Grealy, Lucy. 1994. *Autobiography of a Face*. New York: Harper Collins.

Jayapal, Pramila. 2019. "Rep. Pramila Jayapal: The Story of My Abortion: What it taught me about the deeply personal nature of reproductive choice." *New York Times*, June 13, 2019.

Kaplan, Ann. 2005. *Trauma Culture: The Politics of Terror and Loss in Media and Literature*. New Brunswick: Rutgers University Press.

Karr, Mary. 2005. *The Liars' Club*. New York: Penguin Books.

LaCapra, Dominick. 2001. *Writing History, Writing Trauma*. Baltimore: Johns Hopkins University Press.

Lessing, Doris. 1962. *The Golden Notebook*. New York: Simon and Schuster.

Lorde, Audre. 1980. *The Cancer Journals*. San Francisco: Aunt Lute Books.

Michael, Olga. 2019. "Reading Pheobe Gloeckner's *A Child's Life and Other Stories* at the Time of #MeToo." *Life Writing* 16 (3): 345–67.

Miller, Nancy K. and Jason Tougaw, eds. 2002. *Extremities. Trauma, Testimony, and Community*. Urbana-Champaign: University of Illinois Press.

Moraga, Cherríe L. (1983 original) 2000. *Loving in the War Years*. Cambridge: South End Press.

Nelson, Maggie. 2009. *Bluets*. Seattle: Wave Books.

Oria, Shelly, ed. 2019. *Indelible in the Hippocampus: Writings from the Me Too Movement*. San Francisco: McSweeney's.

Pellegrini, Ann. 2018. #MeToo: Before and After." *Studies in Gender and Sexuality* 19 (4): 262–64.

Pollock, Della. 1998. "Performative Writing." In *The Ends of Performance*, edited by Peggy Phelan and Jill Lane, 73–103. New York: New York University Press.

———. 2005. *Remembering: Oral History Performance*. New York: Palgrave.

Powell, Katrina M. 2008. "Reading, Writing, and Performing Life Writing: Multiple Constructions of Self." In *Teaching Life Writing Texts*, edited by Miriam Fuchs and Craig Howes, 135–142. New York: The Modern Language Association of America.

———. 2018. "Hidden Archives." *Journal of American Studies* 52 (1): 26–44.

Projansky, Sarah. 2001. *Watching Rape*. New York: New York University Press.

Rothe, Anne. 2011. *Popular Trauma Culture: Selling the Pain of Others in the Mass Media*. New Brunswick: Rutgers University Press.

Scanlon, Suzanne. 2015. *Her 37th Year: An Index*. Las Cruces: Noemi Press.

Shapiro, Rebecca. 2019. "Hannah Gatsby Says She Had an Abortion after Rape." June 19, 2019. *Huffington Post*. https://www.huffpost.com/entry/hannah-gadsby-abortion-rape_n_5d0ad164e4b06ad4d25ae954.

Smith, Sidonie. 1994. "Identity's Body." In *Autobiography and Postmodernism*, edited by Kathleen Ashley, Leigh Gilmore, and Gerald Peters, 266–292. Amherst: University of Massachusetts Press.

———and Julia Watson, eds. 1998. *Women, Autobiography, Theory: A Reader*. Madison: University of Wisconsin Press.

Spallacci, Amanda. 2019. "Melancholia as Resistance: Reading Rape Testimonies in Memoir." Presented at International Autobiography Association Conference, Kingston, Jamaica. June 13–15, 2019.

Chapter Nine

Speaking Out, Public Judgments, and Narrative Politics

Researching Survivor Stories and (Not) Telling My Own

Tanya Serisier

The first draft of this essay was written in mid-2018, when I was deep into the drafting of my book, *Speaking Out: Feminism, Rape and Narrative Politics*, a text about the role of survivor stories in feminist politics and cultural change (Serisier 2018). I was working on a section of the book concerned with public judgments of women telling their stories of victimization and, it seemed, approximately nine months after the emergence of the "Me Too" hashtag, that I was surrounded by these judgments. From Laura Kipnis's (2017) *Unwanted Advances: Sexual Paranoia Comes to Campus*, which uses two stories of sexual harassment told by students to make the case that feminism has become "melodramatic" and needs to "grow up" to the public debates around *babe.net*'s publication of "Grace's" story of her date with Aziz Ansari (Way 2018), I found myself overwhelmed by voices declaring themselves "exhilarated" by women's refusal to put up with bad behavior, but "worried" that, once again, angry women had gone too far. I found myself writing about repeated demands for women to take responsibility for their own behavior, to cease painting themselves as victims, and to respect men's right to due process. In short, I felt myself literally swamped by a public discourse accusing women of weaponizing their narratives in order to subvert due process and, ironically, use their stated victimhood to create victims of the men they claimed had assaulted or harassed them. It is from my attempts to respond to this public discourse, and my anger with it, that this essay emerged.

My irritation increasingly led to writer's block. I found myself reflecting on my own experiences and story instead of writing about the reception of women's public storytelling about sexual violence. *Speaking Out* offers a critical reading of feminist and survivor attempts to create political change using personal stories of sexual violence and victimization. It charts the successes and failures of this politics over the last half century, examining public receptions of women's stories, and the ways in which women's narratives of sexual violence, and the women who tell them are, in the words of Leigh Gilmore (2017), "tainted" through dismissing stories as exaggerated or untrue and the women who tell them as untrustworthy and unreliable. As Gilmore notes, even as certain responses to women's stories remain constant, there are historical shifts in the ways in which stories are judged, and I have been interested in the ways in which the "Me Too" era opened up new ways of publicly doubting women as well as created new opportunities for women to tell their stories and be believed. My usual mode of writing about these questions is scholarly, unpacking prominent cases of public speech and judgment using the tools of feminist and cultural analysis. I have been, for reasons I elaborate below, reluctant to draw on my personal story in my academic work. However, as I lived and worked through what I saw as a new cultural moment of judging women's stories, I found I could only return to my usual mode of writing after thinking through my own story, my decisions not to speak about it, and how this has influenced my scholarship.

Here I use my story to think about the contested politics that continue to surround survivor stories. I am interested in the judgments made about narratives, in disincentives to speak publicly about personal experience, in how meaning is made from survivor stories, and, ultimately, in what it means to see our personal stories as political tools. I am interested both in the political effects of women's speech and in what author and survivor Dorothy Allison describes as the "reasons not to tell" (1996, 70). These reasons include disbelief and vilification, but they also include the partial hearings and public judgments that are made of women and their narratives as well as the presumption that the hearers already know what a story means and why a woman is telling it. Ultimately, I argue, many of these judgments are based on the different presumed narratability of women's and men's lives. While men are granted a life story that exceeds specific acts of violence, the biographies of women who tell their stories are reduced to the experience and their decision to speak about it. It is both the telling and response to this telling that constitute the "narrative politics" of survivor stories and sexual violence.

A "NOT THAT BAD" STORY:
TELLING ABOUT COMMON EXPERIENCES

What kept flashing through my mind during my writer's block in 2018 was an incident that had occurred two years earlier, just over a year prior to the explosion of public speech around "Me Too." I was in my last month of working in a UK university before leaving to take a post elsewhere when I received an email from a professor from my days as an undergraduate student in Australia with whom I had had no contact with since I dropped out of that university almost twenty years earlier. It said that he had just discovered that we worked in the same university but in different departments. He was, he said, about to retire, and so was getting rid of several books, including a large collection of feminist scholarship, and he couldn't think of anyone better than me to have it. He also wrote that he was sorry if long ago I had misunderstood his intentions and been offended, but that he had always been interested in my intellect and not in my "physiognomy," a particularly jarring word that I feel compelled to quote in every telling of this story. After receiving the email, I felt the beginning signs of a panic attack, packed up for the day, went home and told my partner. A few days later I deleted the email, and subsequently mentioned it to very few people, and not to anyone I knew who worked in the same institution. A month later I had left the university and the city. Relatively quickly the email faded from my immediate consciousness.

The "misunderstanding" that my professor referred to occurred at the beginning of what should have been my final year as an undergraduate student. At the time I had received some prizes for my work and was expected to go on to graduate study. As with many successful students, this professor alongside others, had begun to take an interest in me after I took some of his classes. I was flattered by the attention and the encouragement and excited by the world that opened to me, as I was introduced to various graduate students through him and, as I saw it, the world of academia. Soon, the professor began to confide in me about his personal and romantic problems, blaming much of them on the cultural disconnect he, as a Latin American, found with middle-class Australian culture, and what he saw as the coldness and stiffness of Australian women particularly. He started inviting me to his house and gradually, after lengthily proclaiming his distaste for the physical remoteness of Australians would first try to cuddle, then grope me and put his tongue down my throat. The first time that this happened, after taking evasive action and then leaving, I convinced myself I had indeed misunderstood. And soon I simply began avoiding the professor and, not too long afterwards, I dropped out of university after failing to submit any of my assignments for that semester due to a crippling anxiety that left me unable to write. The last I heard of him at that time he had convinced a male student I knew not to ask me out by telling him I was a lesbian, a statement that was presumably based on my refusal to continue to communicate with him.

The story of my professor is one I've avoided telling publicly and been reluctant to tell privately, so much so that when I showed the first draft of this essay to some of my closest and oldest friends, they had never heard it. In the remainder of this essay I want to use this reluctance as a way of examining the cultural politics that surround women's narratives of sexual violence and how thinking of them as sites and tools of political contestation, as sites, in other words of "narrative politics," can be useful for us as feminists and survivors. Perhaps the first and most obvious form of contestation is that of direct denial, dismissal, and minimization. The story I've just told is not especially dramatic nor is it uncommon. It is a story that plays out repeatedly with minor variations in universities and other hierarchical institutions and industries with predominantly male gatekeepers in positions of power, as has been demonstrated most recently by the "Me Too" hashtag and the range of industries that have been rocked by allegations of widespread harassment, from Hollywood to yoga. Even the fact that my professor considered himself a feminist, a Marxist, and a postcolonial thinker is not particularly unusual, as numerous highly publicized cases of sexual misconduct in Humanities departments and left-wing political organizations have shown. My professor's depiction of the events, almost twenty years later, as a "misunderstanding," is also not unique. This was not a crude quid pro quo situation of grades for sex; what was offered, and what I lost, was far more nebulous than that. I also never gave a direct refusal, never having been asked a direct question. As a self-conscious nineteen-year-old, I had not been confident enough in my understanding of the situation to be direct.

In addition to being common, the incidents at the heart of this story are "not that bad" compared to other women's experiences, and even to other experiences of my own. The minimizing phrase "not that bad" has, of course, been criticized by Roxane Gay (2018, x–xi), among others, for creating an ever-diminishing set of hypothetical situations that are allowed to be "that bad." She, and many others, including readers of earlier versions of this essay, have asserted the need for feminists to insist that "all encounters with sexual violence are, indeed, that bad." Without denying the importance of this claim, I want to hold on to the "not that bad" of this story by interrogating what is at stake in Gay's insistence. The claim made by Gay is precisely a form of narrative politics. It is an insistence that women's stories of sexual violence matter and need to be heard and taken seriously, a political claim which I argue in *Speaking Out* is at the core of feminist struggles around sexual violence since at least the early 1970s. Feminists have harnessed the affective and political power of women's stories of suffering to change the cultural, political, and legal landscape surrounding sexual violence. Speaking about feminist statistics on violence against women, Andrea Dworkin commented: "We collect statistics not to quantify our injuries but to convince you that our injuries exist" (2005, 14). To this, I would add that we tell stories not to describe our injuries to you but convince you that our injuries should not exist. It is in this sense that telling our stories is an act of political contestation or "transgression" (Alcoff and Gray-Rosendale 1993).

However, it is a form of contestation that seeks to use moral arguments around suffering for its political efficacy. In other words, achieving political effects through stories of suffering can require us to display our trauma and insist that all incidents of sexual violence or harassment are "that bad" rather than asserting that even incidents that do not cause trauma or suffering are, or should be, unacceptable. Ultimately, reliance on narratives of trauma and suffering can become, as Nicola Gavey and Johanna Schmidt (2011) argue, a "double-edged sword" in that they require us to continue to enact and demonstrate our trauma in order to compel political agreement. This can become a demand that women narrate all forms of sexual violence as singularly harmful events, as the narrative climax of a tragedy that is inherently traumatizing because we locate the wrong of the act in our narrated pain rather than in the political assertion that our control over our bodies and sexualities cannot be denied. The former is highly effective but positions us as injured victims rather than political claimants and leaves us open to the counterclaim that the stories we tell are insufficiently traumatic, that they are not "bad enough" to justify the fuss that we are making about them.

It is important to me to not relinquish the "not that bad" of my own story for two reasons. The first is that it reflects my experience, and to insist that women narrate stories in certain ways and with certain affects can itself become a disciplinary force (Serisier 2018). As I discuss in more detail below, this wasn't the worst thing that happened to me during that period, and it was not something that I experienced as a singularly life-altering event. Secondly, we should be able to assert that actions are harmful, wrong, and deserving of censure without requiring that they function as the center of a narrative of trauma. Thinking of our narratives as one way of making a political claim, and a claim that is frequently contested, may help to move away from this trauma logic. It also can, I suggest, assist us in countering other ways in which women's narratives are judged.

TO SPEAK OR NOT TO SPEAK:
DISRUPTIVE NARRATIVES AND EVERYDAY ACTS

The fact that the decision to tell or not tell this story has been significant to me is revealing of a dynamic that surrounds women's narratives. If sexual violence as a topic has been surrounded by a paradoxical combination of secrecy and sensationalism, it is equally true that women's testimony of violence and abuse has been both silenced and represented as inordinately powerful. Indeed, the very assertion of the power of these narratives has been used as a logic for refusing to listen to or believe women's testimony. The archetypal case of this is the law's repeated warnings about the dangers of believing women's stories and the corresponding and enduring myth of the danger of false allegations. Seventeenth-century jurist Matthew Hale's warning that rape, although "a most detestable crime," is "an accusation easily to be made and hard to be proved, and harder to be defended by the party accused, tho never so innocent," remained an element of jury instruction in rape cases until the wave of rape law reforms in the 1980s (Ferguson 1987, 89). But, while the warning might be taken as a simple act of silencing, it can be read as a sign of legal fear of the power of women's narratives and the danger that they will use this power irresponsibly (Larcombe 2002).

Variations on this theme continue to be incredibly influential and they continue to be used to justify distrust of women's stories and claims to have experienced violence or harassment. Early on in my acquaintance with my professor he told me that he had been accused, unfairly in his mind, of sexual harassment by a student. He claimed that his career would never recover and that he was likely to lose his job, claims that were evidently largely unfounded. However, despite the professional resilience of my professor and other men accused of harassment, a firm belief remains in the life-destroying capacity of women's speech, their tendency to wield it irresponsibly, and the consequent need to guard against the destruction of men's fundamental rights. These tropes appear repeatedly in public debates around prominent examples of women's storytelling such as "Me Too" and form part of a larger societal tendency to scrutinize the actions and motivations about women who speak about violence and harm rather than the men who are described as committing it. In a related pattern, media reporting of sexual harassment and acquaintance rape cases are frequently told through the knowing woman and the unknowing man, where women are presented as having known, or being responsible for knowing the consequences of their actions while men are presented as essentially innocent (Lees 1997). For example, she must have known why he invited her to his house for dinner, and the consequences of accepting. If she didn't, she should have. But how on earth could he have realized that she didn't mean for her acceptance of the dinner invitation as an opening for a romantic date? For me, the embarrassment I feel for my nineteen-year-old self and her naivety has been a reason not to tell, but so too has been my concern about what telling my story might "do" to this man.

The construction of women's testimony as "doing" something to the men they speak about is hard to escape, and it is not, I contend, solely mythical. I suggested above that harnessing the political power of women's stories of violence has been a major achievement of Western feminism. These stories do have performative qualities, in that they don't only describe events but act to make individual and collective demands and to, ideally, render the acts that they speak of as morally and ethically intolerable. Women's stories of sexual violence have a capacity to effect political change because they are able to evoke powerful emotions, because they portray evident injustice, and because, in evocatively portraying a social reality that should not be, they can act as a political demand for the world to be different. In this reading, the difference between feminist and survivor activists and legal figures such as Justice Hale is not in their understanding of women's speech but in their evaluation of its potential. While feminists have sought to harness this potential, legal, media, and other dominant social institutions have sought to neutralize it, in part by warning of its destabilizing tendencies, and in part by attempting to "taint" women and their testimony with doubt and distrust.

The latter processes of doubting, denying, and refusing to grant women's stories a hearing have been dissected and confronted by a range of feminist scholars, including Leigh Gilmore in her excellent book *Tainted Witness*, which examines the last thirty years as a "new era of doubting women in public" (2017, 10). The former process of focusing on the destabilizing power of women's speech has been less frequently discussed by feminists, but has, I argue elsewhere, become more frequent in recent years (Serisier 2019). Focusing on the performative power of women's speech has had many benefits for feminists but it can enact a surreal reversal of causal logic, where it is the women's decision to speak which is portrayed as the decisive act in the narrative rather than the act that she is speaking about. Responsibility is, again, removed from the man who does something to the woman and is placed on the woman who speaks about his actions. Rather than responding to what has been done to her, she is seen as doing something to him. Rather than a story about everyday life disrupted by an unacceptable and harmful act, the story becomes one in which these acts are precisely part of normal and everyday life, with the normal functioning of the world only disrupted when women speak publicly. Their speech then acts on men who are seen to be at women's mercy rather than as the initiators of harm against women. The consequences of re-normalization reverses the feminist aim of speaking in the first place, and all too often the consequences become that women themselves are seen as troublemakers. By this logic, my professor was able to complain about the harm done to him by the student who had spoken out even as his career at this and other prestigious universities continued uninterrupted to retirement. Most likely this logic was also implicitly adopted by the university itself, as students who speak out about harassment are judged as a reputational risk to be managed rather than seen as drawing necessary attention to problems within the institution. As Alison Phipps writes, dominant university responses to sexual harassment fall into a pattern of "institutional airbrushing" where students have little individual value and the university sees sexual harassment as something that must be hidden in order to construct a "perfect picture" for applicants and potential funders (2018, 7). And, despite knowing all of this, I continue to feel that the decision to tell this story bears significant weight, so that even when I speak to friends I rarely identify the professor involved and, in the writing of this chapter, I feel tempted to change details to make him less potentially identifiable.

TELLABLE ACTS AND NARRATABLE LIVES: WHO IS GIVEN A MEANINGFUL STORY?

Concerns with the effects of women's speech on men's lives offer a broader insight into the narrative priority given to men and women as well as the relationship that is presumed between their biographies and acts of harassment, violence, or harm. Certain lives are deemed more worthy of narration than others; they are understood as less containable by a single incident and as requiring a backstory and a consequential life to come. When my professor presented himself, he clearly narrated his own biography in a way that presumed that his history of loneliness, living in a foreign culture and being misunderstood, particularly by women, was relevant and worthy of attention. He told it to me extensively as an implicit if not explicit justification for his behavior. The potential consequences to his life of the allegation made against him also loomed large in his narrative while any life story of the unnamed student who had accused him was absent. While this focus may speak to my professor's self-absorption, a focus on the life stories of men before and after the acts of which they are accused is a common feature of public responses to women's stories of harm, and it was replicated in other people I knew at the university who were aware of the allegations. The circumstances in the life of this professor that may have led to his actions or to the misunderstanding, depending on the speaker, were commonplace while speculation about the student was absent. Anecdotes of other things these men have done, families they have, futures that might be erased, are common, and it is frequently presumed that they are the real object of interest in the story. This is particularly true in stories such as the one I tell, where an incident that is "not that bad" is judged as trivial when weighed against the totality of a life.

In her work on storytelling and subjectivity, feminist philosopher Adriana Cavarero argues that biography, or the attempt to construct a single linear narrative out of the diverse conglomeration of moments and events that make up a life, is inherently reductive (2000, 43–44). This reductiveness is exacerbated in narratives where individuals are positioned as the "hero" of the story, their selfhood reduced to a single definitive act or set of actions. This process also occurs in representations of women who speak about sexual violence who, almost inevitably, are defined as traumatized victims or lying villains, or, to put it in Helen Benedict's famous formulation, "virgins or vamps" (1992, 1). I was warned by friends who read early drafts of this piece that it was likely to be read for clues as to who the professor was and that I should be careful with the type and level of detail I provided, as too much or too little would equally enable dismissal of the story. For these well-meaning friends it was largely axiomatic that my narrative would be read as part of his story even as the experience, and my decision to write about it, would be taken as defining of me but not of him. Whereas the story of his life will always necessarily exceed the acts that he is accused of, they envisaged my biography contracting and shrinking to that allegation, that event. These processes are extremely revealing, especially when read in conjunction with the processes discussed in the previous section. As men's actions and responsibilities are minimized, their life stories are granted larger amounts of empathy and hearing. And even as women's speech is registered as singularly disruptive, they are reduced to a walk-on part in someone else's life. This response implicitly asserts that some life stories deserve to be told in full, and some are only significant in terms of their impact on others.

When Dorothy Allison described her "reasons not to tell" the story of her history of childhood sexual abuse, the main reason was her need to assert a selfhood that exceeded the experience of victimization: "I am the only one who can tell the story of my life and say what it means" (1996, 70). This desire to assert the definition and limits of that experience might also be a reason to describe it as "not that bad" without denying its significance. In the case of my professor, it is important to me personally to declare his actions "not that bad" not in order to minimize his responsibility but in order to refuse a reading of these events as definitive in determining the course of my own life, with its heterogeneous interplay of moments, events, and effects. While it is undeniably true that my professor had a backstory and a future that were relevant to what happened, so did I, and I continue to. The immediate context of my life, some of which he knew, also impacted how his acts affected me both then and in ongoing ways. For me, claiming simultaneously that his actions were "not that bad" and "bad enough" means insisting that they were both causally related to and not directly responsible for the fact that shortly after this incident I dropped out of university, unable to complete any of my assessments due to panic attacks and anxiety. I was largely estranged from my family and in the middle of a break-up from a violent partner who was repeatedly breaking into my house and threatening to kill both himself and me. The stress I was under meant that I was barely eating or sleeping and already struggling to work and study. This meant that I experienced the unwanted sexual advances, not only as a significant betrayal but as an action that destabilized the precarious balance of my life. At the time, the university was a refuge and the only area of my life that made sense and was on track. And then it wasn't. The university was somewhere that I had waited my entire life to be and an academic career was something that I'd imagined as a child, and then I left, in a way which might have meant that I was unable to return.

It is the memory of that context that means that when I tell this story I will not tell it as part of his story with me playing a walk-on role alongside the other young woman who accused him of harassment. It is the context that means that I insist that the story is "not that bad" because at the time I was dealing with things that were far worse. And I will not let that incident occupy a central role of trauma. But it is also the context that, paradoxically, has convinced me that my story is worth telling, if only to insist that women's lives, like men's lives, are far bigger and more complex than a single incident even if this is a story that they choose to tell to seek redress. What he did does not and cannot contain either of our life stories. But that simple truth should not be allowed to erase his responsibility and transfer it to my decision to tell the story just as the effects of what he did are not negated by the fact that my life exceeded his actions.

THE MORAL OF THE STORY:
JUDGING THE EFFECTS OF WOMEN'S NARRATIVES

The combined effects of the processes outlined in the above sections on judgments of men's actions and women's narratives are profound. In short, the consequences of men's actions are curtailed and normalized while the potential consequences of women's speech are constantly guarded against, through what Gilmore describes as "tainting" or public doubting. It is, she argues, only in relation to women's testimony of sexual violence that "people feel virtuous, objective and fair when they claim that the conditions that typically initiate and guide" investigations render them moot from the outset (2017, 17). So that the fact that "nobody really knows" whether a woman is telling the truth leads to these cases being labelled as radically undecidable, or merely a case of "he said, she said." Ironically, the presumed public power of women's testimony and its career-ending effects are taken as justification to withhold belief and action. In this way, as Nils Christie (1986) has explained, in cases of social wrong or harm it is far easier to take the side of the perpetrator because all he asks is that we carry on as before and do nothing, while victims demand that we take action and intervene, including in cases involving colleagues, friends, or men whose life stories we know and are invested in. This process is exacerbated by the fact that the outcomes of women's speech are often public and seemingly discrete or identifiable, as in a disciplinary hearing or public shaming. In contrast, the effects of sexual harassment and violence, like the acts themselves, are often privatized, long-term, and enmeshed in the broader life events and narratives of victims and survivors.

To return to my own example, the effects of having been disciplined or, in an extremely unlikely outcome, dismissed for sexual harassment, can be clearly traced to the student who made a complaint. As far as the consequences of my own story, at the point that my old professor wrote to me we were not that far apart in terms of profession and status. He was a senior academic at the end of a relatively prestigious career and I was a junior academic at the beginning of what might well be a similarly successful career. In that sense, no harm done. But this reading rejects and refuses both the actual and potential consequences of that part of my life. It fails to acknowledge the impacts of cumulative experiences of being, or feeling, reduced to "physiognomy" in situations where I was wanting and expecting to be engaged with in ways that recognized my intellect. I was a young woman who experienced my biography, desires, and self being denied by my former partner who sought to control me in our relationship and who would not accept my right to end it. My professor's response to that situation was exclusively filtered through his own neediness, entirely instrumentalizing me. I came out of that year with an anxiety disorder that required psychiatric treatment, a dependency on various prescription and non-prescription drugs to deal with that anxiety, the loss of my place in an undergraduate program at a prestigious university, and a severely shaken sense of confidence and faith in myself and other people.

So, although I am now an academic, I am very aware that I was almost not. My undergraduate degree was delayed and finished with worse marks at a less prestigious university. I left the university to pursue an administrative job and treatment for my severe anxiety. I only just obtained a one-year scholarship for my PhD that enabled me to be funded for a first year and demonstrate my capacity in order to then apply for a second scholarship to finish. My PhD was delayed in part because of ongoing anxiety and other issues and "networking" continues to be a struggle for me as I tend to mistrust social cues in these environments and the motivations of others. On the other hand, my personal history, as with many academics, has motivated my work and fed into the methods and insights of my scholarship, playing a role in shaping its contours and direction. The aftermath of those experiences, and coming through them, also gave me a confidence in my personal strength that I had not previously possessed, and I draw on that strength in my career. I feel both proud and lucky to have an academic career, but am cognizant that universities, and other prestigious institutions, are haunted by absences of those dealing with the complex and ongoing effects of harassment or violence, including those with stories that are "not that bad." I wonder sometimes if the other student who did accuse my professor of sexual harassment is among them, and, indeed, if there are others who were similarly impacted like myself and, similarly, never sought institutional redress.

It is for these reasons that I find public debates and discussions about the effects of women's speech to be deeply impoverished and enraging to the point of paralysis. I was inspired to write this essay to unpack my emotional and analytic responses to these debates, and pinpoint how their performances of objectivity are in fact deeply one-sided. Performative calls to "due process," fairness, and nuance largely refuse to acknowledge that what they are in fact calling for is a return to the standard way of doing things, where due process, fairness, and nuance exist only for those, usually men, on the receiving end of allegations, while those who experience acts of sexual harassment or other forms of harm are allowed to quietly disappear. It is a construction of a fantasy world of fairness ruined by women deciding to speak, rather than acknowledging that survivors' public speech exposes these fantasies and the harms they enable and perpetuate. In the same way that the processes I have described here operate individually, they also operate systemically in universities and other public institutions. Seen in this way, survivor stories are not threats to fairness and due process but attempts to call it into being. Telling them also demands that we imagine the untold stories of those who might have been here but are not or are no longer here, and that we see their lives and narratives as complex, rich, narratable, and deserving of empathy.

SURVIVOR STORIES AND NARRATIVE POLITICS

I am not arguing here against debating the politics or ethics of addressing the wrongs of sexual violence through public speech. I believe that these debates must and should happen as they are a vital part of granting ethical and political consequence to survivor speech. Intervening in these debates through contesting the assumptions that all too often underpin them is a core aim of my writing and research. Here I am concerned with the ways in which judgments of survivor speech reduce a woman's life to a single moment and decision that can be evaluated without consideration of her wider biography, and so found lacking. I am also concerned with the implication that survivor stories detract from a pre-existing state of fairness and due process. To adequately judge the consequences of these narratives requires instead seeing them as an aspiration towards that state and away from one of denial and erasure. In this sense, they are, I insist, a form of "narrative politics" or political contestation. To debate and evaluate the consequences of these contestations is not simply about interrogating them through lenses of doubt and disbelief. It requires also critical attention to the conditions under which they are produced, the ways in which they are and are not heard, and the meanings, interpretations, and framings that they are given. This has been one of the major contributions of the tradition of feminist scholarship on survivor discourse that provides the context for my own work (e.g., Alcoff and Gray-Rosendale 1993, Naples 2003).

In telling the story of my professor and his re-emergence in my life I find myself, as someone who has not previously spoken publicly, reflecting on the ways in which our "reasons not to tell" intersect with and are informed by the processes of judgment that surround those who do speak publicly. A feminist "narrative politics" must consider these judgments alongside the ways in which these stories are incorporated into our wider life narratives. It requires, I think, being willing to understand these events in our lives in non-totalizing ways that still see them as harmful and wrong. It means contesting the characterization of our speech as the disruption or the problem and instead to see it as part of a move towards justice and accountability. And, in terms of stories, it requires a commitment to the equal narratability of women's lives with men's and a refusal to deny women the right to complex, excessive lives that cannot be captured by a single event or incident. This is necessary to avoid the very real absence and erasure of survivors and their stories from our public institutions and public consciousness, and to provide just hearings to our stories and the political demands that we use them to articulate.

REFERENCES

Alcoff, Linda Martin, and Laura Gray-Rosendale. 1993. "Survivor Discourse: Transgression or Recuperation?" *Signs: Journal of Women in Culture and Society* 18 (2): 260–290.

Allison, Dorothy. 1996. *Two or Three Things I Know for Sure*. London: Flamingo.

Benedict, Helen. 1992. *Virgin or Vamp: How the Press Covers Sex Crimes*. New York: Oxford University Press.

Cavarero, Adriana. 2000. *Relating Narratives: Storytelling and Selfhood*. Translated by Paul A. Kottman. New York/London: Routledge.

Christie, Nils. 1986. "The Ideal Victim." In *From Crime Policy to Victim Policy*, edited by Ezzat A. Fattah, 17–30. London: Palgrave Macmillan.

Dworkin, Andrea. 2005. "I Want A Twenty-Four Hour Truce During Which There is No Rape." In *Transforming a Rape Culture*, edited by Emilie Buchwald, Pamela Fletcher, and Martha Roth, 11–22. Minneapolis: Milkweed Editions. Original edition, 1983.

Ferguson, Frances. 1987. "Rape and the Rise of the Novel." *Representations* 20 (Autumn): 88–112.

Gavey, Nicola, and Johanna Schmidt. 2011. "'Trauma of Rape' Discourse: A Double-Edged Template for Everyday Understandings of the Impact of Rape?" *Violence Against Women* 17 (4): 433–456.

Gay, Roxane. 2018. "Introduction." In *Not That Bad: Dispatches from Rape Culture*, edited by Roxane Gay, ix–xii. New York: Harper Perennial.

Gilmore, Leigh. 2017. *Tainted Witness: Why We Doubt What Women Say About Their Lives*. New York: Columbia University Press.

Kipnis, Laura. 2017. *Unwanted Advances: Sexual Paranoia Comes to Campus*. New York: Harper Collins.

Larcombe, Wendy. 2002. "Cautionary Tales and Telling Anxieties: The Story of the False Complainant." *Australian Feminist Law Journal* 16: 95–108.

Lees, Sue. 1997. *Ruling Passions: Sexual Violence, Reputation and the Law*. Buckingham: Open University Press.

Naples, Nancy A. 2003. "Deconstructing and Locating Survivor Discourse: Dynamics of Narrative, Empowerment, and Resistance for Survivors of Childhood Sexual Abuse." *Signs: Journal of Women in Culture and Society* 28 (4): 1151–1187.

Phipps, Alison. 2018. "Reckoning Up: Sexual Harassment and Violence in the Neoliberal University." *Gender and Education*: 1–17. https://doi.org/10.1080/09540253.2018.1482413.

Serisier, Tanya. 2018. *Speaking Out: Feminism, Rape and Narrative Politics*. London: Palgrave Macmillan.

———. 2019. "A New Age of Believing Women? Judging Rape Narratives Online." In *Rape Narratives in Motion*, edited by Ulrika Andersson, Monika Edgren, Lena Karlsson, and Gabriella Nilsson, 199–222. London: Palgrave Macmillan.

Way, Katie. 2018. "I went on a date with Aziz Ansari. It turned into the worst night of my life." *Babe.net*, January 14, 2018. https://babe.net/2018/01/13/aziz-ansari-28355.

Chapter Ten

Professing to Power

Donna L. Potts

On December 11, 1981, my first semester at the University of Missouri, and a week after my father's suicide, I was raped by my German professor. He had invited me over to his house for coffee with his family, presumably to console me for my loss. When I arrived, he invited me in, and as he closed the door behind me, he mentioned that his wife and daughter were in St. Louis on a shopping trip. He then raped me, and on my way out, said: "By the way, I have a lot of power in the department, so it won't do any good for you to say anything about this. Anyway, it's never happened before." He muttered, "No one would believe you."

In retrospect, I recognize that he had been grooming me all semester, inviting me to his office to work on translations of German poems. I had always been good at poetry, good at language, and I assumed he must have recognized that. Good teachers recognize their students' strengths and try to cultivate them. I recall my high school American literature teacher, who gave me a book of early American sayings when I graduated, and signed it, "to Donna, who has a true scholar's mind." I had an inkling of what bad teachers did. My high school teacher who praised my male friend as a "genius" for having read all of the books on the rack in our classroom never noticed that I read all of them too, and he accused me of plagiarism when I used a multisyllabic word in my paper on *King Lear*. "Are you sure you know what that word means?" he asked. His only encouragement to the girls in his class was "you girls should wear shorts more often."

In 2011, I wrote about my rape and its aftermath for *The Chronicle of Higher Education*, in an essay called "For a Victim of Rape, Silence Has No Benefits." In the thirty years that intervened between my rape and my publication about it, I earned a PhD, and am now a professor myself. I teach a graduate seminar on Irish Literature and Trauma, which I am now developing into a book. I served for seven years as a moderator on Pandora's Project, for survivors of rape and sexual assault. In my capacity as Chair of the American Association of University Professors (AAUP)'s Committee on Women in the Academic Profession, I co-authored a report on campus sexual assault, which was published in the AAUP's Redbook, whose documents are included in faculty handbooks across the nation. I have been interviewed with Gloria Allred on NPR, held Sexual Harassment and Assault workshops, and co-organized a state-wide conference on Campus Sexual Assault Prevention. I am also writing a book on Campus Sexual Assault, thanks to a fellowship provided by my university.

Although it would appear from my university funding that I have support for my advocacy and research, I am reminded daily that it *still* often does no good to say anything about rape, nor about the rape culture that enables it. As Judith Herman writes in *Trauma and Recovery*, "It is very tempting to take the side of the perpetrator. All the perpetrator asks is that the bystander do nothing. He appeals to the universal desire to see, hear, and speak no evil. The victim, on the contrary, asks the bystander to share the burden of pain. The victim demands action, engagement, and remembering" (Herman 1992). As I have tried to advocate for students and colleagues who have been victims, and have attempted to comply with the regulations of the Office of Equal Opportunity, I have encountered various forms of disbelief from people who possess the power to change the culture.

When WSU's provost invited me to serve as co-organizer of the state-wide Campus Sexual Assault Prevention Conference in 2014, I suggested to the committee that we include a panel of students. One of the co-organizers, who worked in the Office of Equal Opportunity on another campus, sneered, "Why would we want students? We don't want to hear about their disgust with the system." "Aren't they the ones most likely to be raped?" I responded. I certainly never anticipated needing to argue with a committee of people who were presumably dedicated to preventing student sexual assault, about the necessity of involving students in the conversation.

When a colleague and I shared with a new administrator a long list of cases in which our advocacy for victims had failed, to demonstrate that our current system of responding to sexual harassment and assault is broken, he shrugged and said, "Oh, these are all just allegations. He said/she said." As we sat outside his office afterwards, discussing other faculty senate matters, he stepped out and asked us if we had decided to "stick around and gossip." It occurred to me that the sexist label of "gossip" is often used to silence the truth that women try to speak about violations of their own bodies.

The next day, our student newspaper, *The Daily Evergreen*, published the results of their public records request for the 400-page OEO investigation of former WSU football player Jason Gesser. Despite allegations from multiple women that he sexually harassed them, he was not found guilty of any violations, which WSU's administration quickly tweeted across the nation, eclipsing the college newspaper's painstaking reportage. Shortly thereafter, two women came forward with their stories of attempted sexual assault, resulting in Gesser's resignation as well as the re-opening of the investigation. A massage therapist had reported Gesser to the police for exposing himself, but they dismissed it as a "he said/she said," so he was not charged (Decker 2018). Meanwhile, a member of the WSU Foundation's Board of Trustees made email threats to former administrator Yuri Farkas, who had earlier shared his concerns with the OEO during their investigation of Gesser (Smay and Green 2018).

Two days before the *Daily Evergreen*'s story, Dr. Christine Blasey Ford disclosed to *The Washington Post* that Brett Kavanaugh had attempted to rape her when she was fifteen. She was a psychologist *as well as* a professor, and she would surely prevail, I told myself as I watched the hearing. Relying on her expertise on traumatic memory, she meticulously described how victims respond to trauma, explaining why she could precisely remember some details, such as the way he placed his hand over her mouth to prevent her from screaming, and the way he and his friend laughed uproariously in spite of her anguish.

As she described her experience, she could have been describing mine as well: I could recall my professor's exact words and actions, but I could not recall where his house was or how I got home that day. In "Dispelling Confusion About Traumatic Dissociative Amnesia," Dr. Richard McNally describes how trauma affects a victim's memory:

> Release of stress hormones during trauma fosters consolidation of the experience, rendering it relatively resistant to forgetting. Nevertheless, the mind does not operate like a videotape recorder, infallibly capturing all our sensory impressions. . . . When the details change or fade, trauma survivors still remember the gist of their experience remarkably well. It is easy to see how the capacity for remembering trauma might constitute an evolutionary adaptation, whereas a capacity for forgetting it would seemingly imperil survival. (McNally 2007, 1085)

As much as I identified with and believed Blasey Ford, I soon discovered that Facebook friends (incidentally, all of them male) from my hometown had already dismissed her as a Democratic tool, mocked her academese, poked holes through her painstakingly told story. Even the Democrats among them—one of them a psychiatrist—joked that the entire hearing was only a means of teaching Kavanaugh how to handle the limelight—thereby dismissing a woman's personal trauma as nothing but a paid publicity stunt. I suddenly recalled how, when the psychiatrist was a high school student, he and his girlfriend thought it would be amusing to force me to "go parking" with a friend of his, in the back seat of his car. When I became angry, and got out of their car to walk home down a country road in the dark, they all laughed in much the same way I imagined Kavanaugh and his friends laughing at Blasey Ford.

The men from my hometown believed that Blasey Ford was simply being paid to make allegations against Kavanaugh. They had no concept of the years it took for her to build her career and rebuild her life. To them, her advanced education and large vocabulary made her suspect. They did not understand that she had learned to theorize trauma in part because intellectualization was one way of responding to her own trauma. Excessive intellectualization is a common defense mechanism for trauma victims, because it blocks painful and debilitating emotions (Center for Substance Abuse Treatment [US] 2014). As I listened to her story, I relived my own. I recall my college therapist asking me why I intellectualized my experiences, rather than allowing myself to feel them. In the aftermath of the rape, I struggled with what I now understand to be PTSD. My father's suicide made me question my own purpose in life; if he had taken his own life, finding it not worth living, of what worth was his offspring's life? My rape by a professor I had admired made me question whether I deserved to be in college. If I had been nothing but a body to him, would anyone recognize that I had a mind worth cultivating? My feelings of worthlessness also made it more difficult to leave a partner whose abuse of me began after my father's suicide.

Blasey Ford also spoke of the aftermath of the trauma—how, for many years, she struggled academically, how she never could escape the sound of their laughter at her suffering, and how she had never stopped being fearful, insisting that her new house have two front doors. PTSD can continue for decades, and a variety of trauma triggers can set it off, bringing back strong memories and making the victim feel that she is re-living the trauma. Triggers can include sounds, sights, smells, sensations, or thoughts that remind the victim of the traumatic event in some way (Triggers 2019).

These aspects of her story mirrored my own, and because they are so painful, they are aspects I have rarely discussed. When I was in graduate school, I took a seminar from a professor—a woman—whom I greatly admired. Because Samuel Johnson was her primary research interest, I sought in her the support that had been denied me earlier. I felt obligated to glean as much from Johnson's wisdom as I could. Johnson wrote, "Depend upon it, that, if a man *talks* of his misfortunes, there is something in them that is not disagreeable to him; for where there is nothing but pure misery, there never is any recourse to the mention of it." He likely believed that women's misery should not be aired. "Public practice of any art, and staring in men's faces, is very indelicate in a female," he said. As for a woman preaching, it "was like a dog walking on its hind legs. It is not done well, but you are surprised to find it done at all."

Johnson writes in an era when women had virtually no access to formal education, and were regarded as intellectually inferior to men. He writes, "A man is in general better pleased when he has a good dinner upon his table, than when his wife talks Greek" (Samuel Johnson 2019). Yet even the generation of teachers before me still clung to this notion—thus, my high school English teacher, who doubted that I could really know the multisyllabic words I used in my essays, while considering it the girls' responsibility to please him by wearing shorts. Women were, and are, considered to be more appropriately the objects of the male gaze. They had best not ever gaze at men. Furthermore, they dare not demonstrate expertise, but rather, help to further men's expertise.

Kate Manne's *Down Girl: The Logic of Misogyny* explains that women, as a historically subordinate group, are expected to provide feminine-coded goods and services: attention, affection, admiration, sympathy, sex, and children. Men, on the other hand, are expected to take masculine-coded perks and privileges: "power, prestige, public recognition, rank, reputation, honor, 'face,' respect, money and other forms of wealth, hierarchical status, upward mobility, and the status conferred by having a high ranking woman's loyalty, devotion, respect, etc." (Manne 2017, 130). Women's historically subordinate position helps to explain why Kavanaugh was permitted a display of outrage when his privilege was threatened by Blasey Ford's testimony, as well as my male Facebook friends' mockery of her narrative as mere preparation for his role on the Supreme Court. My rapist's power and prestige necessitated that my rape narrative be suppressed in favor of his continued career trajectory. Ever since I was a teenager, I was enculturated to suppress my fear and disgust in deference to men's desires—from the night when my friends presumed I was obligated to engage sexually with a teenager I barely knew, to the day when a minister from my church stalked me, grabbed me, and kissed me in front of our house, and my mother dismissed my panicked account by saying "but he's a preacher."

Leigh Gilmore's *Tainted Witness: Why We Doubt What Women Say About Their Lives*, examines how and why women's stories are *tainted* to discredit them: "to contaminate by doubt, stigmatize by association with race and gender, and dishonor through shame, such that not only the story, but the person herself is smeared." Gilmore observes that

> the discourses about rape that circulate within rape culture undermine women's testimony. Rape discourse casts doubt on women as credible witnesses to their own harm, and on claims of rape in general. Through rape discourse, women who bring forward accounts of sexual violence are turned into tainted witnesses before the law and in courts of public opinion. (Gilmore 2018, 2)

Even as I write, a Connecticut woman named Jennifer Farber Dulos remains missing, likely murdered by her husband, who recited his revenge fantasies to her over the years of their increasingly troubled marriage. Despite his and his girlfriend having been videoed depositing thirty plastic trash bags containing her bloody clothes as well as sponges used to clean up her blood, Fox News and her ex-husband's lawyer, Norm Pattis, relied for an explanation on Gillian Flynn's *Gone Girl*, in which a woman fakes her own murder to retaliate against her husband for a sexual relationship with his student. Tellingly, neither the novel nor the film based on it address the power imbalance in the husband's inherently nonconsensual relationship with his student, but rather, portray him as an innocent victim of female wiles. Likewise, despite documentation of threats of violence by Fotis Dulos, his lawyer could argue that Farber Dulos had staged her own murder or committed suicide out of revenge. Pattis claimed that she has a "pretty florid imagination and motives to use it to hurt" his client (Vigdor 2019). Gilmore's *Tainted Witness* predicts his response: "When the witness is a woman, and especially when the harm includes sexual violence, she will be subjected to practices of shaming and discrediting that preexist any specific case" (Gilmore 2018, 5).

My graduate seminar on Irish Literature and Trauma includes books that serve to illustrate this concept. Roddy Doyle's *The Woman Who Walked into Doors* features Paula Spencer, a protagonist whose physical and sexual abuse by her husband is twisted into blame of her. The bruises that register her abuse are ignored by hospital staff, who are content to believe she caused the bruises herself, by getting drunk and walking into doors. Paula reflects that her best years were when she was ten to twelve, before puberty arrived. As soon as she develops breasts, she learns to feel shame about her body, to feel dirty. She recalls the look on her mother's face, after her bath:

> It's one of the only bad things I can remember from my childhood, that expression on my mammy's face in the bathroom, like I'd done something absolutely dreadful, terrible to her. . . . She'd been robbed—that was what she'd thought when she saw my breasts starting; her little girl had been taken from her. (Doyle 1997, 18)

Paula is aware that her older sister Carmel has been sexually abused by their father; puberty represents an initiation into nonconsensual sex. Moreover, the shame transcends familial relationships. Society—both school and church—makes her feel shame: crude remarks about female bodies are ubiquitous, women are constantly objectified, even by authority figures such as teachers and priests. When her teacher touches her inappropriately, she thinks, "There was nothing exciting about it, a grown-up man feeling me, feeling me while he was correcting my mistakes. . . . The ones that weren't perverts were either thick or bored or women" (Doyle 1997, 31). The female mind requires correction through male control of her body. As she is perceived as attractive by men, she is likewise regarded as nothing but a body, whose mind is not worth cultivating.

Doyle's very title expresses the way in which victims of trauma are blamed and pathologized. The medical profession as well as the community are content to believe that Paula has simply walked into doors, because it allows them to avoid challenging patriarchy, to accept the truth that her husband has been abusing her. They all prefer to look the other way: "The doctor never looked at me. He studied parts of me, but he never saw all of me" (Doyle 1997, 23). Not surprisingly, Paula's husband Charlo eventually begins to display a sexual interest toward his own daughter—which is the breaking point at which Paula throws him out. While she is incapable of valuing herself enough to leave him out of self-interest, she knows how to manage the role of self-sacrificing mother, throwing him out only when he threatens to harm her daughter.

Recent interpretations of Title IX have insisted that harassment and rape must be addressed because women deserve an equal opportunity to education. My rape by a professor convinced me that despite my quest to cultivate my mind by enrolling in a university, I was ultimately nothing but a body to be exploited by powerful men. When I reported my rape to a university psychiatrist, he merely shrugged and said, "I'll bet a lot of men are attracted to you," and then he offered to prescribe antidepressants.

On the Tuesday after the rape, I had to take a final from my rapist, who had jokingly mentioned the day before the rape that we could use our Saturday session to discuss the upcoming final. I ended up earning a "B" for the class, despite my strong academic performance all semester. I wondered if it was because I had not cooperated with him, but remained stone-still, paralyzed, during the rape. I wondered if I had been too traumatized to do my best on the final. I lost confidence in my intellectual ability, and I did not fully regain it until after I had earned tenure and published a book and four articles.

I told my closest friend, who was also my roommate as well as a student of German who would later marry her German graduate teaching assistant. She remained silent as I described what happened. I uneasily tried to believe that she was too shocked by my narrative to comment, but years later, when I was being interviewed for *More* magazine about the rape, she was called and asked for her reaction. "I told her I didn't believe you, but now I do," she said. She could not believe that a "nice" father figure like Ernst Braun would rape anyone, but she could believe that her own best friend, whom she had known since childhood, would lie to her.[1]

For me, the trauma greater than rape was that my own best friend did not believe me, that my own mother had no reaction whatsoever to my story of rape, and when I described the psychiatrist's reaction to my story, said only, "Well what did you expect him to say?" My youngest sister, who did not know about the rape at the time, never bothered to read my narrative in *More* magazine, or at any rate, she never bothered to comment on it after I sent it. My mother asked, "Why don't you just get over it?" As I write this essay, I am fully aware that the people who are presumably closest to me will not bother to read it.

Immediately after the rape, I ended up moving in with my boyfriend. I was afraid to sleep in the duplex I shared with three other students, particularly after we discovered the phone line had been cut. In retrospect, I think my boyfriend cut it. He was eleven years older than I, and he had left an ex-wife and three children behind to follow me from my hometown. I never asked him to leave, and I recall being disappointed when he announced his plan. But because he had already erupted in jealous anger when I suggested I wasn't ready for commitment, I did not dare tell him. There was no way for me, an eighteen-year-old college student, to tell a grown man what to do. He then decided to enroll in college and major in English too, and he continued all the way to a PhD. He began verbally abusing me, never missing a chance to tell me I was stupid. When he borrowed my books for class, he would even mock the notes I had taken in the margins of the books. Years later, I found comments like, "Oh, God!" written under my painstaking notes in the margins of the paperback novels I had loaned him for class.

On one trip back to our neighboring hometowns, he asked his mother if he could have his father's gun. She gave it to him. Back in Columbia, Missouri, he enjoyed pulling the trigger on the gun, which was not loaded—and laughing at my startled response. "You're so stupid. You thought it was loaded?" he would laugh. About a year after I moved in with him, he told me if I ever tried to leave him, he would track me down and kill me. He then began writing my phone number on bathroom walls, using a fake name: "For a good time, call Leeza." I was kept awake at all hours by men calling with obscene propositions. Because I did not find the constant phone calls funny, he accused me of lacking a sense of humor—the usual charge against feminists who raise any objections to rape culture.

In retrospect, I understand that his antics were a way of breaking me down psychologically so I would tolerate even more abuse. In *Coercive Control: How Men Entrap Women in Personal Life*, Evan Stark coined the phrase "coercive control" to describe the ways an abuser "might dominate and control every aspect of a victim's life without ever laying a hand on her." Coercive control "is an offense to liberty that prevents women from freely developing their personhood, utilizing their capacities, or practicing citizenship." Abusers continually monitor or control their victims' routine activities of life, particularly those traditionally associated with women—like parenting, homemaking, and sex (Stark 2007, 124). Abusers control how they look, what they eat, what they wear, who they communicate with, until all escape routes—family, friends, community—are sealed off and freedom cannot exist. My abuser insisted on choosing my clothes for me, and gradually cut off my contact with family and friends. When I was in my early twenties, he taunted me, "You're really getting old and unattractive. If you left me, nobody else would want you."

He then began placing ads in magazines, which I later found in a drawer while packing my belongings to leave him. The ads referred to me by the name "Fluffy," a woman with a presumably insatiable sexual appetite and no mind of her own. One evening a group of men arrived at our door, and they raped me. Tears were streaming down my face, and they were laughing. He might well have told them it was a fantasy of mine, but more likely, they didn't care about my fantasies—only about their own.

Leigh Gilmore's *Down Girl: The Logic of Misogyny* explains that when women challenge patriarchy, by seeking power and prestige, thereby trespassing on men's historical turf, they are subjected to retaliation. Women who presume to challenge the system, even by walking in public by themselves, demonstrating control over their own bodies, historically the possessions of men, face many forms of retaliation—catcalling, harassment, sexual assault, rape, and even murder (Gilmore 2017, 217).

I suppose my pursuit of a PhD, which entailed a quest for intellectual independence, must have represented a threat. As his death threats escalated (I knew he was a veteran, but he began claiming he had worked as a paid assassin in Vietnam), I began to arrange an escape. I applied for graduate school at Washington State University, and I was accepted on a fellowship. I took a Greyhound bus one morning, intent on never coming back. However, I did not understand that escaping the abuse was only the beginning. I could not escape the trauma so easily. I went to a women's shelter, where I was given a checklist to fill out to determine the extent of the abuse. I checked nearly every single box—from verbal to physical to sexual abuse—except for the box for attempted murder. He had threatened to kill me, but he had never actually attempted it.

Because they had no room for me at a shelter that night, some graduate students offered to take me in. I was allowed ten sessions with a counselor, and I used them up in one semester. Desperate for therapy, for antidepressants, for any kind of relief, I applied for a study on depression at Barnes Hospital, but I was turned away because I was severely depressed, and their study focused on moderately depressed patients. I didn't do well in my graduate classes, and I failed the qualifying exam twice. I eventually had to return to the University of Missouri, feeling safer because I learned that my abuser had moved on to a new victim, another graduate student, and would likely not bother me now.

Universities were not equipped to deal with the kind of trauma that women experience, and they still are not. Intimate partner violence is potentially deadly, but the women who seek help continue to be ignored. Writing about the murder of University of Utah student Lauren McCluskey, Gillian Friedman notes that "nearly half of dating college women report experiencing violence and abusive dating behaviors. Girls and young women between the ages of sixteen and twenty-four experience the highest rate of intimate partner violence, almost triple the national average, according to the Bureau of Justice Statistics" (Friedman 2019). She also wonders if the issue is that women are often not believed; even after Lauren showed screenshots of Melvin Rowland's sex offender status, the police still dismissed him as a threat and never bothered to check his parole status.

I knew Lauren McCluskey. She was from Pullman, Washington, where I live, and her parents are professors at Washington State University, where I teach. I have a daughter the same age, who graduated from high school the same year as Lauren. When I heard the news, I thought, *she could have been my daughter, my student.* She could have been me.

Rowland lied to Lauren about his name, his age, and his background. As soon as she learned the truth, on October 9 (Tanner 2018), she broke off the relationship. The most dangerous time for a woman in an abusive relationship is when she leaves (Mitchell 2017). Tragically, the police did not recognize Rowland's threats, stalking, and extortion in the weeks prior to the murder as abusive.

Yet other students recognized it. On September 30, they told a residence hall official that she was in "an unhealthy relationship with an older man who was controlling her" (Murdock 2018). He had also discussed bringing guns to campus and giving McCluskey a gun. Beginning on October 12, she made repeated efforts to get campus and the Salt Lake City Police Department (SLCPD) to recognize she was in danger. She told police he was a convicted sex offender who extorted money from her by threatening to post intimate photographs of her, had threatened to kill himself, peeped through her window in the residence hall, and attempted to lure her out of her dorm (Murdock 2018). Lauren and her friend told police that Rowland had been trying to get access to a gun—which is against the law for a convicted felon, especially one on parole, to possess. They told police that he had impersonated a supervisor at the university police department. She was receiving text messages, supposedly from his friends, telling her he was dead (though later examination of his phone revealed that all of the messages were coming from him) and that she should kill herself. The police failed to recognize any of these acts as acts of violence.

Physical abuse is often what most people think about when we use the term "domestic violence," but abusive partners often escalate rather quickly from emotional abuse to physical abuse. "When you report four major crimes, blackmail, being in possession of a weapon as a convicted felon, impersonating an officer and stalking and you don't even talk to the potential suspect, that's a serious problem," said Jim McConkie, the attorney for the McCluskey family (Gehrke 2019).

In a recent letter to the University of Utah administration, Matt and Jill McCluskey noted, "Responsibility for assessing Lauren's level of personal danger was entirely placed on Lauren, despite the fact that she had just ended a manipulative relationship and despite her numerous attempts to report elevating concerns to the UUPD." The McCluskeys' letter noted that each time their daughter called campus police "it was like the first time . . . Lauren was asked to frame her concerns anew, repeatedly respond to the same list of questions, and fill out the same forms" (Curtis 2018).

Ninety-six percent of college women understandably do not report sexual victimization, largely because of fears about how they may be perceived or might not be believed. But Lauren called the police at least twenty times. Her murder was preventable (Fisher et al. 2000). The University of Utah's report said the campus police force was not trained to recognize or respond to possible interpersonal violence; didn't know how and wasn't expected to check on a suspect's parole status; tended to communicate with victims by email, phone, or text rather than in person; and didn't ensure important information was followed up on when assigned officers were off duty. There was no action in McCluskey's case in the days before she died because the assigned detective was not working or had other duties. Because of a "general lack of knowledge in the area of relationship violence," the McCluskeys observed, campus police saw the situation as a "low priority." In Lauren's case, housing staff considered but did not file a report with a campus system designed to track and respond to such situations, and did not pass the information to university police. University police did not open a formal investigation until seven days later (Reavy 2018). Despite the mishandling of McCluskey's case, which led to her murder, the university nonetheless gave three university employees of the Department of Safety awards for how they conducted themselves before and after Lauren's death.

The Lethality Assessment Program (LAP), already adopted by 46 police departments around Utah, uses eleven questions to help identify victims who are likely to be killed by a partner. Those victims are then immediately connected to more help. Among the questions that Lauren would likely have answered "yes" to are the following: "Have you left him/her/them? Does he/she/they follow or spy on you or leave you threatening messages? Do you think he/she might try to kill you? Does he/she have a gun or can he/she get one easily? Is he/she violently or constantly jealous or does he/she control most of your daily activities? Does he/she follow or spy on you or leave threatening messages?" (Lethality Assessment Program 2005).

Lauren was also the victim of sextortion, when Rowland threatened to distribute private photographs in exchange for money. Sextortion is widely recognized as a form of sexual exploitation, coercion, and violence, as is voyeurism ("Sexual Violence Surveillance" 2009).

The Domestic Violence Hotline's recently released 2017 Impact Report showed a 74 percent increase in number of contacts indicating that firearms played a role in their abuse ("A Year of Impact: National Domestic Violence Hotline" 2018). Jill McCluskey suggested prosecution for the person who gave Rowland, a parolee, a firearm (McCluskey 2018), and Rowland's threats to bring a gun on campus should have been addressed.

As the McCluskeys wrote, "This situation cries out for accountability beyond updating policies and training and addressing [campus police department] understaffing by hiring five new department personnel." It calls for disciplining the people who failed Lauren. It calls for caring enough to listen to victims. Lauren's parents are now suing the University of Utah in a $56 million civil rights case, alleging that campus police could have prevented their daughter's killing—and that Utah's president, Ruth V. Watkins, was irresponsible in insisting otherwise. The lawsuit alleges gender discrimination, claiming that police and other university officials didn't prioritize Lauren's concerns because she was a woman; they viewed her as "unreasonable, hysterical, hypersensitive, paranoid" and acted with "irrational gender stereotypes." In addition, the police department has struggled with a culture of treating female officers poorly. One officer told the lawyers that her male coworkers would pee in her work bag. Another said that her male colleagues refused to believe a woman who reported that she was raped (Romboy 2019).

When I was in college, I met with a university therapist and described the abusive relationship I was in. When I discussed the possibility of leaving my abuser, he disagreed, arguing that "He's your rock. He's your support." He saw me only as a hysterical young woman, because I had recently lost my father to suicide, after which I had been raped by my professor. In retrospect, I understand that he probably did not believe I had been raped or abused; most women are not believed. He thought my problems would be solved by having an older male protector. While the gun that my abuser used was not loaded, in Lauren's case, the gun was loaded, as it is for so many women: 50,000 women world-wide are murdered by intimate partners, according to a recent UN report (Cole 2018).

After I completed a PhD and began working at Kansas State University, I was asked by my colleague, who had recently founded an undergraduate feminist group called "Ordinary Women," if I would like to come to talk to the group about my experiences as a woman in academia. As my various traumas flashed before my eyes, I told her I couldn't possibly do that. One reason I couldn't do it was that I thought feminists were supposed to be strong women, and I knew I was not strong. A close friend of mine had commented, knowing nothing of my history, "I could never be raped. I'm too strong a presence." One night, however, out to dinner with a group of those feminists, I found the courage to mention my rape. Their stunned, empathetic response taught me they were there to support me, not to judge me, and that rape had nothing to do with strength. It would take another twenty years for me to talk about everything—to utter the phrase "gang rape" and to write about it in *CHE*. Linda Martin Alcoff's *Rape and Resistance: Understanding the Complexities of Sexual Violation* examines how rape has been used as "a key element of social terror," used to "demoralize, demobilize, and weaken subjugated communities" (Alcoff 2018, 37).

I had the greatest difficulty accepting that my abuser, who received money from the men who raped me, was trafficking me. When I first raised the issue, while being questioned by a researcher at Barnes Hospital as to whether I had ever been involved in any exchanges of money for sex, her stunned response convinced me I should stay silent. Prostitutes are much more likely to be criminalized than their male clients. They are often presumed to offer sex for money of their own free will, although studies have shown that in the vast majority of cases, some form of coercion is involved. In the recent case of Jeffrey Epstein, his under age victims were redefined as women and as prostitutes, tainting the witnesses while preserving the perpetrator's reputation (Watkins 2019). Moreover, his subsequent suicide means that his accusers will never have the opportunity to face the accused. Conspiracy theorists have been quick to assume that one or another rich and powerful man was responsible for his death in prison—when the true conspiracy is patriarchy itself. It is either the case that rich and powerful men protected him, or that male prison officials chose to ignore their high-profile inmate long enough for him to evade justice.

As the years went by, I found ways to talk to my students who had themselves been victims of domestic abuse, sexual violence, and trafficking. One of them said, "My parents wouldn't believe me when I told them my husband was abusive—until he tried to run me over with his car in our driveway." Another said, "I was raped in high school by a family friend, but my parents were religious and didn't believe in abortion. Thank God I had a miscarriage." I began to consider it an obligation to profess, because they needed to know that strong women, women who had succeeded in their careers, were victims too, and they were not alone. My teaching of Irish Literature and Trauma reinforces my and my students' awareness of how trauma victims are pathologized, how they are disproportionately female, how public policy deeply influences personal lives, how the state operates to control women's bodies.

However, I am still faced with the fact that when confronted by a powerful man, I, a strong, successful woman, still have a story that means nothing. I tried reporting a fellow participant at a conference I regularly attend, a man who regularly assaulted or attempted to assault the women participants, to the president of our organization, and he laughed and said, "You wouldn't believe how many women he's run off." I learned that women's presence at conferences means nothing compared to that of one powerful man. When I mentioned his behavior to an older woman, she assured me that he used to do that to her, as though she were relieved that he had moved on to younger women. She told me she had been afraid to confront him, because he was a reviewer for *Poetry* magazine. I am not sure why she felt compelled to continue to include him in the annual poetry readings she organized. I finally decided that, rather than avoid the opportunity to read, I would email him and warn him that if he ever did anything like that again, to me or any other woman, I wouldn't hesitate to call the police. He never attended another conference.

A colleague of mine, with a PhD from a top university and a book publication with another top university, reported a senior colleague who groped her on two separate occasions under the table at search committee meetings. But when she reported it to the appropriate campus office, the director asked only, "How were you dressed, and why did it take you so long to report?" He interviewed the men at the table, all of whom said they saw nothing—because of course it happened under the table. The case was dismissed by the OEO. Everyone from the dean to the president had heard her story (she cited it as the reason for her departure, when she was asked in an exit interview administered by the dean), but she was the one forced to find a job elsewhere, while he was promoted to department chair and then to associate dean, and will undoubtedly one day be dean.

I recently became department chair, and during my interview, the dean asked me whether, given my advocacy and activism on campus, I would be able to take a neutral stance if I were chosen as chair. Leadership positions in academia have traditionally favored the maintenance of a neutral stance, and they have not surprisingly been held by men. Since becoming chair, I have indeed felt that I had no choice but to advocate for women on campus: women who had endured domestic violence from their partners who were also on campus; women who were disproportionately in non-tenure-track ranks, and thus afraid or unable to challenge a variety of forms of exploitation; female graduate students harassed and even assaulted by male colleagues. If my role is to remain neutral, how can there ever be a more favorable climate in academia for the sizeable proportion of women in it? Apathy is a privilege that women cannot afford.

As I write, Dr. Blasey Ford still faces death threats for her testimony, whereas Brett Kavanaugh is safely installed on the Supreme Court, where he will likely be entrusted with making decisions about women's bodies and reproductive choices for many decades. All he had to do to destroy Dr. Blasey Ford's allegation was to express indignation that a woman tried to ruin his career. Jess Row, writing for the *New Yorker*, observed of Kavanaugh's tirade that he "stripped the rhetoric of self-defense down to its most basic layer: I'm right, you're wrong; she's lying, I'm not; she remembers nothing, I remember everything. For his supporters, this apoplectic behavior under oath was not only persuasive; it opened up that vein of reflexive empathy that conservatives often reserve for white men in positions of power" (Row 2018).

He merely had to perform indignation (he later confessed that he was advised that a show of anger was his only hope of securing the position); she had to bare her soul. Although I know that a woman, no matter how successful, will be ignored when she is pitted against a powerful man, I continue to speak, with more urgency than ever. Kavanaugh's confirmation to the Supreme Court reminds me that survivors' stories can now go viral, but the disbelief surrounding them is all the more viral. Alcoff warns that we must develop an awareness "of the specific convention by which the credibility of accusers is judged," and in particular, the phenomenon of reverse empiricism, which "involves decreasing the presumptive credibility of the very groups and individuals who have a direct experience of the problem," and "projecting onto those who have experienced sexual violation the inability to rationally judge or assess anything or anyone in related domains of inequity forever after" (Alcoff 2018, 48). Rape victims may be deemed incompetent to judge a case of possible rape—and may be denied the right to serve on a jury, as I have twice been. Survivors must nonetheless keep telling their stories.

NOTE

1. I would eventually learn that he began sexually abusing one of his own daughters when she was only three years old. She assured me he was not a good father: "I was his property at that time, as he liked to remind me. He was a purely evil man, I think the proper term is psychopath. . . . He was a monster."

REFERENCES

Alcoff, Linda Martin. 2018. *Rape and Resistance: Understanding the Complexities of Sexual Violation.* Cambridge: Polity Press.
Center for Substance Abuse Treatment (US). 2014. Trauma-Informed Care in Behavioral Health Services. Rockville (MD): Substance Abuse and Mental Health Services Administration (US); Treatment Improvement Protocol (TIP) Series, No. 57, https://www.ncbi.nlm.nih.gov/sites/books/NBK207201/.
Cole, Diane. 2018. "UN Report: 50,000 Women A Year Are Killed By Intimate Partners, Family Members." NPR, November 30, 2018. https://www.npr.org/sections/goatsandsoda/2018/11/30/671872574/u-n-report-50-000-women-a-year-are-killed-by-intimate-partners-family-members.

Curtis, Larry. 2018. "Murdered Utah student's parents disagree with review, say death could have been prevented." https://kutv.com/news/local/-u-of-u-students-parents-disagree-with-portions-of-independent-investigation.

Decker, Casey. 2018. "Massage therapist says Jason Gesser exposed himself to her." https://www.krem.com/article/news/local/whitman-county/massage-therapist-says-jason-gesser-exposed-himself-to-her/293-596377854.

Doyle, Roddy. 1997. *The Woman Who Walked into Doors*. Penguin Books, Kindle Edition.

Fisher, Bonnie S., Francis T. Cullen, and Michael G. Turner. 2000. "The Sexual Victimization of College Women." National Institute of Justice, https://www.ncjrs.gov/pdffiles1/nij/182369.pdf.

Friedman, Gillian. 2019. "What really happened to Lauren McCluskey? The inside story of her tragic death." *Deseret News*, May 30, 2019. https://www.deseretnews.com/article/900073116/lauren-mccluskey-university-of-utah-death-me-too-murder-sexual-assault-investigation.html.

Gehrke, Robert. 2019. "Gehrke: It's time for the University of Utah to accept its failures in Lauren McCluskey's murder." *Salt Lake City Tribune*, July 3, 2019. https://www.sltrib.com/news/2019/07/03/gehrke-its-time/.

Gilmore, Leigh. 2018. *Tainted Witness: Why We Doubt What Women Say About Their Lives*. Columbia University Press.

Herman, Judith. 1992. *Trauma & Recovery—the Aftermath of Violence*. New York: Harper Collins.

"Lethality Assessment Program." 2005. https://lethalityassessmentprogram.org/about-lap/how-lap-works/.

Manne, Kate. 2017. *Down Girl: The Logic of Misogyny*. Oxford University Press, Kindle Edition, 130.

McCluskey, Jill. 2018. https://twitter.com/jjmccluskey/status/1062469103926108160?lang=en.

McNally, Richard J. 2007. "Dispelling Confusion About Traumatic Dissociative Amnesia." Mayo Clinic Proceedings, September 2007, 82(9): 1083–87. https://www.mayoclinicproceedings.org/article/S0025-6196(11)61370-0/pdf.

Mitchell, Jerry. 2017. "Most dangerous time for battered women? When they leave." *Clarion Ledger*, January 28, 2017. https://www.clarionledger.com/story/news/2017/01/28/most-dangerous-time-for-battered-women-is-when-they-leave-jerry-mitchell/96955552/.

Murdock, Sebastian. 2018. "Lauren McCluskey Sought Help Against A Dangerous Man. She Still Died." *Huffington Post*, December 28, 2018. https://www.huffpost.com/entry/lauren-mccluskey-university-of-utah-domestic-violence_n_5c268d9ee4b08aaf7a905aef.

Reavy, Pat. 2018. "Report: University of Utah police understaffed, but student's murder may not have been preventable." *Deseret News*, December 19, 2018. https://www.deseretnews.com/article/900047256/officials-release-details-of-independent-investigation-into-lauren-mccluskey-case.html.

Romboy, Dennis. 2019. "Parents of slain student Lauren McCluskey sue University of Utah for $56 million." *Deseret News*, June 27, 2019. https://www.deseretnews.com/article/900077182/lauren-mccluskey-parents-sue-university-of-utah.html.

Row, Jess. 2018. "Why Is Being Held Accountable So Terrifying Under Patriarchy?" *New Yorker*, November 30, 2018. https://www.newyorker.com/culture/culture-desk/why-is-being-held-accountable-so-terrifying-under-patriarchy.

"Samuel Johnson." 2019. *SamuelJohnson.com* https://www.samueljohnson.com/.

"Sexual Violence Surveillance." 2009. *CDC.gov*. https://www.cdc.gov/violenceprevention/pdf/sv_surveillance_definitionsl-2009-a.pdf.

Smay, Ian and Dylan Green. 2018. "Records show numerous allegations of sexual misconduct against Jason Gesser." https://dailyevergreen.com/36274/news/records-show-numerous-allegations-of-sexual-misconduct-against-jason-gesser/.

Tanner, Courtney. 2018. "Lauren McCluskey's parents disagree with the University of Utah's claim that her murder could not have been prevented—and they want university staff disciplined." *Salt Lake City Tribune*, December 20, 2018. https://www.sltrib.com/news/2018/12/20/lauren-mccluskeys-parents/.

Vigdor, Neil. 2019. "'Revenge Suicide Hypothesis' Offered by Lawyer for Estranged Husband of Missing Woman." *New York Times*, July 2, 2019. https://www.nytimes.com/2019/07/02/nyregion/jennifer-dulos-missing-connecticut.html?searchResultPosition=3.

Watkins, Ali. 2019. "Jeffrey Epstein Is Indicted on Sex Charges as Discovery of Nude Photos Is Disclosed." *New York Times*, July 8, 2019. https://www.nytimes.com/2019/07/08/nyregion/jeffrey-epstein-charges.html.

"What Are PTSD Triggers." 2019. *WebMD.com.* https://www.webmd.com/mental-health/what-are-ptsd-triggers#1.

"A Year of Impact: National Domestic Violence Hotline." 2018. *TheHotline.org.* http://www.thehotline.org/wp-content/uploads/sites/3/2018/06/2017-Impact-Report-DigitalFINAL.pdf.

Chapter Eleven

Beaches, Books, Baseball, and Being One of the Guys

Katherine Chelsea

Twenty-four hours after I woke up naked and bleeding in the bed of the man who raped me, I found myself bobbing in a shark cage above five hundred feet of the bluest water I'd ever seen.

I'd spent the previous day in a daze, still in shock that my virginity had been extinguished in such a blaze of fear and pain. The cage rose with the swells and collapsed back into the trough with a satisfying crash. My fingers clenched around the bar until my knuckles glowed white and my naked legs kicked to keep myself vertical. My heart pounded and I waited for fins to slice through the surf or phantom shapes to sharpen into missiles that would crush the skimming turtles in a great surface-shattering launch.

I thought the sharks would be the most dangerous part of that trip. I was wrong. Leaving my drink unattended while I went to the bathroom was far more dangerous.

In the weeks to come I would suddenly recall the feeling of sheer help-lessness under an unfamiliar and heavy body. I would remember his hands around my neck and the awful realization that he was getting off to my pain. I would remember the nausea of soreness and the shock of blood as I sat up as soon as he headed to the bathroom, the quick scanning of the dim, messy room, the surreality of my sandy softball t-shirt crumpled on a stranger's floor. I would remember dressing myself faster than I ever had, electrified as if my life depended on it, and stumbling to the front door in a blind haze.

My jagged memory has edited the footage of those fourteen hours and that house and that man. I have snapshots of that run out of that house. Somewhere I ran into a plumeria tree. Perversely, one bloom got caught in my hair, tucked behind my ear as if placed there by a lover. I ran barefoot in a daze. At one point I almost got hit by a car and the driver cursed at me. I wanted to sob, apologize for being in the way. I ended up at the beach and sat on a pristine stretch of white sand. A beautiful family asked me to take their picture and their toddler asked why I was crying. The parents moved on and asked someone else to take their picture instead.

There was blood on my shorts so I swam for a long time and half-hoped a current would drag me out so I wouldn't have to tell my mom what happened.

I assumed I would know what to do and do what I was supposed to but I swam and showered and brushed my teeth and showered again and swam again and I hated myself for it but I couldn't stop. In a rare cogent moment I laughed at the cruel irony and cognitive dissonance of experiencing such profound sadness in such a beautiful place. I felt guilty for being miserable in paradise.

Shock. Shark cage. My lifelong bucket list item achieved and I felt nothing. It was just a blank swath of memory. I got on a plane. I came home. My puffy-eyed boyfriend was waiting with sunflowers at baggage claim at LAX. We drove in a blind haze to the Santa Monica Rape Treatment Center. There were locks and buzzers and strict hierarchies of space and kind receptionists with gentle voices. I couldn't help but think of *The Handmaid's Tale* as I was assigned a lady protector and we walked as a little solemn pair across the street. We passed two other pairs of sunken-eyed girls, two other keepers of our genitals.

The blur of the cozy reception area (snacks, paperwork, tissues, paperwork, pillows, paperwork) and the stark horror of the exam room (tiny closet, hyperventilating as I took my clothes off, the soothing technician's voice as she ran the black light over me to assess the bruises). The hard exam table. Wondering whose shrieks those were. Biting down on my hand as the doctor whom I told myself was not there to hurt me but could not help but recoil from as she inched her tools inside of me. Taking a break while they brought me a heated blanket. Wrapping myself up like a burrito that had to be opened on one end so it could be poked and prodded. Answering the nurse's questions about my favorite books that I knew were intended to distract me but that I appreciated nonetheless. Hearing my voice break on the last syllable of "mockingbird" as they swabbed my torn anus.

Clothes back on but I'm still dripping sweat and my heart beats like a hummingbird. Back to the exam area. Writhing to get away from myself and the sensation of recent penetration even though I know it was well-intended. More paperwork, more forms, more fliers, more folders. Everything put-together and professional and institutionalized.

Calendarizing. Last period. Schedule a checkup for every four weeks. When does school start? Do you know if your school insurance covers therapy? That's okay. We'll find someone for you. Here are the pills. Take this one with food or you'll vomit and don't take this one with food or you'll vomit. Drink a lot of water and don't be alarmed when they turn your pee brown. Here are some more folders to explain the side effects. They're all terrible but necessary. Gentle adjusting of glasses and soft voices grow softer. Because of the extent of the tears in your vagina and anus, you're at a higher risk for HIV, so we'll make sure you do the checkups every three months for the next year. Are you going to report? Are you ready to fly back to Hawai'i every few months to go through the process of depositions and identifications and testimonials? Can you do it?

The institutionalization of it all just killed me. Thousands of people before myself had gingerly sat in this same seat, bruised, tormented crotch and all, and been handed these same navy folders and wondered what the hell they were going to do now. We were part of a process that was there to help us, which I knew I should be grateful for, but I could not help but loathe the necessity of this process. I hated that thousands of people had sat in this same chair.

I always assumed that I would know what to do if I found myself in that unthinkable situation. It's so easy to assume you know what you're doing until it happens to you. When you are a hypothetical victim you are alert, rational, and thinking ahead to the steps that must be taken, the people that must be called, the tests that must be done. When you are an actual victim you are paralyzed and want nothing more than to feel clean again as soon as possible. The steps seem insurmountable. The people are alien. And the tests are terrifyingly invasive.

I left my three-year career in the entertainment industry to enter a Literature PhD program, and had naively hoped that a four-day solo backpacking trip to Hawai'i would rejuvenate and re-inspire me in the short few weeks between my Los Angeles life and my San Diego life. I'd gone to Oahu in search of confidence. I returned to California completely derailed. Like a great white shark devouring a turtle, the feeling of suffocating helplessness returned whenever some small reminder set me off and shattered the calm surface I'd been determined to maintain. I was diagnosed with anxiety, depression, and PTSD the week before I turned twenty-five. I moved to San Diego the day after my first therapy appointment. I started my program. I would not be eligible to see a therapist at school for two more months.

Grad student orientation fell on my birthday. Thousands of strangers crowded into an auditorium and I couldn't breathe and I couldn't focus on what the various chancellors were saying and I couldn't take it anymore and I tried to walk like a normal person until I felt that I was far enough away from my new colleagues to run away in my business casual attire and not worry about being seen. That afternoon I swam in the ocean for three hours.

I was surprised by what set me off. I was simultaneously agoraphobic and claustrophobic—exposed, vulnerable, caught, detached—but I was also in new, hard classes and trying to make new, cool friends and pretending that my brain was a productive, absorbing organ.

I wanted to feel normal. I pretended to be fine.

I tried to track my triggers with anthropological interest on a long email chain to myself with the subject line "progress," ever the optimistic academic, believing that every observation and every experience was fodder for self-improvement and creativity and life lessons that could benefit someone else (I hoped. I hoped so hard.). Books and the beach kept the bad stuff at bay, but new bad stuff (or regular old stuff that now seemed bad) reared its ugly head every day. I showered in the dark and couldn't make eye contact with men at the grocery store and lost ten pounds in a month. My familial-inculcated stance on premarital sex just felt laughable now so I had sex with my boyfriend and cried after he left.

The classroom and the library, my lifelong havens, became additional battlegrounds of memory. I felt like my loves of language and literature were turning against me, dredging up new sources of unwanted reminders. I hated the self-help books' calming covers and innocuous titles (or rather, I hated the necessity of them). I especially hated (or rather, hated the accuracy of) self-help statements that were eerily precise. Erin Carpenter's *Life Reinvented* proved to be truly marvelous, but I had to set it down after reading "Survivors may only see themselves through others' eyes; they view their value as what they can do for others, rather than seeing their own intrinsic value as individuals. They often act like 'people-pleasers' and go out of their way to fit in. They are described as givers and caretakers, often thinking of others' needs before their own" (Carpenter 2014, 50). Teaching was the only time I felt some semblance of self-esteem because I knew I was helping my students; when I was not in a position to help others I felt utterly worthless.

I learned that part of the standard post-rape depression stems from previous sources of comfort becoming new sources of stress, catalyzing feelings of loss. I felt like I was mourning my old self as things that used to provide joy just provided unwelcome indications of the newly carved sense of difference between my Before Self and my After Self, setting them on opposite sides of an insurmountable chasm the size of the Grand Canyon. During one of my first grad seminars I learned that the French expression for "orgasm" is "le petite mort." My Before Self would have marveled at the intricacies of language; my After Self wondered at the parallels between death and sex and death and the opposite of orgasm.

It is impossible to escape mentions of rape in literature. It is everywhere, even (especially) in the places I didn't want to see it or think about it or consider the possibility of it existing. I abhorred rape as a plot device, loathed it as a tragic backstory, resented it when it was perceived as the turning point that turned someone from sweet to shattered. *Harry Potter* is the comfort blanket that I have always wrapped around myself when sick, sad, or scared;

about one month after the rape I slammed *Half-Blood Prince* shut, fuming, and wondered if Merope Gaunt had raped Tom Riddle Senior. Were Fred and George selling love potions the way that some asshole had sold my rapist date rape drugs? Would Mad-Eye Moody say it was my fault for not practicing constant vigilance?

Panic rose as I started reevaluating every book I had ever read. How many potential rapes had I not noticed? Why was this so normalized? I felt like I was viewing everything through a new lens that kept me on-edge and terribly over-aware. This unwanted alertness salted old wounds and opened fresh ones. I wondered if I was overreacting and overanalyzing, then wondered if I was noticing things that had always been there, then felt guilty for my own obliviousness. Had I missed friends' cries for help? Had I failed to recognize the signs that I now could not escape in myself? What else had I missed?

During my first quarter of teaching I taught the Bible and my students laughed at incest and I cried for Dinah in a corner of our campus Starbucks during a ten-minute break between classes. I learned that the best prevention of panic attacks in three-hour graduate seminars was forcing myself to write all the countries in alphabetical order. The harried pages of my notebook from my first theory class look like the ramblings of a lunatic: "Marquis de Sade? (Afghanistan, Albania, Algeria)" . . . "Freud anal stage (Bahamas, Bahrain, Bangladesh)" . . . "Eagleton rape of Clarissa . . . (Cambodia, Cameroon, Canada)."

Even though I sometimes felt like academia was drowning me in reminders, I was grateful for my tendency to overanalyze; it helped me maintain some semblance of objective distance. The morning after, when I sat on the beach, I felt like a forensic criminologist as I examined my own bruised and bloodied body and mentally drafted the report I would give the RTC doctors. In the two weeks I spent at my mom's house before I moved, I scoured a pile of books and articles, desperate to find answers about my own body and the memory that I feared I could no longer trust. Alice Sebold's *Lucky* (1999) became the Rosetta Stone that allowed me to translate myself, and her line "You save yourself or you remain unsaved" became the mantra that I wrote obsessively in my journal and whispered to myself as I fought back panic attacks in the bathroom between classes. I tried to predict triggers and evaluated them with exhausting cost-benefit analysis methods from high school economics. My childhood best friend gave me a book about the Japanese art of *kintsugi* (repairing broken pottery with gold), and I was so touched by her beautiful metaphor that I immediately dove into more art history books. I learned about trauma studies and considered the parallels between depictions of soldiers and rape survivors in literature. I learned about screen memory and marveled at how I had failed to recognize this obvious concept in children's literature and vowed never to be that ignorant again. I would see better, think harder, and be a better advocate for characters who needed one.

But was it enough to advocate just for characters? How could I use this to advocate for real people too? How could I, a straight white person, use my position of privilege to empathize with and create a better world for those who do not benefit from antiquated prejudices? I clung to critical thinking with clawed desperation.

Literature had molded me and saved me countless times, and I knew that I had to rely on it now more than ever. It wasn't so much a life raft as it was an anchor; old books reminded me of the person I was when I first read them and new books offered the possibility of change. I could get through it. Books would get me through it. I forced myself to journal every day, which sometimes manifested as broken country-list fragments that resembled my seminar notes, but occasionally included slim glimpses of my mental status. Most of the time I just wrote someone else's quote that more succinctly expressed what I was feeling.

October 10, Chad Harbach's *The Art of Fielding:* "Literature could turn you into an asshole: he'd learned that teaching grad-school seminars. It could teach you to treat real people the way you did characters, as instruments of your own intellectual pleasure, cadavers on which to practice your critical faculties" (Harbach 2011, 328).

October 22, George Eliot's *The Mill on the Floss*: "They had entered the thorny wilderness, and the golden gates of their childhood had forever closed behind them" (Eliot 1860, 224).

November 1, Tolkien's *The Hobbit*: "'Go back?' he thought. 'No good at all! Go sideways? Impossible! Go forward? Only thing to do! On we go!'" (Tolkien 1937, 69).

Before I left for Hawai'i I'd been deep into my second novel and had idealistically imagined revising my draft on a beach somewhere, free from distraction. Of course that plan had been derailed. There were a few optimistic moments after school started when I opened the draft and stared blankly at the screen, wondering at this new feeling of paralysis. The creative well had gone dry. I could write objective analytical essays just fine, but now I struggled more than ever to do something that had always been a tremendous source of joy. I worried that I was losing myself. I wondered how much more of myself I had to lose before I could fix myself. I wanted to be alone and write, then hated being alone; I wanted to be around other people and talk, but when I was around others, I couldn't wait to be alone. I couldn't write and I couldn't think and I couldn't get away from what I didn't want to think about. As an extrovert who gains energy from the presence of her friends, feeling incapable of socializing left me even more tired and drained. I only felt energized by taking care of others, but being around them required extra social batteries that I did not seem to possess and so could not recharge.

Experiencing this process during the #MeToo movement was surreal and horrible and validating and exhausting. Each day we relived someone else's trauma and hurried to categorize what was acceptable and what was not. My former entertainment colleagues, with whom I did not share my experience, eagerly texted me updates about men we'd loathed working for as they made painfully overt efforts to ingratiate themselves to women they'd abused and hoped to prevent from coming forward. The texts' tones were satisfied, jovial, as if they were sharing juicy gossip to satiate me in my dry ivory tower. I could not help but wonder what my life would be like if I were still in LA, an unraped virgin who could read about Harvey Weinstein without knowing how his victims felt. Maybe I would have already lost my virginity to my loving boyfriend and considered it a wonderful experience rather than a traumatic event. At my three-months-post-rape mark in November, during the Louis C.K. week, I contracted a horrible flu that unfortunately mirrored the symptoms of HIV that manifest three months after contact. A segment on Roy Moore played in the waiting room while I waited to find out if I was HIV-positive and I wished I could talk to the girls he'd hurt and ask them if they ever got over it.

November 20 entry, Pat Conroy's *The Prince of Tides*: "Rape is a crime against sleep and memory; its afterimage imprints itself like an irreversible negative from the camera obscura of dreams" (Conroy 1986, 483).

My former industry pretended it was set aflame but was put out by crocodile tears. I was outraged but not surprised by the ease of hiding behind half-assed hashtagged solidarity. Like any well-intended movement, #MeToo could not prevent the misappropriation and manipulation of the signs and signifiers that were supposed to grant power to those who needed it. The master's tools could not dismantle the master's house.

Social media became even more exhausting than usual, but during broken insomniac nights I couldn't stop myself from scrolling blearily through others' opinions: strangers, celebrities, entertainment friends, academic friends, Friends Who Knew, Friends Who Didn't. In December, during my first finals week, Matt Damon received considerable criticism for saying that sexual assault occurs on a spectrum. The group chat of entertainment friends lambasted Damon and agreed with Alyssa Milano's "it's the micro that makes the macro" Tweet, but the more recently formed group chat of Friends Who Have Also Been Raped (a helpful and sadly necessary outlet where we shared memes about depression that we couldn't share with Friends Who Have Not Been Raped) quietly agreed with Damon's contention that "there is a difference between . . . patting someone on the butt and rape" (Eppolito 2017).

In this group chat, I am the only one who worked in the entertainment industry; during my three years working in television, I had my butt "patted" by my bosses and coworkers more times than I could count. I had my ass grabbed and my breasts ogled and offers to "hang out" at male bosses' and coworkers' homes. My coworkers "surprised" the youngest member of the office by taking me to a strip club when I thought we were going to a bar. I was told that I should be honored to hear "locker room talk" about my female coworkers because it meant that my male coworkers considered me "one of the guys." Male coworkers "accidentally" rubbed against me in tiny kitchens and elevators and male bosses asked me to bend over more slowly and wear shorter skirts. At my last job my direct supervisor "sexted" me as he sat five feet away from me, smiling. Shaken, I went to the EVP and showed him the texts, and he laughed and said I should be flattered.

Those experiences and the dudes who perpetuated them all certainly emerged from the same primordial ooze. Those micro and not-so-micro aggressions were demoralizing and unwarranted, but I rank these different violations on a spectrum that ranges from "I think about this every day and it makes me feel disgusting" to "I think about this every day and now I have panic attacks and PTSD." The "micros" felt like I was being slowly waterboarded, as if my tormentors were trying to break down my resistance drip by drip; rape made me feel like I was drowning. Both types of violations leave you reevaluating all your decisions and wondering at what point you supposedly signaled that you wanted that attention and hating that no one cares that you absolutely did not want that. They leave you in a frightful state of self-loathing. I cannot speak for every person who has experienced these, but for myself, the spectrum of impact is very real. I could get through the micros but I wasn't sure if I could get through the macro.

January. "Me too" gave way to "New year, new me" and none of it felt sincere anymore, but I couldn't tell if everyone else thought that or if I was just viewing things with my new pessimistic lens. I was certain, unfortunately, that rape had become the elephant in the bed of my relationship, and that relationship was crumbling under the weight of it. Of course we'd had other issues before all of this happened, but those pressures felt magnified under dying-rose-tinted glasses. My boyfriend had been wonderfully helpful in the preceding months, and I could not have been more grateful for the compassion he demonstrated when I woke up gasping and needed to be held. We both felt guilty and sad and tried to overcompensate and we both failed. I felt like he could do better; he had a life to lead and driving two hours to see me was not helping him. I broke up with him on January 14 (after R. Kelly, before Bryan Singer) and felt relieved that I wouldn't drag him down anymore. I think we both felt relieved that we didn't have to try anymore.

It was my fifth month of living in San Diego. I still broke into a sweat when a male student entered my tiny office for office hours. After five months of bulimia I was back to my sophomore-year-of-high-school weight and I couldn't stand the sight of myself in the mirror. I had tried confiding in a school friend who told me I was a bad feminist for not reporting the rape. Therapy helped, but with the time restrictions posed by grad school and the necessity of working multiple jobs, I had to choose between making a therapy appointment (and spending money) or keeping a tutoring appointment (and getting paid). I still could not sleep and spent broken nights researching everything I needed answers for.

Learning that I was not alone both helped and hurt. Statistically, three in four rapes go unreported; for every person who was braver than I was, there were three of us who were hurting in silence. I learned that the feeling of frozen helplessness I had experienced during the part of the attack when I was conscious was called tonic immobility, "a state of involuntary paralysis. . . . In animals this reaction is considered an evolutionary adaptive defense to an attack by a predator when other forms of defense are not possible" (Russo 2017). I cried at the irony when I learned that sharks manifest this behavior. I cried at the validation that what I was experiencing was not uncommon: ". . . those who experienced extreme tonic immobility were twice as likely to suffer post-traumatic stress disorder (PTSD) and three times more likely to suffer severe depression in the months after the attack than women who did not have this response. . . . [Tonic immobility] has been observed in soldiers in battle as well as in survivors of sexual assault" (Russo 2017). Heidt et al.'s 2005 "Tonic Immobility and Childhood Sexual Abuse: A Preliminary Report Evaluating the Sequela of Rape-Induced Paralysis" found that 52 percent of female undergraduates who reported childhood sexual abuse also experienced this paralysis. Fight or flight is not an option for those who are powerless to do anything but play dead.

Thankfully, I was not sexually abused as a child, but I grew up with a violent dad whose outbursts targeted his children, especially the oldest (me) who was willing to take it to spare the others. With something like poisonous nostalgia I remembered evaluating the cost-benefit analysis of a Dad Meltdown: trying to evaluate the source of his anger, determining if I could stop it and if I could stop it within the necessary time limit before the eruption, trying to keep him as calm as possible to neutralize the situation, looking for the nearest exit point for the younger ones, preventing myself from expressing emotion in case it aggravated him. My siblings and I have always jokingly referred to ourselves as "war buddies," and as I revisited my favorite books that depicted war veterans, I could not help seeing the same exhausting alertness, the same constant scanning for danger, the depletion of self-worth provoked by the perpetual willingness to sacrifice yourself. Just as *Mrs. Dalloway*'s veteran Septimus Smith was rendered powerless by "this gradual drawing together of everything to one center before his eyes, as if some horror had come almost to the surface and was about to burst into flames," (Woolf 1925, 15) I felt paralyzed by the sensation of constant, immovable threats hovering around me. I could not control them. I could not avoid them. My only sense of self-preservation was motivated by my need to protect those who needed my help; there was no one else to save now, and I did not always feel worthy of being saved, or capable of saving myself.

The first therapist I saw in November marveled that I was "doing so well" and congratulated me on the survival skills that I had acquired from growing up with an abusive dad, as if she were a job interviewer lauding an unexpected asset on a candidate's CV.

Reading depictions of rape in literature felt strangely voyeuristic, but I could not stop myself, driven by some sick curiosity to see how others wrote about it. I wondered perversely if I could tell the difference between depictions written by people who have experienced it and people who have not. I felt weirdly compelled to learn more about depictions of it in books and movies and TV shows and music. Exposing myself to these depictions never yielded positive results; I was either disappointed by unrealistic, unsympathetic portrayals or horrified by those that hit home with chilling accuracy. Immersion therapy failed me, but I felt a strange duty to be knowledgeable about a club in which I had reluctantly assumed membership.

As I dove in, I again wondered about the possibility of actual change within my former industry. Relatively recent rape-featuring works of literature that have been adapted and received considerable commercial and popular acclaim include *Deliverance* (1970), *The Color Purple* (1982), *The Green Mile* (1996), *Game of Thrones* (1996), *Atonement* (2001), *The Kite Runner* (2003), and *The Girl With the Dragon Tattoo* (2005), and as I reread and rewatched these I struggled to reconcile my understanding of how rape functions as a device for characterization. Why do books that contain rape become prime fodder for adaptation? Is taboo titillating? How is gratuitous violence towards women treated differently than gratuitous violence towards men? Are raped women of color ever presented with the possibility of agency? As I paged through "less overt" depictions in my worn copies of *Gone with the Wind* (1936) and *A Streetcar Named Desire* (1947) I marveled at the fact that my education in these texts had failed to mention *very* overt representations of rape. As I rewatched *Sixteen Candles* (1984) and *Back to the Future* (1985) I hated myself for not recognizing problematic aspects of these films the first time I watched them, then remembered that I first watched them in middle school. By not recognizing these as problematic, had I rendered myself complicit in my own undoing? My thoughts turned to the future and the children I plan to eventually have. How will I teach them about depictions of rape? How will I teach them to recognize what is problematic? I hated that I used to so dearly enjoy what I now saw as egregiously, offensively wrong, then felt guilty that I had ever enjoyed them in the first place.

Of course, this is by no means an isolated twentieth- or twenty-first-century phenomenon. The prototypical Sleeping Beauty, Zellandine (c. 1528), was impregnated in her sleep. We see rape as a plot device in *The Wife of Bath's Tale* (c. 1387–1400*)*, *The Rape of Lucrece* (1594), *Titus*

Andronicus (c. 1588–1593), and *The Spanish Gypsy* (Middleton, 1621). Helen of Troy and the Sabine women were rape-able pawns in a chess game over which they had no control. Empires rise and fall with the objectification and destruction of women's bodies. Rape is used as a reasonable basis of revenge and justification for an honor killing: women are raped so that men may act.

This idea bothered me to no end. What constitutes an empowered rape victim in literature, and how can we emulate that example in real life? Is an empowered rape victim someone who seeks revenge on or makes peace with her rapist? Is a "positive" depiction of rape one in which the female victim successfully avenges herself? Is Lisbeth Salander's act of tattooing "I am a sadistic pig, a pervert, and a rapist" on Nils Bjurman the level of unattainable badass revenge to which we should aspire? When the legal system (or our personal limitations that prevent us from accessing the legal system) fails us, what options remain?

Reading and researching (and it felt so blasphemous to admit this) were not enough to fix myself. I knew I needed to make friends and learn how to make eye contact with men and feel like a normal twenty-five-year-old. My therapist asked me to brainstorm helpful outlets of socialization and I immediately decided on softball. I hoped that playing in a slow-pitch coed league would help re-socialize me around men in an environment where I felt confident and capable. Fast-pitch softball had dominated my life from age four to eighteen; my love for the game and my long history with it are sewn into the scars on my knees and shins, the creaky, crooked ankles and fingers that have been sprained dozens of times, and the scar tissue that has decorated my brain since my first concussion. For the first time I realized that dealing with softball injuries had introduced me to the negotiations of the relationship between body, memory, and trauma that I now struggled to reconcile on a much more extreme scale. Since I had already proved that I could deal with that as a teenager, shouldn't it be easier for me to deal with it as an adult?

I signed up for a local league and was assigned to the pink team, which felt strangely appropriate. As I entered the bleachers where my new pink-clad coed teammates gathered I felt pre-game adrenaline mixing with pre-meeting-new-people jitters and mingling into anxious butterflies. How long had it been since I last approached new team members at the start of a new season, something that I used to consider a thrilling opportunity to make friends in a place that I loved? I remembered how Harry felt walking through the Dursleys' house for the last time: "It gave him an odd, empty feeling to remember those times; it was like remembering a younger brother whom he had lost" (Rowling 2007, 44). As I played catch (with a man!) for the first time in years I felt my muscles readjusting to old harmonies and began slinging the ball faster with each throw until my partner was shaking his stinging glove hand. I hid a grin. It felt nice to be good at something again.

Once I stepped out on the diamond I knew I'd made the right decision. I could marvel at my body's reflexive reactions instead of being afraid of them, and the roots of these actions—the thousands of hours of games and practices and workouts—were cause for pride, not shame. For nearly half a year I'd shied away from my own memory, reeling from everything I wished I could avoid; I recoiled from sensations that reverberated with potential triggers, launching not so much a preemptive strike as a preemptive block. As I ran to second base I felt awash in welcome, unblocked nostalgia, recalling the thousands of times I had run that same route in hundreds of cities, sweltering heat, pouring rain, surprising hail, drifting ashes during fire season. I claimed second as my position in t-ball and played it all through high school and travel ball, learning it like a language and loving it like a friend. As I settled into my old position on this new field, I felt like myself for the first time in months.

I went the entire length of our first game without dwelling on the rape, and realizing that afterwards brought such bittersweet joy that I wanted to weep. Seventy minutes had never felt so short.

Over the next eleven months, my softball skills earned my new teammates' respect, and while it was easy to make new friends in this environment, I had a harder time forcing myself to attend the post-game bar ritual. I told myself that short-term discomfort was necessary for long-term healing; forcing myself to talk to male teammates became a sort of immersion therapy where I learned how to negotiate the process of re-socialization and handle triggering environments. I forced myself to laugh at their accusations of paranoia as I covered my drink at the bar and brought my own to team parties. As I grew closer to my teammates and was praised for being "one of the guys" they stopped filtering their conversations around me, and I found myself in another locker room like that I'd unwillingly entered at my production company.

In Los Angeles, I had been afraid to speak out, worrying that calling out my coworkers or bosses would prevent my advancement in the company or cause me to lose good standing with potential recommendation writers. I hated how cliché it was and spent hours replaying conversations in which I added in things I wished I'd had the guts to say the first time, when they would have mattered. My silence had rendered me complicit in my own undoing, but I would not make that mistake again.

In the "locker room" of a slow-pitch softball team, I was bound to no career-oriented restrictions, and in my angry state I could not care less if my blunt calling-out of misogynistic comments offended my teammates. My male teammates laughed when I was "triggered" (they used it facetiously) by some inanely sexist comment and launched into a scathing lecture, but I felt satisfied that I was no longer silencing myself. They rolled their eyes when "angry feminist mode was activated" (the left fielder's words), but I hoped that this time I would be the one waterboarding and slowly breaking them down. I was so determined to fix this very frustrating aspect of dudes with whom I mostly enjoyed hanging out. In hindsight, perhaps the amount of effort I was devoting to "fixing" them should have indicated that it was a lost cause, but I was determined to maintain these friendships. We spent the summer going to Padres games and barbecues and bonfires; I spent the summer naively hoping I could turn them into feminists—or at the very least, less naïve perpetuators of rape culture.

September opened with Les Moonves stepping down and Christine Blasey Ford speaking out and Soon-Yi Previn defending Woody Allen. I celebrated my birthday at a bonfire with my teammates and they made Kavanaugh jokes and I retorted bitterly, feeling exhausted by the guys and betrayed by the girls. I ran into the dark bay and swam until our fire was a tiny spark and my muscles shook with cold. Exactly a year before, I'd gone swimming after grad school orientation and wished that a current would just drag me away. I was stronger now. I was fiercer now. I would not let myself be dragged.

I settled into the rhythm of the new school year: Friday nights were for softball and the post-game bar ritual, Sunday nights were for team bonfires, every other night was a reading night. Even as the fall air temperature sank to California Cold (fifties at night) and the water felt even colder, my Sunday swims in the dark, shallow bay felt oddly insulated and safe and cathartic. I was back to a healthy weight and handling PTSD, school, two side jobs, and conferences, and almost felt like my old self. I was preparing a dissertation on tomboys and found it fitting that I had been drawn to figures who gain agency through sport. I submitted the abstract for this chapter on November 26, 2018, planning to write about how "devising my own healing process is a tremendous privilege. For most of my life I have been defined by my loves of literature and softball, and now the two are working together in ways I never could have imagined. I intend to save myself as best I can, and I hope that my own process helps someone who needs it."

December 14 was the last day of the academic quarter and our last game of the season. It had been sixteen months since the rape, which none of my teammates—whom I now considered my best friends in San Diego—knew about. I felt like my life was under my control again. I went to a bar with these friends every Friday and felt like a Normal Person who could talk to a male stranger without having a panic attack. (Nothing romantic—I was definitely not at that point yet—just enough small talk and friendly conversation to make me feel like a Normal Person.)

We won our last game and I felt rather satisfied that even after pulling an all-nighter to perfect my last essay, I had gone 4–5 and made a diving catch that left both knees bloody but victorious. Our usual bar was hosting a Christmas party, so the group voted to go to a trendy place downtown, and we caravanned over and all tried to park near a male teammate's apartment. I was not pleased with this plan; not only were we sweaty and dirty (and in my case, bloody) and would probably be rejected from or looked down upon at an overpriced Gaslamp establishment, but I was also exhausted and felt obligated to put in face time at our victory celebration, and in order to sneak out early I would have to walk a few blocks by myself back to my car in an unsafe area. I held my keys slotted in my clenched fist as I power-walked to the bar and told myself I would stay for an hour.

The new bar's patio was aglow with Christmas lights but freezing, and I wrapped my hands around my Earl Grey to keep warm. I was definitely too tired to drink, too tired to be out at all, and dehydrated after chugging needed caffeine for the past twenty-four hours. I had to tutor at 8 a.m. the next morning, then drive one hundred miles north for my mom's company Christmas party. At exactly an hour after my arrival, I announced my intent to depart, played off the cries of "party pooper," and accepted an offer to be walked to my car by the teammate whose apartment I'd parked near. As we weaved past sketchy-looking individuals on dark streets I felt grateful to be walking with a man. When we got to his apartment he asked if I wanted water and to see his dog (not unusual—I had stopped by his apartment before just to play with her), and I accepted. When we went inside he pushed me down on his couch and tore off my sweatpants and shoved himself inside me.

My exhaustion dissolved as adrenaline kicked in and my thoughts roared furiously ("not again," "how could you let this happen," "SAVE YOUR-SELF OR YOU REMAIN UNSAVED") and I asked him to stop and then screamed for him to stop and tried to push him off of me and then shut down as I realized he knew I was asking him to stop and he kept hurting me.

I wish I remembered this in snapshots as well, but there were no foreign substances poisoning my bloodstream, no Rohypnol nor even alcohol, just electrified fear and confusion. I had thought of him as a goofy friend for nearly a year. He never demonstrated an ounce of attraction towards me—he made fun of me all the time and I was happy to have a platonic male friend who never demonstrated any interest in me. I needed that. And now it was gone.

I remember again asking him to stop in a voice that sounded like a whimper and him telling me that he knew I wanted it. I remember his dog climbing onto the couch as he was thrusting into me and some foolish part of me hoped that this would somehow make him realize he was doing something wrong but he kept going and hot tears trickled down my cheeks. I remember wondering if he was going to kill me. I remember thinking "if I leave this apartment alive I don't know how I'm going to go through it all again." I laid there wondering what I had done wrong to make this happen again and hating that the score was now 1–2: Consensual Partner 1, Rapists 2.

Sixteen months of work and "progress" emails and controlling the gradually decreasing panic attacks. Sixteen months of waking up gasping, finally getting to the point where I could almost sleep through the night, pushing myself to make male friends, forcing myself into self-prescribed immersion therapy where I told myself I had to learn to feel comfortable so that I could feel normal again. Months and months of work. Gone.

I thought I'd done everything right that night. I didn't drink. I didn't walk by myself. I trusted a male friend with whom I'd been alone before.

As if on autopilot, as if I'd already rehearsed for a terrible part in a play that I did not want, I sat up gingerly when he went in the bathroom and dressed like my life depended on it and got away from that place as fast as I could. As I ran numbly to my car I thought of a chillingly bloodless post-assault passage from Audre Lorde's *Zami*: "I thought it was all pretty stupid, and he got cum all over the back of my dungarees" (Lorde 1982, 105).

Just as I had the first time, I showered and scrubbed him out of me until I finally felt empty and brushed my teeth and threw up out of disgust and brushed my teeth again and showered again and cried in a small ball on the floor of the shower and wondered how I'd let myself get to this point.

Being raped by someone I'd considered a friend for nearly a year was much worse than being raped by a stranger. I considered telling our teammates, our mutual friends, the people who had gotten me through a really rough time without knowing how big a role they were playing in my life. Friday night slow-pitch softball with platonic male friends had truly helped me. And now it betrayed me.

I have never felt so stupid and so conflicted. I thought I couldn't report a friend. I mentally scanned through eleven months of interactions, trying to recall if there was ever a time when I expressed anything that could be perceived as an iota of interest towards him (nope) or if he ever expressed anything remotely romantic towards me (Maybe? Had I misread things? Was it my fault?). I couldn't report a friend. But he had demonstrated that he wasn't a friend. Maybe I had somehow indicated something romantic towards him at one point that I could not remember? Maybe he thought it was a misunderstanding and it was my fault for not communicating clearly enough that I did not want to have sex with him? But I had cried and said "stop" and "please stop" and "I don't want to do this" multiple times. There was no way he could interpret that as consensual sex. I had clearly asked him to stop multiple times and he had clearly chosen to ignore me. He did not see me as a friend. He did not see me as a person.

This time I knew what to do and still let myself down and took six showers before I went to the doctor. Once again shame enabled illogical conclusions ("I can't cancel the shark cage because I'll have to tell them I was raped." "I can't not go to my mom's Christmas party because then I'll have to tell her I was raped."). I couldn't put my family through that again. I couldn't put myself through that again. Once again I did not report it. I got the antibiotics and Plan B and all the necessary measures we have created to minimize collateral damage and those that this affects. I shielded myself with the tools that would guarantee this was something only I had to deal with. No one else needed to know or be affected by it.

Once again I dove into research, looking for an explanation for something I never would have predicted from someone I'd considered a platonic friend. Courtney Fraser's excellent "'Ladies First' to 'Asking for It': Benevolent Sexism in the Maintenance of Rape Culture" helpfully delineated the difference between benevolent sexism (women are pure and we must protect them) and hostile sexism (women are trying to control us and we must put them in their place) (Fraser 2015, 141–203). One of Fraser's headings, "'I Know You Want It': How Benevolent Sexism Constructs Consent" reminded me horribly of Rape 2. As Fraser describes, the idea that women are "pure" also suggests that we do not necessarily lack sex drive, but lack the ability (or the permission) to express desire because it renders us less "pure." It deprives us of our voice.

I did not get a kit done this time. I regret that every day.

In May 2019, twenty-one months after Rape 1 and six months after Rape 2, a school friend (who knew about both of them) told me to stop being miserable and afraid of men and go on a date. "Just go on a Bumble date. Tell me where you're going and text me every twenty minutes. You need this." (I wondered how many conversations about me my friends had behind my back about this.) I downloaded the app and grudgingly agreed to go on a date once the school year ended. I matched with a few guys, marveling at the dating app format and the ease with which life stories are condensed into emoji-filled bios. After matching with a guy whose profile said he read books, we texted about Vonnegut, dogs, and *The Office* for a few weeks before agreeing to meet at a restaurant not far from La Jolla (I Yelped and Google Street Viewed before I agreed—well-lit, close parking, looks safe, sent friends the address, got their approval).

Preparing for a date was far more stressful than preparing for a final exam. How honest should I be? How selectively do I need to curate my autobiography to seem normal? What if he flat-out asks me how many sexual partners I've had? How do I answer that? Would it be more devastating to tell him up front and have him reject me because of that? Or should I wait until he knows me better and then tell him and then be rejected? What if I like him? What happens then? At what point do I tell him what happened to me? Should I just have sex with him to prove to myself that I can do it? What if I slept with him and then told him what happened and he thought I was raped because I was too forward or promiscuous? Should I wait until we've had sex at least once so that I know what it's like to have sex with a consensual partner who does not think of me as a raped person? Will I ever be able to have a relationship? What if I have a boyfriend again someday and I really like him but then I tell him and he dumps me because of it?

He was nice and held my chair for me and made me feel surprisingly comfortable as I forced myself to order wine and try to suppress the maelstrom of thoughts (Watch your drink. Can't get up. What if that's what he was intending? I told my friends where I am and they have me on Find My Friends so I should be fine right?). We talked for a while about innocuous TV shows, but then he mentioned *House of Cards* and Kevin Spacey and I could feel myself putting up defenses and "activating angry feminist mode" and wishing I could apologize and then feeling furious that my default setting was apology. The blush rushed to my cheeks and I clenched my hands around the bottom of my seat and wondered if he noticed. I brought up #MeToo and hoped that I could soon retire my masochistic "immersion therapy" technique. He said all the right things. He seemed genuine. My hands unclenched, but I maintained constant vigilance.

I had sincerely hoped that by the time I finished writing this I would have achieved some new level of progress. I hoped to end this chapter on a helpful note that would encourage survivors that they are not defined by this. No one wants to be defined by this, and we can choose not to be. I am uncomfortable with using the word "survivor" to describe myself—it connotes a kind of bravery that I do not feel I always embody—but will gladly use it to describe my friends who have also been raped. My friends are pillars of strength who encourage me to keep going; their survival skills demonstrate the bravery and wisdom that I hope to someday master. I prefer to think of myself as a Person Who Is Getting Through It.

Whether you are a new survivor or a fellow Person Who Is Getting Through It, or someone who loves someone who is, you probably know that this journey is incredibly, painfully difficult, but it is not impossible. I have changed in ways that I hate—I am more judgmental and pessimistic, more suspicious of everyone, less hopeful about things I never even doubted for myself before—but I have also grown and become more capable in ways I never could have anticipated. As I approach the ripe old age of twenty-seven, I remind my students that as the highs get higher, the lows get lower, but our lowest lows enable us to better appreciate our golden highs. Books, the beach, and baseball/softball—loves by which I have always defined myself—became both invaluable companions and inadvertently painful accomplices. The people who love you and the hobbies you love sometimes experience collateral damage by a journey you cannot control. You remember it at the most inconvenient times: walking past your mom's plumeria tree, a classmate jokingly asking you how you lost your virginity, running into Rapist 2 at a restaurant when you're at a friend's birthday dinner. Constant vigilance is exhausting. Predicting triggers is exhausting. Preventing yourself from encountering reminders is impossible.

I still feel like I am divided into a Before and After self, but my After self can do more than the Before self could. Rape is not a life sentence. It is a pothole, a deterrent, a horrid detour on the path to self-actualization, but it is not what defines me. I am defined by whom and what I love, and that is something that cannot be taken away from me.

REFERENCES

Carpenter, Erin. 2014. *Life Reinvented*. Denver: Quantum Publishing Group.

Conroy, Pat. 1986. *The Prince of Tides*. Boston: Houghton Mifflin Company.

Eliot, George. 1994. *Middlemarch*. Edited by Rosemary Ashton. New York: Penguin Classics.

Eppolito, Sophia. 2017. "Here's what Matt Damon said about #MeToo, and the backlash that followed." *Boston Globe*, December 19, 2017. https://www.bostonglobe.com/arts/2017/12/19/here-what-matt-damon-said-about-metoo-and-backlash-that-followed/PNOjcVddMV9rQ13eqsDm4I/story.html.

Fielding, Chad. 2011. *The Art of Fielding*. New York: Little, Brown and Company.

Fraser, Courtney. "From 'Ladies First' to 'Asking for It': Benevolent Sexism in the Maintenance of Rape Culture." *California Law Review* 103, no. 1 (February 2015): 141–203. https://doi.org/10.15779/Z38MV66.

Harbach, Chad. 2011. *The Art of Fielding*. New York: Little, Brown and Company.

Heidt, Jennifer M., Brian P. Marx, and John P. Forsyth. "Tonic immobility and childhood sexual abuse: a preliminary report evaluating the sequela of rape-induced paralysis." *Behaviour Research and Therapy* 43, no. 9 (September 2005): 1157–1171. https://doi.org/10.1016/j.brat.2004.08.005.

Lorde, Audre. 1982. *Zami: A New Spelling of My Name*. Berkeley: Crossing Press.

Milano, Alyssa. (@alyssa_milano). 2015. "Dear Matt Damon: It's the micro that makes the macro." Twitter post, December 15, 2015. https://twitter.com/alyssa_milano/status/941840663087218689?lang=en.

Rowling, J. K. 2007. *Harry Potter and the Deathly Hallows*. New York: Scholastic.

Russo, Francine. 2017. "Sexual Assault May Trigger Involuntary Paralysis." *Scientific American*, August 4, 2017. https://www.scientificamerican.com/article/sexual-assault-may-trigger-involuntary-paralysis/?redirect=1.

Tolkien, J. R. R. 1982. *The Hobbit*. New York: Ballantine Books.

Woolf, Virginia. 1990. *Mrs. Dalloway*. New York: Mariner Books.

Chapter Twelve

The Past Is Always Present

Social Media and Survival

Lee Skallerup Bessette

Trauma is never linear.

This is one of the reasons rape victims are so rarely believed when reporting their rapes to the police—the story changes, moves in and out of time, with the victim not necessarily behaving in a way that would openly suggest that she had just been raped, been forever traumatized and changed. Those moments immediately and soon after the moment become strange movements in time, and while the further you get from the trauma, the rape, the more linear time may become once again, it never fully hardens into a beginning-middle-end narrative, because the trauma can intrude on the present at any moment.

Jenny Elkins calls it "trauma time" (2003, xiv) while psychologist Robert D. Stolorow posits that

> it is the ecstatical unity of temporality—the sense of stretching along between past and future—that is devastatingly disturbed by the experience of psychological trauma. Experiences of trauma become freeze-framed into an eternal present in which one remains forever trapped, or to which one is condemned to be perpetually returned through the Portkeys supplied by life's slings and arrows . . . all duration or stretching along collapses, past becomes present, and future loses all meaning other than endless repetition. (2003, 160)

I struggle to tell this story, to make sense of it, because when I first told it, first used the word "rape," I wasn't always greeted with sympathy, with empathy, or with compassion. And those who did offer such support, I often ended up hurting in the end. I was unable to accept the gifts they were giving, choosing instead to keep breaking things since I was so broken. I struggle even today to forgive the sixteen-, seventeen-, eighteen-, nineteen-, and twenty-year-old me for what I allowed to happen to me, how I responded, and how I hurt people I loved and who loved me.

I want to start with a triumph, with a happy ending. I can control where the narrative starts and ends, even if I couldn't always predict or control what happened in between. At any rate, I can shape it, try to shape it, narrate it in a way that leans towards triumph, away from trauma. In July of 2018, I started a job as a Learning Design Specialist at Georgetown University. Less than ten years previous, I had been in a contingent faculty position teaching writing at a rural state comprehensive institution serving some of the poorest zip codes in the country. In less than ten years I went from nowhere and being nobody, to being at one of the most prestigious universities in the country, if not the world.

I accomplished this largely through blogging and my presence on social media, specifically Twitter. I once tweeted that I wrote myself into existence, which isn't actually that far from the truth. I live-tweeted and live-blogged my life as a contingent instructor, a precariously-employed researcher, a mother, a wife, a coach, a woman trying to navigate towards success in academia. I started writing on my personal blog, and then on Inside Higher Ed, and then for ProfHacker. I gained a reputation as a voice for those who did not feel they could speak themselves given their precarious positions within academia, as someone who amplified voices who otherwise might not get heard. I was an advocate for adjunct faculty, for "non-traditional students" and the institutions that serve them, for the invisible majority of faculty and staff working at said institutions.

On Twitter, I found like-minded educators, other critical pedagogues, and my teaching shifted dramatically and drastically. They helped me to be brave enough to try peer-driven learning, an approach that empowered the students to decide how they would meet the learning outcomes of the course. I decided to experiment with ungrading, focusing instead on process and reflection, rather than product. For the first time in my career, I had a positive feedback loop to draw from, and a community of support and practice.

Twitter also reminded me what it was like to have your words read, seen, heard, understood, and appreciated. My first career choice was journalism, and I don't remember never not writing. Academia had temporarily taken away my love of writing through the process of trying to publish peer-reviewed articles. I had been brutalized by Reviewer 2 and faculty who could never find fault with what I said but instead with how I said it, that I was too emotional, too personal, not formal enough. When I took risks on my blog, while there would always been a few haters in the comments, I had many more who would reach out to me, privately and publicly, thanking me for my work. They would thank me for taking the risk, for helping them to be more brave.

Through Twitter and my blog, I re-wrote my story, my career as a triumph. We deal with our traumas when we are ready, when the triumphs feel solid enough to withstand the onslaught. My triumph was not yet solidified, not yet strong enough to withstand the onslaught, when, three or four years ago, I discovered that my rapist had been following me on Twitter for an undetermined amount of time. I was at my daughter's ballet class, waiting among the other dance moms (who always make me feel awkward and ill-at-ease because of my status as an outsider) when I got a notification of a new follower on Instagram. I recognized the name immediately. He had tried to friend me on Facebook years previously and I hadn't recognized the name at first. But when I realized who it was, I blocked him immediately, vowing that I wouldn't forget. Now, here he was yet again, trying to follow me on Instagram. I was shaking in the waiting area, trying not to lose my composure in front of the other moms who were happily chatting about running half-marathons or the crafts they did with their kids.

How did he find me? I admittedly have an uncommon last name, so if he was looking, I wasn't hard to find. But why was he even looking for me? I had blocked him on one platform. Why was he looking for me on another? How did he even know I had Instagram?

Panic set in when I realized where he knew my Instagram from. I went to Twitter to search for him in my followers list. At this point, I had 8,000 or 9,000 followers and didn't screen my new follower notifications. His last name is as distinct as mine, and after a few minutes of frantic searching, I found him. He was indeed following me on Twitter. In a panic, I blocked him immediately. There's no real way to know when he had started following me. But it was clearly not in the beginning, as he wasn't that far down my followers list. Yet he was a few pages in which meant that he had been following me for some time.

My mind was racing, spinning. I held it together to drive my daughter home, but broke down once the kids had gone to sleep. Why was he following me? How did he find me? Why was he looking for me? Did he happen upon me because I tweeted about the Montreal Canadiens? Or because I participated in education-related chats and he was (to my horror) a teacher himself?

I felt violated all over again, with him invading my life, my space, my self, on Twitter. It had happened almost exactly twenty years previously, when I was seventeen, and here I was, back to feeling small and powerless and alone, isolated even. How do you even start to articulate to anyone the trauma, the re-traumatizing? Wasn't I to blame, anyway, having lived so publicly on social media, not locking down my social media, not paying more attention to who follows me, not being more careful?

I was back to where I was when I couldn't even name what had happened to me as being rape. He was my boyfriend, after all. I had said yes once, twice, a few times, before it turned into a *do we have to*, into a *no*, and then into *please, no, please*, into silently accepting that it was going to happen and it was easier if I didn't put up a fight. The emotional manipulation gradually increased so imperceptibly that suddenly I was no longer in control of myself, of my life. But when I finally shared with others outside the relationship what was happening to me, I was told I was exaggerating, that it wasn't that bad, or, as my mother put it, "We all have problems."

On Twitter, I felt alone and exposed. It was somehow worse, because I didn't know when he had started following me, how he had found me, why he was following me, and how to protect myself beyond simply blocking him, which felt both somewhat empowering but also really disappointing. I was alone in my panic, in my grief. While my community on Twitter rallied around me and my decision, there was little else they could do to help protect me. I wasn't worried about my physical safety. I was worried about my emotional and psychic safety, the part of my life that I felt like I had the least control over. After all, that was a boundary he had time and time again violated. I had broken up with him, refused to get back together with him, cut off all further contact with him, moved cities, provinces, entire countries, and he couldn't take the hint that he was not welcome in my life.

I didn't want him on my Twitter, the space that had changed everything for me. He was the antithesis of everything I had built over the intervening twenty years. But even as I hit "block" on Twitter, I immediately felt a twinge of doubt and shame. Why aren't I over this? Why should it matter twenty years later?

I had consented to be public, but I had not consented to him having any sort of piece of my life, all these years later. He didn't have the right to know about my life, the trauma and the triumphs. I did not, had not consented to that.

In the back of my head, I think I worried about what other boundaries he felt he was entitled to cross with me, even after all this time and space. I was trying to re-write myself, and here he was trying to insert himself back into the narrative. I may have told and retold my social media ascension story so many times, but this story, of when I was seventeen, going on eighteen, is one that I very rarely tell. Partially, it is because I am still ashamed, ashamed of myself for even getting into a relationship that devolved into rape and abuse. I also feel ashamed that I still feel ashamed. I feel ashamed because even though I know it was rape, I still have trouble calling it that because of how our society typically understands rape—a stranger violently abducting and then raping someone. Rape is too rarely construed as occurring with an intimate partner with whom you have consensually had sex with previously. Too often that's not termed "rape." It's termed "being difficult."

I was seventeen. I was broken from years of first physical and then mental abuse at home. I felt unlovable, broken beyond repair. When he showed up in my life, he represented an opportunity to be loved and feel love. I wanted so badly to feel deserving of that love and sex was the way I was to earn that love from him. I was a virgin and scared and desperate. The first time wasn't rape. But it devolved into rape. I didn't know that it was never really about the sex but about the power he had over me, to coerce and control me. He was such a master manipulator that after I finally broke up with him, my mother grounded me and forbade me from seeing any of my friends, but allowed my now ex to visit me at home, to try and convince me to take him back. She believed I treated him unfairly, unjustly, that I deserved to be punished for what she perceived I had done.

One night when I came home from one of our dates, everyone was asleep and I knew I'd get in trouble if I woke anyone up, but I didn't care and stood in a scalding hot shower until I had drained the hot water tank. I secretly hoped I would get in trouble, so that I could finally tell someone what was happening. Another night I completely left my body, worried instead about all of the bug bites I was certain to get on my back as he had his way with me outside on the grass next to the park I played in as a child. That summer when I was seventeen, about to turn eighteen, I had to have my appendix removed, checking into the hospital on Monday and coming home on Friday. I wasn't allowed to do anything because of my recovery, but I was allowed to take a walk with him where he raped me in the park while I tried not to cry, worried that my stiches might pop. But it had been so long since we had sex and didn't he come and visit me in the hospital and he didn't want to get angry with me but he would.

One time, I tried to talk to him about my reluctance to have sex again and as often as we were having it, to try to explain to him that when I say no, I mean no, and to stop. He stopped short and angrily asked if I was accusing him of rape. The word hung in the air and I hesitated before reassuring him that, no, that wasn't what I was saying, don't get mad. I don't even remember if I had articulated it in my own head that it was rape, because I didn't want it to be rape, so I was surprised that he had said it. Looking back, did he already know what he was doing was wrong, as quick as he was to accuse me of accusing him? But my hesitation was all it took for him to fly off the handle at me, berating me, and then crying and apologizing to me. But it never got any better. And I never brought it up again.

I told no one, too ashamed, too scared of what people would say, would think. Didn't they all already see me as broken, and thus this just confirms my status, my being, my identity? I didn't feel worthy of help or sympathy, but I also didn't want to face their derision or dismissal. I didn't have a clean narrative, I wasn't an ideal victim, the violence was so gradual that I struggled to say this is when it became rape. Was it that night I was finally driven to take the shower? The night I left my body? The night after I came home from the hospital? The first time I said no and he didn't listen and I dismissed it, but then it just kept happening? When I finally found someone I thought I could trust enough to tell the truth to, it was a relief to finally say the word out loud. Even then, even now, the name doesn't feel right, but the trauma was real enough. The violation was real enough. The lasting effects are real enough.

I know from experience that violence doesn't have to be physical to hurt, to wound, to cripple, to kill. While my father had an explosive temper and was physically abusive, it was my stepfather and then my mother whose words cut as deep as the blows. My boyfriend-rapist never hit me, but manipulated me instead with words and physical intimidation. It's still trauma, just without the physical bruises and scars. Before I left Montreal for good, I was always worried that I would run into him, that he would physically intrude into my life. So I lived for a time with a constant, low-level sense of dread. Luckily, for me, it never devolved into outright paranoia, but it did feed my anxiety. My ADHD brain was unable to let go. I was always hyper-focused on what I could or should be doing to keep myself safe—travel in groups, make sure someone always knows where you are, don't go to the bathroom alone. Boys always tease that girls apparently can't pee without company, but the truth is that we have been taught since birth that it is unsafe to do so, even if we couldn't articulate it.

And so these same lessons we learned to avoid getting raped or assaulted, we transfer to the digital environment. The onus is still on us to keep ourselves safe. Then we are blamed when inevitably it isn't enough. We don't want to feel like we need to be protected. But it is clear that whatever we can do ourselves isn't enough to keep us safe. I chafe against the unfairness of it all, the injustice, but I cannot articulate what justice would be. Did what he did warrant going to jail, being labeled a sex offender for life? Would it have been justice for me to be dragged through the mud by my friends, my family, my community, and the justice system, had I spoken up, insisted on prosecution? Would justice have been him even acknowledging what he had done and apologizing?

What is fair here? What is justice?

When I discovered that my rapist followed me on Twitter, I wanted to share, connect on social media and simultaneously in that moment wanted to delete everything and hide. It was all because of him. He didn't ruin sex for me, nor would I let him ruin social media for me, the place where I had become myself, found friends, found my career. I resented the reminder that I wasn't "over it" or that perhaps I would never be completely past this event. I didn't think about him or the times he raped me and manipulated me very often anymore. But they were a part of who I was and who I had become. As much as I carried the memories of what he did to me with me, always, that was the only part of him I wanted in my life. I wanted him to be a memory. And now I had the power to say no.

A year after I had finally found the strength to break up with my rapist, I moved away from home for university. I didn't just move away from home, though—I moved out of my mother tongue, choosing to go to a Francophone university. I wanted to re-write myself in a new language, a language I had learned in school, but one that I wasn't yet immersed enough in to recreate myself. I broke from my home language, my home culture, and hopefully, myself. Could living in a new language mitigate the trauma of myself? Could I find and write and read and speak a new and different and better self?

I was a first-generation college student, studying in a second language. My trauma made me flee, run away, escape, and I found myself learning how to articulate myself in a new language. And, over five years, I re-wrote myself in French. College is as much of a journey of self-discovery as it is a formal educational experience, and my own journey through language and literature reshaped me fundamentally. The poetry of Anne Hébert, gorged with imagery that dealt with the violence and marginalization that women face, became the eventual topic of my dissertation, poetry I would probably not have discovered had I not gone to a French university.

> They lay me down, they drink me;
> Seven times I know the tight grip of bones
> And the dry hand seeking my heart to break it (Hébert, n.d.)

I found in Québécois literature and poetry and culture language to help me articulate what had happened to me, how it happened to me. The Québécois feminists, informed by the French feminism of Cixous and Irigaray and Kristeva, but also by the history of Quebec, nourished my heart and my soul and gave me life and light and permission to write myself, to question the world that had been presented to me as a *fait accompli*. Nicole Brossard, Marie-Claire Blais, Hébert—these women showed me new and different ways to tell stories, to find agency, to push back, to grow.

I also found exiled Haitian author Dany Laferrière, who wrote and re-wrote his life and his trauma in a series of quasi-autobiographical novels. He wrote ten books, calling it his *autobiographie américaine*, describing his life, in non-chronological order, from his early childhood in rural Haiti, to being a young teenager in Port-au-Prince, to being a target of the dictatorship because of his writing, to his arrival in Montreal, and finally his observations about a new life, in exile, in North America. I was drawn in at first because of his deceptively simple prose, which would unfurl new layers and meaning each time you read it. And then I re-read it again through the lens of the works that came after. He dealt with all kinds of trauma with a deftness I could never hope to replicate: the trauma of living under a dictatorship, the trauma of losing your father to exile, the trauma of exile, the trauma of racism, and even the trauma of Montreal winters.

He started writing before he knew his narrative would arc towards triumph and not tragedy. When he finished his *autobiographie américaine*, finally ready to deal with the trauma of his father's absence and madness from living in exile, he was writing from a place of clear triumph, his place in literature and in Québécois culture firmly established. And then he set about re-writing his already-published books, exploring ever more deeply the traumas he was examining through retellings and reimaginings that included movie adaptations. And then, after almost a decade, Laferrière published two new novels in rapid succession, two new retellings of his life. The first, titled *Je suis un écrivain japonais/I am a Japanese Writer*, has the author imagining himself, losing himself, in Japan and Japanese culture, following Basho on his journey north. The next novel, *L'Énigme du retour/The Enigma of the Return*, is a complete retelling of his life, but this time through the lens of how his father's exile and death shaped his life. He finally asks the question, on behalf of his father, whose body he is returning to Haiti, can you go home again?

In French, there is a verb tense called *le present historique*; in French, you write history in the present tense, not past tense. The past is always immediate, present, active. I had been drawn to that immediacy in his narratives, in how he wrote and rewrote his life. I was also drawn to how he sought to collapse, or at least interrogate, fixed borders and identities, with the dedication at the beginning of *Je suis un écrivain japonais* reading "A tous ceux qui voudraient être quelqu'un d'autre/For everyone who would like to be someone else." Those words spoke to me in a way that made me feel like this book was written for me; I had long wished I could transcend who I was, shaped by trauma. In response, I wrote about how he sought out Japan to distance himself from his own trauma before finding the strength to articulate his experience, and I saw my moving away, moving languages for university, as my way of seeking distance, seeking a new way to tell my story.

Laferrière was trying to get to a deeper truth about his own life, his own identity, his own trauma. But now I know about trauma time, and how trauma reshapes how you experience time and memories. Is Laferrière really using the *present historique* or is he living in that present when he writes? The author/narrator of the novels often starts by getting into the bath and floating off into the memories and narratives that follow. The bath is a time machine, allowing him to sink, literally and figuratively, into his own past. I related to that immediacy of his writing, his moving in and out of time, of getting lost in time, and then trying to write his way out. Our traumas weren't the same, but I was drawn to the way he explained and experienced his reality.

Amy E. Robillard (2019) writes in her book *We Find Ourselves in Other People's Stories*, as she tries to narrate through her own trauma, "We build our stories from stories that have come before, and the stories we build become resources for others who hear or read our studies and draw upon them in some way" (29). In Laferrière's books about growing up under a dictatorship as a child, he describes voraciously reading whatever he could get his hands on, but also how he listened attentively to the fragments and pieces of stories everyone else told his grandmother and then himself. Speaking stories was dangerous, with the threat of disappearing always looming, a threat that finally came for Laferrière as he narrated the realities of the dictatorship as a newspaper writer. He built his stories from what came before, the tradition of the *lodyans*, his grandmother and the community he grew up in, the streets of Port-au-Prince. And then he wrote his own stories, that I found, that I made meaning from, that helped me speak my own truth and story.

Robillard goes on to say, "The work we study is rarely accidental. We do not stumble upon a subject and decide, willy-nilly, to study it" (2019, 77). This is clear to me in my choice of authors to study, to write about, to explore and examine in depth. An extension of that statement could be: what we teach is rarely accidental as well. After I received my PhD, I started teaching writing and, if there was one mantra I held in my head while I taught, it was "trust students." I would trust students about their experience with and through writing, about their reasons they were late or missed class, about anything. My default would be to trust students and their articulation of their experiences. I would trust and respect their words in ways that others had not trusted and respected mine.

I would create a "safe space," a much-maligned term that nonetheless describes what I wanted them to feel when they were in my class: trusted, empowered, valued—in a word, safe. I wanted them to be safe to be themselves, to give them the space that social media had provided to me when no one else ever had—not the classroom, not my home growing up, not even my beloved pool and swim team. When nowhere is safe, then you can either cower or cry out. I chose to cry out, as is my nature, and for once, on social media, people heard me and came to me. In turn, I would come to them, my students, in our classroom and let them be who they were. Or, at least, I would create a space where they could start to figure that out.

I had no formal training in writing pedagogy, like most people who earn their PhDs in Literature and find themselves in front of a classroom of students. I had never read bell hooks's *Teaching to Transgress* or Paulo Freire's *Pedagogy of the Oppressed*, didn't know what critical pedagogy was. In the pages of the textbook I was required to teach, I found out about "The Banking Concept of Education" and realized how wrong I had been for the first part of my career as a teacher (2014). I realized that bringing my whole self to the classroom, that being vulnerable, that believing and valuing my students was radical and necessary for them, even if I had come to the approach mainly by accident and through my own necessity.

I was teaching students in Eastern Kentucky who were quite unlike me. I grew up middle-class and was "the best and the brightest"—I excelled at school, generally followed the rules, and I was rewarded for it. What I could offer had value in our education system and in our society. My students grew up in isolated rural areas, attending "failing" schools. The lucky few went to the flagship state university. Then there were the ones who came to our school. They were motivated to "get a degree" because they wanted a better life for themselves, but often had little motivation or direction beyond that.

When you teach freshman writing, students inevitably disclose varying degrees of personal information, narratives, and trauma. The students I taught, particularly in developmental writing, often had their trauma based in the schooling they received. Grades were not what was earned but instead what was doled out arbitrarily to those who were favored because their parents had influence or they were good at sports. Teachers weren't educators but instead enforcers who picked favorites and picked on those who struggled, who didn't fit in. School was just another place where the injustices and inequities of their daily lives were reinforced. They went to school because they had to. They survived school because they figured out some way to get through, to survive, to endure.

Their narratives about themselves were heavily informed by external sources: they were poor, stupid, incapable, hicks, rednecks, hillbillies, ignorant, backward. This was the popular narrative about people living in Appalachia, largely informed by popular culture, often reinforced by people from the community, but also their realities of poverty, addiction, and abuse. I wanted to give them stories, language to create a different, more robust narrative for themselves, to begin the process of writing themselves into existence. Their past was always present, and instead of seeking to suppress it, to deny it, to erase it, I sought to help them narrate and rewrite it.

I knew I had to change my teaching. I couldn't carry on as I had anymore, coercing my students to learn. I was going to learn with them, with their consent, within the strictures of the institution. There would be no manipulation, no assertion of authority for them to submit to. At least, I would try. I would, for in a few classes at least, try to show students there was another way to learn, another way to be in the world. The hardest part was getting the students to trust me. They didn't believe my proclamations that we were going to learn this way, that I wasn't going to just go back to the old way, disappointing them. "Don't give us hope," they were implicitly saying, "only to take it away." They also didn't believe that they could learn under different circumstances. What about rigor? What about motivation? We spent the first few classes reading ("the only readings I will assign to you this semester," I would tell them) about learning, about motivation, and about the coercive nature of modern schooling. I was the first person sometimes who had ever asked them the following questions: "What do you want to learn? And, what do you already know and love?"

They flourished. The projects they produced were thoughtful, creative, engaging—beyond anything I could have assigned or contained in a rubric. I had my students write op-eds about how to improve their schools, with some even having published their pieces in their local papers. They wrote blogs, posted their projects, and shared their work. And I encouraged and praised their work. I saw them gain confidence in their writing, pride in the work they produced. I wanted them to feel safe enough and supported enough to take risks themselves. Many of them did. Many of them thanked me for encouraging them, empowering them, enabling them. I would tell them that whenever they would tentatively, nervously ask me, "Can I do this?" I would inevitably almost always say, "Yes, and let me help you get there."

The patience, the forgiveness, the compassion, the empathy I should be able to show my younger self is instead focused on the students I teach, who are the same age as I was when I was falling apart. Gendered expectations aside, I embrace my role as a confidant, a mothering figure to the students I teach. It's complicated. I sometimes fear that I am in danger of reinforcing gender norms, setting up the expectations that all their women professors fulfill the role I eagerly take on. And yet it is meaningful work to me, work I am good at, and work that I enjoy. It is work that if I don't do, I oftentimes wonder, who will? Who will help these students survive and thrive in college?

I abandoned conventional grading, instead asking them to assess themselves based on criteria we developed together. I wanted them to focus on process, not product, to see and understand education as an iterative, continuous process, and not just something that ends after a 15-week semester. I wanted them to know that grades were not something to be held over them as a reward or punishment, but instead a necessary evil we could work to circumvent. Their worth, I wanted them to understand, was more than a letter grade on a paper. I helped them to embrace collaboration rather than competition, moving beyond their conception of "group work." I invited them to bring their whole selves into the classroom, into the work, into the reading, into the learning, to make it meaningful, to make it matter to them. The students, in turn, wrote moving reflections on the process, about how my class had opened their eyes to what education and learning could be. They were often harder on themselves than I would ever have been, pushing themselves in ways I could never have asked or even imagined. I taught hundreds of students, read hundreds of these reflections, and yet it never felt like it was enough. It was one class, one drop in the bucket in their long lives as students, one instance of consent in a lifetime of coercion.

There are those who were critical of my peer-driven, ungrading approach to teaching, saying it didn't adequately prepare students for the "real world," that I was coddling them. But my students were all too well-acquainted with the so-called real world outside of college already—working multiple jobs, caring for family members, dealing with mental health issues, food insecurity, and homelessness. How is a competitive, coercive environment in school preparing them for the real world?

I think I just answered my own question.

I became a faculty developer and technologist, based on my experience in the classroom, my experience with Twitter. I now help faculty incorporate technology into their teaching, enabling them to develop their digital fluency skills so they can help their students. If I teach the teachers, then I'll be able to reach more students. I also now teach classes in digital studies, in technology, in digital fluency. And I watched as Twitter fundamentally changed (Stewart 2014). I already knew Twitter could be an unsafe space for some, especially Black women (Crockett 2014) and other POC (I. 2015), but it escalated while I was making my career shift. Personally and professionally, I had experienced all the good social media could bring, could be. I wasn't sure anymore if my narrative would be one of the last. I knew, myself, how exposed and vulnerable we all are on social media of any kind. But then came the trolls, the incels, the swarming, the doxing, the bots, the Nazis. I changed my narrative, how I taught these skills. I showed people resources about locking down their accounts, their digital identities, how to better protect themselves. I offered them critical resources from a feminist and racially conscious perspective, tried to get them to think about the digital beyond a simple colonialist narrative of expansion and conquest.

But I am still haunted by the question: Are we teaching to the world we want, or just preparing students to be complicit and accepting of the world that exists?

This situation is much like all of the messages women receive about being tough enough to handle the sexism, the microaggressions, the violence that we face from the time when we are just kids. "We all have problems," my mother said to me. These messages, these lessons, these hard-knocks are all just a reality that we have to accept and figure out how to survive, a list which sadly includes rape, sexual assault, and online harassment.

But what if I'm not interested in mere survival, but instead interested in how we can all thrive? I not only want to protect my daughter, but eradicate the threats altogether. It shouldn't fall on her to protect herself, or me to equip her for survival, but to work to confront those things that would seek to do damage to her. I want to confront them head-on rather than cower behind ineffective protective measures.

School shouldn't be something that is just endured. And womanhood shouldn't be something that is just endured.

A rape is never just a rape, a single incident. There are conditions in place that facilitated the act of violence. The rape ends, but those conditions do not. They remain, all around you, all the time. Social media has brought them out, brought them to the forefront. But women always knew that the violence and the misogyny and the entitlement culture have been there. School too often remains a coercive force, too, teaching us to comply, that power comes from forcing others to comply. We're not given the language to narrate our stories, our realities, our traumas. We're told our experiences don't matter, aren't valid, and we are convinced to keep quiet, to minimize our pain, to silently accept what everyone understands as fate.

But I refused that fate. I found authors who refused that fate. I sought to help students refuse that fate. We struggle through feeling "undone, done in, breakable, collapsible as we experience a failure of meaning" (Robillard 2019, 73). And I triumphed. But that doesn't mean that my past is behind me. Because sometimes, unexpectedly, your rapist follows you on social media, and the only power you have is to block him, and you do, but then find yourself right back where you started twenty years earlier.

REFERENCES

Beauchamps, Zach. 2018. "Incel, the misogynist ideology that inspired the deadly Toronto attack, explained." Vox. Accessed October 27, 2019. https://www.vox.com/world/2018/4/25/17277496/incel-toronto-attack-alek-minassian.

Crockett, l'Nasha. 2014. "'Raving Amazons': Antiblackness and Misogynoir in Social Media." Model View Culture. Accessed July 3, 2019. https://modelviewculture.com/pieces/raving-amazons-antiblackness-and-misogynoir-in-social-media.

Elkins, Jenny. 2003. *Trauma and the Memory of Politics*. Cambridge: Cambridge University Press.

Freire, Paulo. 2014. *Pedagogy of the Oppressed*. New York: Bloomsbury. Kindle.

HASTAC Staff. 2015. "Gender Bias in Academe: An Annotated Bibliography of Important Recent Studies." Accessed July 24, 2019. https://www.hastac.org/blogs/superadmin/2015/01/26/gender-bias-academe-annotated-bibliography-important-recent-studies.

Hébert, Anne. n.d. "The Tomb of Kings: Translation Poetry Generator." Accessed August 18, 2019. https://poetrygenerator.readywriting.org/.

hooks, bell. 1994. *Teaching to Transgress*. New York: Routledge.

I., Izzy. 2015. "The State of Online Harassment: Decentering Whiteness and Colonization." Model View Culture. Accessed July 3, 2019. https://modelviewculture.com/pieces/the-state-of-online-harassment-decentering-whiteness-and-colonization.

Laferrière, Dany. 2009. *Je suis un écrivain japonais*. Montreal: Boréal.

Robillard, Amy E. 2019. *We Find Ourselves in Other People's Stories*. New York: Routledge.

Stewart, Bonnie. 2014. "There's something rotten in the state of Twitter." The Theoryblog. Accessed July 3, 2019. http://theory.cribchronicles.com/2014/09/02/something-is-rotten-in-the-state-of-twitter/.

Stolorow, Robert D. 2003. "Trauma and Temporality." *Psychoanalytic Psychology* 20 (1): 158–61. https://doi.org/10.1037/0736-9735.20.1.158.

Chapter Thirteen

Claiming Conclusively

Speaking Back to Campus Title IX

Courtney Cox

I cannot pinpoint when I realized that my undergraduate advisor's interactions with me were inappropriate just as I cannot recall the first time I heard of the #MeToo movement. What I do know is that the two have become inextricably bound for me, encapsulated in a kind of tension that compels me to both vacuum my story inside of myself and simultaneously scream it out. I came of age in a confessional society, an environment that carves out a safe space for victims to share their stories, expectant that in the telling, the reaction will be of consequence. Yet, when the stories we tell topple the social order, when speaking out has lived consequences, with this comes the pressure to stay silent.

The protocols of campus Title IX and those of the #MeToo movement are grounded in the same realities of hegemonic oppression and misogyny. However, they are conducted with opposing exigencies. Title IX complaints are bounded entirely by the regulation of protocols and procedures. Without a nuanced understanding of the rhetorical construction of academic institutions and the development of Title IX protocols, the potential for recovery and repair is limited. The #MeToo movement, in contrast, has provided the impetus to reflect on my experiences, to legitimize my trauma, and, ultimately, to seek out avenues to fight for change. Through #MeToo and the resulting online discourse, discourse is relatively unregulated. In order for stories of sexual misconduct to avoid generalization and move past abstractions, we must invite a nuanced understanding of the obstacles and impossibilities placed before survivors who are able to share their stories to enact change as well as the realities of survival. Within this chapter, I share my story as an example of the tensions that lie between Title IX and #MeToo.

Title IX Report Narrative Introduction: Filed April 2018

    When I first met Dr. D., I was a first-semester freshman enrolled in his Honors Cultural Anthropology general education course. I was struck by the enthusiasm of his lectures, the dire importance of the discipline, and his attention towards me. Within weeks, I changed my major to anthropology, and in the midst of transitioning from high school to college. Finding an invested and attentive mentor like him was integral. New to the college environment, I had no frame of reference to measure his investment in me, the time we spent together, and the unequivocal trust I grew to have for him.

    During those four years of college, I spent countless hours in his office, orienting myself to the discipline of anthropology and asking more and more questions. And, as I did so, I also tried to brush certain things aside. There were the comments he made about my breasts. There were his invasive questions about my personal life. I wrote these things off. After all, perhaps personal boundaries were less valued here. Perhaps all of this was due to the nature of studying archaeology itself, a subdiscipline of anthropology that demands students and professors spend a large amount of time spent outside of the class visiting sites and completing field work.

    Dr. D. showed me overt favoritism along with several other female students in the department. This led to rumors and resentment from my peers. Oftentimes the two of us would go on trips alone—to meet with faculty members, to visit nearby archeological sites, or to visit his alma mater. No inappropriate physical conduct took place during these times. However, in hindsight, his investment in me and the sheer amount of time alone that I spent with him, a much older male professor, was inappropriate. I'm grateful for what he taught me about the discipline. But if I had been aware of the implications of our relationship, I would have kept my distance.

My hard drive is full of shrapnel.

I keep a copy of my Title IX narrative in the main folder of my computer documents, lingering at the bottom, the only file that is not meticulously organized. I tried my best to make the text look pretty: fully justified, Garamond, size 12 font. There were 1,445 words in all, and I shined each one over and over again in my re-writing. I emailed the file as a PDF, adding the note, "I would like to be kept anonymous." On the phone with the Campus Conduct Coordinator, a woman I never actually met, I was told that my request for anonymity would not be granted, as had previously been promised. "We can't issue a non-contact order if your name isn't included. Plus, he'll know it was written by you either way. Since you've shared this with us, you cannot revoke now." My assurance of anonymity had been central to my decision to report and, although I had anticipated my claims would be supplementary, I was thrust into the center of the narrative, free-falling without protection.

Still, so often, I remember the beginning. Dr. D.'s office was on the bottom floor of the science building, an unsightly space on my otherwise charming campus. Constructed in light red brick, dimensioned into unforgiving rectangles, the tiles of the lobby echoed through the space as I entered it. When you descend the stairs to the basement, you are greeted by the smell of formaldehyde as it wafts from the biology closet. The space is marinated in this scent, and even when the dissected carcasses are disposed of, the chemicals braid themselves in the air and linger. This smell troubled me at first, but as the semesters passed and I spent a majority of my time here, my nose adjusted, and the scent was as welcome as fresh air. Entering his office, you pass through a windowless door, plastered with our state's Archaeology Month posters on both sides. His name was printed at the bottom of this poster, and in both entering and exiting, you were immediately aware of his influence, of the weight his name carried, of his ascent in the university.

Despite the male-dominated tendency of archaeology, my department was composed of almost exclusively female students. My freshman year, the major was new and the department was small, with only one full-time faculty member teaching the dozens of female students: Dr. D. Faculty members in other departments called us "Dr. D.'s Harem," a name that was certainly apt. Due to the nature of archaeology, we often spent time completing field work, sometimes travelling on weekends, finding ways to fill the monotony of scorching afternoons deep in our test units when the only sound, otherwise, would be the metallic clink of trowels against the river mud.

By the end of my four years, I swear that I knew all his best stories, told breathlessly as we crossed the Midwest for field work, conferences, or visits he hand-selected me for. I had started college with no interest in archaeology, but after enrolling in his general-education course my first semester, I was so fundamentally changed by his lectures, the magical ways of thinking that he fostered in his students, that I changed my major from English to anthropology by Labor Day. I had made up my mind quickly, all at once, not concerned that my major-intensive classes would mostly be taught by one man. At best, Dr. D. is controlling, demanding, and egotistical. At worst, he is misogynistic, manipulative, and endlessly powerful at an institution that had little protective pathways in place for its students. He was networked, dedicated, and singular in his control over the department and our futures. When I think of my first semesters as his student, I hear the echoes of what one fellow student stated plainly and often: "For the next four years, he will be my god."

I attended a strict and very traditional liberal arts college. Because so many boundaries were established for us—visiting hours, same-gender housing, a no-alcohol policy—we were not expected to negotiate our own. When I say that my body was not safe around him, I realize that this is a new thought, and at the time, I thought of our intimacy as protection, dedication, commitment to my future. Because Dr. D. taught the majority of my courses and I had little preparation for what college mentoring should be like, it seemed like comments about my body, lingering physical contact, and endless commentary on my personal life were normal, if not a reward for my scholastic excellence. I would bristle, though, at shaming comments about how I looked, concern about how others would perceive me because I was petite and effeminate. *I just don't see how people are going to be able to take you seriously, Miss Cox.*

As I progress in my remembering, I find myself stingy in the sharing of details. I tire of thinking of him, wrestle with the knowledge that in my telling, I once again become pressed to the center of the story. Much like I felt in the process of reporting to Title IX, I feel the pressure to make the details concerning *enough* to be worth reading, while also maintaining the kind of stable ethos necessary to wager a complaint. In *Down Girl: The Logic of Misogyny*, Kate Manne explains the troubling paradox victims often experience in the process of reporting, stating that a victim "is liable to be perceived as at once self-dramatizing and self-important, and at the same time, wan or maudlin" (Manne 2018, 225). In choosing to speak at all, I must justify my reasons for doing so, while also maintaining the kind of critical distance of an unbiased observer. Too much emotion and I become an oversensitive pansy. Too little affect and the trauma is proven to be of little consequence. With each claim I make, I must be prepared to justify, contextualize, and demonstrate that the effects are measured. In doing so, I must renegotiate my relationship with my trauma, make it persuasive, anticipate the intentions of my audiences. Despite the fact that my Title IX investigation has come to a close, it has fundamentally changed how I am able to tell my story.

Perhaps this conditioned response is why, as I write this, I do not want to focus my story on this man, and I find myself backspacing many of the details. Yet I cannot tell the story of my experience in reporting without providing the impetus for doing so. As I type the story above, I tell myself that I wanted this, that at the time I benefited from his favoritism. I tell myself that boundaries are formed in negotiation, and I did not do my part to maintain distance. I wonder to myself if this story is one worth telling at all, if I am over-sensitive and perhaps casting blame where it is not deserved. I justified for years that my harassment was not worth reporting because I was not physically assaulted. And, I now do not know how to continue the telling of my story amid the guilt of "What if?" I tell myself that I should have been grateful things were not worse for me, that I did not fall into the horrors I've heard only after the fact. I tell myself that my gratitude should have been enough to keep me silent, and still, no matter my complaint, when I tell my story, I often feel I am speaking into a vacuum that does nothing more than erase my voice as soon as I speak.

As an undergrad, I told my English advisor first, not sure of what I intended the telling to *do*, why the words found their way from my lips. After Dr. D. had made an openly sexualized comment about my body at a public archeology event, I had made a decision not to meet with him alone in his office. I was president of the Anthropology Club for which he was, of course, advisor, and so when it came to planning events, I resolved to email him to secure approval for upcoming campus events. Likely aware of my choice, Dr. D. refused to answer my emails. I went on with my planning, defiantly, and after seeing a flyer for an event he had not formally approved, Dr. D. told my peers, "I'm going to rip that bitch a new asshole," before laying into me about my abhorrent disrespect. This bubbling of rage and anger filled me with fear, and although his threats were likely metaphorical, the effects were entirely physical, raising goosebumps on my arms and prompting paranoid avoidance of the stark science building which housed most of my responsibilities.

So much of my identity was enmeshed in the anthropology department: it was where I worked, the locus of most of my classes, and where the bulk of my friends resided. I had retained an English minor and worked on the campus literary journal, however, meeting a kind mentor in another department in the process. We had weekly editorial meetings, and one week I found myself lingering in his office. "I don't feel safe working in the archeology lab anymore," I began. All the while I was paralyzed by the fear that in voicing my complaints, I was admitting that I wasn't smart enough to complete the work, that I didn't have the rigor to graduate from my program. Yet when I heard my own voice speak the story aloud, I realized that I already had the words for how I felt. Still, I second-guessed each one, worried about the notion that I might sound ungrateful.

My English advisor had sharp and darting eyes, a father who took these concerns seriously. "When you talk about him, you are shaking," he said. He felt paternal, surely, and as such, acted as though he could make it cease to exist. I was a junior then and he supported me in my decision to quit my assistantship with the anthropology department. The topic seemed unavoidable and boiled over in meetings with my cultural anthropology mentor, followed by psychology research directors, and then the dean of the School of Sciences. No one seemed surprised exactly, and I wondered why prior action had not been taken and at what moment Dr. D. had been identified by each of these mentors as aggressive and unsafe. In each of these admissions, I kept my distanced composure. However, in the breach of normalcy, I could almost feel his shadowy and unrelenting presence take form alongside each meeting, creating cracks between the bookshelves and the pristine diplomas of my trusted mentors.

I became an expert in avoidance, and I found ways to survive the last year and a half of college. My mentors were supportive, willing to listen, able to join me in carrying the weight of my claims, but no one offered me support in making a formal report. In conversations, the well-intentioned question circled back: "Is he not being nice to you?" Yet, each time my fears were dismissed as trivial, they became as Denise Riley explains in *Impersonal Passion: Language as Affect*, felt as psychosomatic effects, manifested in a type of material reality that altered my ability to relate to others in this sphere (Riley 2005). These sorts of questions were aimed at dismissing my concerns, reinforcing the beliefs that I had already been fostering for years that my concerns were trivial and that I simply wasn't tough enough.

Now that some years have passed, I shuffle between self-blame and condemnation that my mentors were not able to help me report Dr. D. at that time. I resent that they were not able to fill in the gaps of my story and that they did not have the bureaucratic know-how to navigate my complaints. Yet, as Judith Butler asserts, "The subject who speaks hate speech is clearly responsible for such speech, but the speaker is rarely the originator" (Butler 1997, 34). Given the context of my alma mater as a restrictive environment, perhaps my mentors understood that this institution fostered this kind of reactive inappropriateness. I now understand that this response is systemic, reflective of not just my department, my brick and ivy institution, but instead the pressures of higher education to guard the politics of the workplace. Rebecca Solnit writes of the tendency for those in power positions to lose the ability to mirror others' emotions, to key into their empathy and compassion (Solnit 2018). Although these facts allow me to come to terms with the reasons for why my veiled complaints may not have induced action in the faculty members that I respected, they do not quell my own guilt. I wish I could have known the right words to incite meaningful action. Perhaps due to the complexity of navigating the university system, my mentors were able to silo their concerns and thus justify not interfering in a situation where a colleague acted in ways that were harmful to his students.

After graduation, I ran from the entire discipline, slowly, but in hindsight, with the kind of trajectory that made sense. I turned down my best anthropology graduate school offer at a school that would have made everyone I've ever known proud of me. I moved home and enrolled in an emerging master's program for an interdisciplinary English degree in Digital Publishing. I was proud of this decision, but when Dr. D. discovered my plans to attend graduate school in English, he told me that I needed to reject the offer and hold on to my job in the local coffee shop for the next year and save up to reapply to archaeology programs. I had been ashamed to tell him my postgraduation plans, or maybe just uncomfortable. "I guess you don't need to talk to me anymore now that you don't need anything from me," he said, a comment that I tried to ignore with a smile.

I graduated summa cum laude, moved to a new state, and started graduate school. Yet I began to receive sporadic Facebook messages from Dr. D., despite the fact that we were not digital friends. In time, I hear secondhand that he intends to make sure I don't pursue a PhD in English. "What a waste that would be," he tells my former fellow students. When I receive his messages, sometimes I answer, politely though distanced. When I do not reply, his messages seem to grow increasingly angrier. Each time, his messages enter my Facebook inbox with the abruptness of a shovel as it digs into soil, ripping open the stratified layers of the ground beneath with a quick jump on the head of the spade. When I open his messages, I take a deep breath, reminding myself that the cognitive circuits for physical and emotional pain are the same. My body revolts. I am shaken. In retrospect, I soothe myself with Judith Butler's theoretical assertations that injurious language operates, in some ways, like physical assault (Butler 1997). I am wounded, summoned, reminded. I block his messages, feeling safe that I cannot be reached. In order to make it through the next day, I tell myself that it's the depth of my own pride that makes me afraid. I remind myself that he is a good man and that he is not ashamed of me. He simply cannot understand why my life did not go according to his plan. I tell myself that trauma is not relative, that I need to toughen up. I convince myself that I'm projecting, that it's my guilt in knowing I let him down that makes me feel so uncomfortable. Although he resides in another state and could not, logically, physically harm me, these communications become a kind of violence due to the conditioned response of fear and shame that they evoke within me.

Despite his misguided efforts, I enroll in a doctoral program in English, begin teaching, and marvel at how *young* my students seem. I often wonder what they would do if they found themselves harassed by a professor, if they would be able to recognize it as such, and what I would do if they asked me for help. As I begin to teach, I think of Dr. D. much more often because when I face my first-year writing students, I realize their vulnerability and how it must mirror that of the students still enrolled in his classes.

Near the close of the my first year enrolled in my doctoral program, I hear from a friend in the Anthropology department at my undergraduate alma mater that a student is organizing colleagues to report Dr. D., that she's in contact with the Title IX coordinator. I procure her email address, tell her that I want to support her however I can. This student is older than me, having graduated before my freshman year. Although I hardly knew her, I had wanted to be like her. She told me that nine females from the department would be reporting, that the Title IX coordinator had told her that we could submit anonymously. I felt empowered, the part of something momentous. When I spoke with this other student, she was unapologetic in her rage, calling him an asshole and unafraid of the repercussions, despite residing in the same city as Dr. D. and working in the same field. I hated that her experiences let her become something feverish and fierce, while I mostly remained docile and afraid, thinking of the implications of this choice. I began trying to write about it all, feeling a kind of block that was previously unfamiliar to me. I did not know how to tell the story of years in a matter of paragraphs. I tried my best to be ambiguous, to shroud myself in a kind of vague protection.

To write at all, I had to prod at the shrapnel still lodged in my body, and as the numbness began to subside, I tentatively examined the aftereffects of a trauma I had not legitimized for many years. Lynn Worsham writes that trauma results in our prior ways of existing and understanding being over-whelmed, "leaving the individual or community without the means to make the event intelligible, controllable, and communicable. Thus, the traumatic event cannot be assimilated or experienced fully at the time of its occurrence, but only belatedly" (Worsham 2006, 173–74). In the work that I had done in assimilating my experience, for me, the choice to report was not a choice at all, but an inevitable compulsion that brewed over years of avoidance. How-ever implicitly, these unspoken and unarticulated stories of a life I had run from still had a hold on my own lived experience in the present. In the process of writing, I felt both empowered and ungrateful, strong and whiney in my complaint.

My Title IX communication that followed was at best disorganized and at worst triggering and irresponsible. In the process of reporting, I was told that there had not been a Title IX office when I was a student. This meant that reporting years before would have been impossible. After sub-mitting my narrative and being told that my report would not be kept anonymous, I was not given a reason why, nor the ability to request that my file remain anonymous. "I want you to know that this decision makes me feel unsafe," I told the Title IX coordinator, a woman who seemed put out and frazzled with having to deal with me. The communications with the coordinator took place almost entirely by email. She was terse, vague, and her messages were riddled with typographic errors and informality, further making me feel like I was little more than an inconvenience. In my one phone call with her, I asked when Dr. D. would be made aware of our case. "We'll have someone go and talk to him in person. We wouldn't conduct matters this serious over email." I wondered then why my claims were met with such informality, and he was given the benefit of formal consideration when he was the one under investigation.

Through this scattered and unprofessional communication, I found a de-terrence in my will to protest because I felt as though my claims were not met with even a gesture toward politeness. Each response seemed a bit gruffer than the one before, and I felt increasingly guilty that this woman, whose job it was to coordinate this process, had to be pulled into the messiness of this story. Much like the kind of deterrence that Dr. D. had invoked in filling me with self-doubt and checking up on me after graduation via demanding and terse messages, as I waited for the inevitable contact, I began to feel like I was the culprit through the process of reporting.

The other former student who I had been in contact with informed me that rather than nine students as I had been previously told, only three of us had followed through and sent in our testimonies. The definitiveness of the process surely had silenced the majority, I marveled, as I wondered to myself if I would have reported knowing that my story would need to carry so much of the focus. Rhetorically, it seemed, the processes of Title IX worked much like those of an abuser. In one of her poorly composed emails, the Title IX coordinator explained that the university was bringing in an outside private investigator. He would contact me to set up an interview in a matter of weeks. They would be in touch.

After I made the decision to report Dr. D., someone close to me asked, "Why now?" After all, I was a graduate student at another institution, and I had not seen him in years. "Have you considered the effects on your career?" What a pity it would be, the person seemed to suggest, if my decision to report my professor impacted my future academic livelihood. In my own mind other thoughts took hold. Imagine working without stopping to breathe, barreling through graduate school, and then not being able to find a job because you spoke out against something long buried in your past, about a person you didn't have to see again. Imagine taking a job where I'm condemned for being harassed by my professor. Imagine how it feels to report the most important mentor of your college career, fighting against it with every fiber of your being, knowing the futility each step along the way, yet knowing that you have no choice. I don't have to imagine.

As I waited for my formal interview with the private investigator, I came to terms with all of the ways that my reactions to my decision to report were contradictory, as Sharon Crowley explains in *Towards a Civil Discourse: Rhetoric and Fundamentalism.* In the process of reporting, I was experiencing an entire disarticulation from the ideologies and beliefs that I had built in a formative part of my life, and in a sense, I had become comfortable being uncomfortable. Crowley explains that "disarticulation might require abandonment of an entire ideology or even a hegemony" (Crowley 2006, 79). In the process of reporting, I realized that the institution was not there to protect me, and both as a student and an alum, I was valuable to the institution only in terms of my compliance and my silence. I had expected to feel a release from the years of fear and guilt that I had carried with me. Instead, I felt embarrassed that I had spoken up at all. Rather than taking my claims seriously and making me feel as though Dr. D. was the one being investigated, I felt rigid, as though I was being punished for the audacity of speaking out at all. I was inconveniencing them, I told myself as I waited. Speaking up for myself, taking steps away from a sexually harassing and unkind bully seemed like a betrayal to the whole institution.

To quell this blocking guilt, I sometimes remind myself of the last time I returned to my college campus. I was there for just one night, staying with a friend who had not yet graduated. At this point, I had not considered reporting Dr. D., but the pervasive attempts he made to contact me made me uncomfortable. When I arrived on campus, I entered through the side gates, seeing his car parked in the reserved space where it always had been, instantly recognizing his license plate and realizing that, despite it all, so little had changed in my absence. Still so much was the same, and still, I was afraid on the off chance of running into him. This was the kind of fear that made me want to turn my car around, cross state lines and return home. Even before I began my report, I was no longer welcome on the campus that had been my home for four years.

During the hour-long phone call with the private investigator, I paced around my apartment, trying to resist my inclination to be likeable. He was nice enough, a retired cop who seemed to be both rooting for me and entirely out of his depth in the questioning. I had the feeling that he wanted to be liked, too. After introducing himself, the first question he asked me was if everything in my narrative had been true. This was an easy one: "Yes, of course." The questions that followed were more leading: "Were you offended at the time, or is this something new, maybe with all other discussion over sexual harassment in the media?" There was no simple answer here, as I cannot disengage myself from the cultural context. I told him that I had reported him to faculty in three departments while a student and that no action had been taken. The media surrounding #MeToo had not directly impacted my memories or the way that thinking back on them had made me feel. "No, the surrounding cultural context has had no impact on my ability to feel and respond and take action," I answered. This question was too simple for the complexity of my actual response. There was no way that I could have answered it well.

We recounted the story I had submitted months prior, probing questions were asked, and I remained as measured and terse in my answers as possible. Mostly, these questions were harmless until the investigator inquired: "I hear that your advisor tended to give the most inappropriate attention to women who were petite, brunette, and physically attractive. Would you consider yourself to be meeting all of these descriptions?" This was a question that had no safe answer, and I knew that in either response, I would be discredited. I wondered, then, how he pictured me, the voice on the other end of the line, and realized that no matter my response, this was the moment when the verdict was decided. I wish I could tell you that I said, "Could you please explain to me why the way I look justifies my harassment?" But I think I just said, "Yes."

Before we got off the phone, the investigator told me that he was glad I was a teacher, that he could tell I cared a lot about my students. He told me that my students were lucky to have me, and this was the moment that I began to cry. Once I hung up the phone, I knew that my chapter had closed and that the matter was out of my hands. As hard as this phone call had been, the waiting was harder. When I followed up, asking about the decision of the report, the curt coordinator told me that "the private investigator is on vacation. He'll finish the report when he is back." Almost six months after my initial narrative was filed, I received a final terse email including an attachment of the final report with little more than a "Sorry that we forgot to tell you that a decision was made weeks ago." The affect was flat, I was sure, and the apology was just a formality.

I opened the report without meaning to, scrolling through the ugliness of the words contained within. In the case files against my former advisor, the closest mentor I have ever had, a man I once revered like a father, you could read the stories of him forcing students to sleep beside him in hotel rooms, a man who shamed, intimidated, and belittled the women in my department. Although support had been found for my claims, the entirety of the case was filed "inconclusive." My file was discussed last, select portions pulled into the final report. I read Dr. D.'s one-sentence retort to my claims: "She is an extremely vain individual." One sentence and the entirety of my claims were discredited.

The first time I wrote this essay, I tried to force a happy ending. How neat it would be if my story ended here, with my readers rooting for me, and my future seeming bright, diverging further and further from what I've written above. It's a likeable enough arc: girl is mistreated, girl uses her writing to build the strength to make change, girl reports abusive advisor, Title IX investigates, nothing changes, yet the girl is empowered by the strength of her own words. I want to tell you that in the filing of the report, I was able to label my fears as inconclusive and trust in the processes, come to agree with the verdict. But I simply do not have the words.

I hate that this is my story to tell. Sometimes I regret making my report, and I wonder if I had known from the start that the case would be ruled inconclusive, if I would have continued with my participation. I think of his family sometimes—his children almost my age and his wife—and feel guilty if they had to learn about his behaviors and see this man differently. I wonder why it's easier for me to humanize their relationship with him than my own. I spoke, and nothing was really changed at all.

Here is the thing, though: sexual misconduct is predicated on the expectation of silence, so when we do find the occasion to speak up, there is the expectation that the weight will be lifted. Sometimes silence can feel safer, especially when one has the expectancy that speaking up will enact change. And it doesn't.

It's only half a lie if I say I am grateful that I have gained the administrative literacies to enter into this process, and that through this process, I know that my alma mater has been changed. If I had not received Title IX training at other universities and encountered peers who had already made contact through this process, I would not have known how to report, just as I had not as an undergraduate. The actual process of reporting sexual misconduct at my alma mater was buried within administrative barriers and seemed disconnected from the faculty members who could be advocates for their students. When I go to the school website, I see "Title IX" linked to one of the drop-down menus for the first time. For students who don't have the mentors to point them in this direction, they may be able to find resources on their own. Although I mourn for the students who will inevitably go through this vulnerable and intrusive process, I take comfort in the fact that the pathways are more accessible now so that, ultimately, these incidents will be less prevalent. Through the positioning of this information, hidden institutional barriers are removed and I choose to take this pathway to access, at the very least, as a type of victory, however small.

Rather than letting the fear continue to tense my body, making me rigid and unworthy as I stand in front of my own students, I choose to relearn that vulnerability does not mean weakness and try to excavate as much kindness as I can here. Although we tend to talk about sexual harassment and abuse in abstractions, without a systemic view into how and why gendered atrocities linger, changes are improbable. The #MeToo movement provides the initiative for a greater understanding of the rhetorical implications of abuse: how it fits into our institutions, lingers within embedded social situations, and stigmatizes survivors within harmful archetypes of what it means to be a victim. The movement cannot and should not stop with online testimonials and trending hashtags, however. Instead, we must approach the tactics and trajectory of the movement and address the tensions with the realities of standard reporting procedures. What the #MeToo movement ultimately invites us to add is the power of our narratives, to take control of them by whatever means necessary. Doing so has the potential to topple the cemented nature of institutions and to bring greater transparency. But, in the end, I don't need a Title IX ruling or heavy university mandates to legitimize my trauma. Instead, I continue to gain strength in finding new ways to speak back.

REFERENCES

Butler, Judith. 1997. *Excitable Speech: A Politics of the Performative.* New York: Routledge.

Crowley, Sharon. 2006. *Towards a Civil Discourse: Rhetoric and Fundamentalism.* Pittsburgh: University of Pittsburgh Press.

Manne, Kate. 2018. *Down Girl: The Logic of Misogyny.* Oxford: Oxford University Press.

Riley, Denise. 2005. *Impersonal Passion: Language as Affect.* Durham: Duke University Press.

Solnit, Rebecca. 2018. "Easy Chair: Nobody Knows." *Harper's Magazine*, March 2018. https://harpers.org/archive/2018/03/nobody-knows-3/.

Worsham, Lynn. 2006. "Composing (Identity) in a Posttraumatic Age." In *Identity Papers: Literacy and Power in Higher Education*, edited by Bronwyn T. Williams, 154–69. Salt Lake City: Utah State University Press.

Index

About the Editor and Contributors

Dr. **Laura Gray-Rosendale**, President's Distinguished Teaching Fellow and director of STAR English for "at risk" students, teaches classes in autobiography, rhetoric, composition, popular culture, and gender issues. She has published a wide range of books including *Fractured Feminisms* about feminist theory and practice as well as *College Girl*, a memoir about sexual violence.

Dr. **Lee Skallerup Bessette** is a learning design specialist at the Center for New Designs in Learning and Scholarship (CNDLS) at Georgetown University. She previously blogged for *Inside Higher Ed* and *ProfHacker*, and her writing has also appeared in *Women in Higher Education*, *Hybrid Pedagogy*, *The Journal for Interactive Technology and Pedagogy*, and *Popula*. She is currently writing two memoirs for Wilfred-Laurier Press and another for Blue Crow Press. She has a PhD in comparative literature from the University of Alberta.

Hélène Bigras-Dutrisac is a PhD student in the Department of Women's Studies and Feminist Research at the University of Western Ontario. Her current research, titled "Blogging and Online Journaling in the Age of the #MeToo Movement," focuses on articulations of sexual trauma in online journals and blogs, asking how survivors mobilize these spaces to creatively express, process, and/or politicize their experiences. She has presented her work at several conferences, including: "Applied Baudrillard," "Beyond Life Itself," and "Coding, Decoding, Recoding." She has also published an article titled "Unintelligible Lives: Trauma, Embodiment, and Trans Identities" in *To Be Decided*: Journal of Interdisciplinary Theory*.

Dr. **Lynn Z. Bloom**, Emerita Board of Trustees Distinguished Professor and Aetna Chair of Writing at the University of Connecticut, has also taught autobiography and creative nonfiction, and directed writing programs at the University of New Mexico, the College of William and Mary, and Virginia Commonwealth University. She learned the essentials of writing from Dr. Seuss, fun; Dr. Strunk and E. B. White, elegant simplicity; University of Michigan professor Art Eastman, nitpicking revision; and Benjamin Spock, during interviews for *Doctor Spock: Biography of a Conservative Radical* (1972), "If you don't write clearly, someone could die." These precepts inform the heart, soul, and human voice of her teaching and writing, including *Writers Without Borders* and *The Seven Deadly Virtues and Other Lively Essays* (both 2008), the feminist *New Assertive Woman* (1975), and nearly 200 articles—many on auto/biography, composition research, disability studies and teaching. Her current work focuses on creative nonfiction—memoir, essays, writing about food, travel, medicine—that people love to read—and write, also the subjects of her 2013 Fulbright in New Zealand. Her most recent essay is "The Slippery Slope: Ideals and Ethical Issues in High Altitude Climbing Narratives" (*Assay*, September 2019); the research included a flight around Mt. Everest via Buddha Air.

Dr. **Ari Burford** is a senior lecturer in women's and gender studies at Northern Arizona University (NAU)—which is located on stolen Diné and Hopi land. Their PhD is in literature from the University of Arizona. Ari is currently looking for a publisher for their book-length memoir entitled *Finding Them: A Queer Girlboi's Journey Recovering Memories of Incest and Living to Tell About It*, a book about healing, accountability, despair, survival, feminism, genderqueer existence, and finding their way into embodiment and joy. At NAU they created the queer studies minor, and they teach courses on writing as resistance, healing, queer literature and film, feminism, intersectionality, and queer and trans resilience. Their published creative work "And Then with a Spin I Am Boy Again" and "The Day I Was Seven and I Kept Her Safe" appear in *Cahoodaloodaling* and *Entropy*. Their articles "'Her Mouth is Medicine': Beth Brant's and Paula Gunn Allen's Queer Erotics as Decolonizing Methodologies" and "Cartographies of a Violent Landscape: Helena María Viramontes's and Cherríe Moraga's Remapping of Feminisms in *Under the Feet of Jesus* and *Heroes and Saints*" appear in *The Journal of Lesbian Studies* and *Genders*. Whenever possible, Ari loves dancing on the beach with their mustache made of glitter.

Katherine Chelsea is a PhD student at the University of California, San Diego. Her research focuses on Victorian gender, children's literature, and sporting culture. Her first novel was published in 2015.

Courtney Cox is a PhD student in the Department of English Studies at Illinois State University, where she specializes in rhetoric and composition. Courtney is an interdisciplinary scholar, with background in anthropology, sociology, and digital publishing. Her research interests focus upon feminist rhetoric, critical literacies studies, and critical ethnography toward the aim of institutional intervention. Courtney is assistant editor of *Rhetoric Review*. Her creative poetry and prose have been published in several journals, but you can read more of her work on Title IX and institutional critique in *enculturation*.

Dr. Sally J. Kenney is the Newcomb College Endowed Chair at Tulane University where she is the executive director of the Newcomb Institute, a professor of political science, an adjunct professor in public health, and an affiliated faculty member of the Law School. She has written about comparative employment discrimination, the European Court of Justice, and judicial selection, focusing particularly on women judges (see https://newcomb. tulane.edu/content/sally-j-kenney-phd). For the last nine years, she has turned her attention to preventing sexual assault on campus, teaching an interdisciplinary course on rape. She has also worked to start a prison education program in the Louisiana Correctional Institute for Women.

Marissa Korbel's writing has appeared in *Harper's Bazaar*, *Guernica*, *Bitch*, *The Manifest Station*, *Mutha Magazine*, *Under the Gum Tree*, and *McSweeney's*. She contributed to the anthologies *Burn it Down* (2019), *Only Light Can Do That* (2017), and others. She writes a monthly column, "The Thread," for *The Rumpus*. Korbel received her Bachelor of Arts degree from Mills College, and her Juris Doctor degree from Lewis and Clark Law School. She works as a public interest attorney in support of campus and minor sexual assault survivors, and lives in Portland, Oregon, with her partner and child.

Dr. Melinda A. Mills is associate professor of women's and gender studies, sociology, and anthropology; coordinator of women's and gender studies at Castleton University; and a visiting instructor in the Women's and Gender Studies Department at the University of South Florida. Her research interests focus on multiracial identity formation; interracial relationships; race, class, and gender in popular culture representations; and women's responses to street harassment. Forthcoming publications focus on health, wellness, and womanism; trauma and transformation; and black women's experiences with street harassment. Her award-winning first book, *The Borders of Race*, examines the lived experiences of multiracial people of various racial combinations. Dr. Mills is currently completing her book manuscript on multiracial people in romantic relationships.

Dr. **Donna L. Potts** is a professor and chair of the English Department at Washington State University, where she teaches Irish literature, including a graduate seminar on contemporary Irish literature and trauma. She is the author of three books about literature—*Howard Nemerov and Objective Idealism* (Missouri 1994), *Contemporary Irish Poetry and the Pastoral Tradition* (Missouri 2011), and *Irish Environmental Writing: The Wearing of the Deep Green* (Palgrave 2018)—as well as one book of poetry, *Waking Dreams*, and the editor/co-editor of three books. From 2012 to 2019, she served as a moderator for Pandora's Project, for victims and survivors of sexual abuse and assault. She has written about rape and gang rape for *Chronicle of Higher Education*.

Dr. **Katrina M. Powell** is professor of English and director of the Center for Rhetoric in Society at Virginia Tech. She teaches courses in rhetorics of social justice, feminist autobiography, and research methodologies, and her research focuses on displacement narratives and human rights rhetorics across transnational contexts. She is the author of *The Anguish of Displacement* (UVA Press 2007, funded by a National Endowment for the Humanities Fellowship) and *Identity and Power in Narratives of Displacement* (Routledge 2015), editor of *"Answer at Once": Letters from Mountain Families in Shenandoah National Park* (UVA Press 2009) and *Practicing Research in Writing Studies: Reflexive and Ethically Responsible Research* (with Pam Takayoshi, Hampton 2012). She has also published in *JAC: Journal of Rhetoric, Culture, and Politics*, *College English*, *College Composition and Communication*, *Biography: An Interdisciplinary Quarterly*, and *Prose Studies*. Her current work focuses on the dissemination of displacement and refugee narratives and the ethical dimensions of archiving those narratives in alternative spaces. With a fellowship from the nonprofit Voice of Witness, Powell is conducting an oral history titled *Resettled: Beginning (Again) in Appalachia*, to be published by Haymarket Books.

Dr. **Tanya Serisier** is a senior lecturer in criminology at Birkbeck College, University of London, and completed her PhD in 2010 in comparative literature and cultural studies at Monash University, Australia. Her thesis "Shahrazad's Daughters: Telling Stories in Response to Sexual Violence" investigated the feminist political practice of "speaking out" as a literary and cultural practice, with a focus on the speaking position of survivors. She has continued to publish in this area, most recently in her monograph, *Speaking Out: Feminism, Rape and Narrative Politics* (Palgrave Macmillan 2018), which develops some of the themes first explored in her thesis. The book is the first critical account of "speaking out" about sexual violence as a central element of feminist politics. *Speaking Out* argues that feminist belief in the transformative potential of women's personal stories of violence has been both highly successful but also produced unresolved ethical questions and political limitations. She has also published more widely in the history of feminist responses to sexual violence and the cultural politics of sexuality, violence, and the regulation of sex. Previously, she has rarely used autobiographical material in her own work, but, as she explains in the "Personal Statement" included in her monograph, her research interests arise from her own personal experiences with sexual violence and with feminist politics around it.

Lena Ziegler is a third-year PhD student in rhetoric and writing studies at Bowling Green State University. Her research interests include sexual violence, sexuality, the rhetoric of consent, and political rhetoric. Her dissertation will focus on the normalization of sexual violence in heterosexual romantic relationships. She holds an MFA in creative writing from Western Kentucky University with a concentration on fiction and nonfiction. She is an editor and co-founder of the literary journal *The Hunger*. Her fiction chapbook *MASH* was published in 2019 with The A3 Review and her first novel *Him & Her* was a finalist in the Autumn House Press 2018 Fiction Contest. Her work has appeared in *Indiana Review*, *Split Lip Magazine*, *Dream Pop Press*, *Red Earth Review*, and elsewhere.